D1418121

Time Alone With God

by

Tom Hufty

Albury Publishing
Tulsa, Oklahoma

Time Alone With God
ISBN 1-57778-092-2

55422 Trabue Lane
New London, Missouri 63459

Published by ALBURY PUBLISHING
P. O. Box 470406
Tulsa, Oklahoma 74147-0406

INTRODUCTION

After many years in ministry and "growing up" as a Christian son, husband, and father, I know that the most important time of my day – every day – is the time I spend with God. The challenge this presents, of course, is not just making the time, but even more, how to spend that time. There are many wonderful devotional books, but many of us need more than just a good story and a Bible verse. We need something that will "provoke unto love and to good works" (Hebrews 10:24 KJV).

Years ago, when I was asked to write a column in our church newsletter, I had no idea the extent to which God would use these simple teachings. After years of trial and error, I devised the 4-R method: Read, Reflect, Respond, and Remember. This encourages the believer to read a Bible verse; reflect upon it with a story, illustration, or teaching; respond to thought-provoking and challenging questions (the "faith without works is dead" principle); and finally gives a "takeaway" or one-liner to meditate upon during the day.

It is my prayer that this devotional will be a blessing to you as you seek a deeper, richer relationship with God. Whether you use it for your individual devotions, with your family, your friends, a Sunday school class, or a Bible study, I believe the truths contained in this book will bring a new excitement to your *Time Alone With God.*

Dedication

To my best friend, my beautiful wife, Rhonda. No one in all the world has helped me love Jesus more or encouraged me to spend *Time Alone With God* more than you. And to my children, Zac and Mackenzie. No one provides better illustrations than you guys.

ACKNOWLEDGMENTS

Thanks to all the people at Pleasant Valley church who read my thoughts for years. Thanks to all the people at Hannibal-LaGrange College who are still trying to figure me out. Thanks to all the great folks at Albury Publishing. And thanks to Walker and all you guys at Awe Star. You're Awesome!

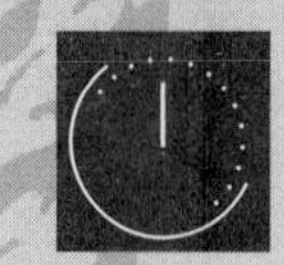

The Joy of Belonging to Jesus

Read

I have told you this so that my joy may be in you and that your joy may be complete. — JOHN 15:11.

Reflect

I was an active teenager. My dad used to say, "Son you're involved in everything but the girls scouts and you buy cookies from them." The reason? I wanted to feel like I belonged to something. The night I graduated from high school an award was given to a guy and girl of the graduating class who were the most active in organizations and school activities throughout their high school career. The award wasn't much, twenty-five dollars as I recall. I remember sitting there with my mind in neutral, waiting to get my diploma, when they announced, "And the boy participation award for 1974 goes to Tom Hufty." WHAT? I couldn't believe it. I walked onstage, received my envelope, and walked off the platform beaming. All the kids around me wanted to see my check. It was a great day. Later that evening, my dad came up to me and said, "Son what does that award mean?" I told him, "Dad, it means that if I hadn't been involved in all those activities I would have been valedictorian." He didn't believe me.

It's great to feel like you belong to a group of people. But it's even greater to feel like you belong to Jesus. When you commit your life to Him there is an eternal connection that takes place. You belong to Him forever and He will never let you go. Jesus said, "I give to them eternal life and they will never perish and no one can snatch them out of my hand" (John 10:28).

Respond

We can join any number of groups and still not feel like we belong. Only belonging to Jesus brings us everlasting peace and security. He is the only One who can satisfy our need to belong for now and eternity. Do you have this eternal sense of belonging? If not, ask Jesus into your heart right now! If you already belong to Him, but you feel far from belonging, open your heart to Him and be restored.

Remember

When you know Jesus personally, you belong to Him and heaven will be your home.

Fellowship With God

Read

Therefore, there is now no condemnation for those who are in Christ Jesus. — Romans 8:1.

Reflect

If God were to come to earth right now in bodily form, do you think He would hang out with you? Do you think He likes you? Oh, I know He *loves* you, but does He *like* you? Your answer to that question says a lot about what you think of yourself and what you think of God.

For many of us, we think God wouldn't want to hang around us because of our past sinfulness. We haven't come to grips with the extent of His forgiveness, even though we have repented. We can't help but think He must still be a little bit angry with us. The fact is, every reason God had to be disgusted and angry with us was dealt with on the cross. His forgiveness is so complete that He not only loves us, but He can like us as well.

Now, it could be that the paragraph above didn't tell you anything you don't already know. It could be that you still feel God is ticked at you over your sin. You still feel condemned. Why? Perhaps you have not taken Him at His Word. It might be that you are measuring your acceptability to Him on the basis of your past performance. Take a closer look at today's verse: Therefore, there is now no condemnation for those who are in Christ Jesus. If He's washed you clean, you're clean!

Respond

It's amazing to me that God wants to have a relationship with me. In fact, He wanted that relationship with me so badly, He removed everything that could come between the two of us. Even when I sin, He encourages and strengthens me to repent, overcome it, and go on. Get alone and praise God for His love and acceptance of you. Confess to Him the times you have not taken Him at His Word. Ask Him to help you resist temptation today. Now, go out there today and let Him hang out with you!

Remember

God not only wants a relationship with you, He wants to have fellowship with you.

Will You Listen?

Read

In the past God spoke to our forefathers through the prophets at many times and in various ways, but in these last days he has spoken to us by his Son. — Hebrews 1:1-2.

Reflect

Voices are interesting — unique to say the least. I remember well my dad's voice coming from the stands when I played baseball during my childhood and teen years. I could recognize his voice above the rest of the crowd. Today I watched videos of my son when he was about four years old. Boy, has his voice changed over the years! God's voice is interesting too. He spoke to Elijah in what was described as a still, small voice. Job described His voice as thunder. David described His voice as powerful enough to break the cedars. One thing for sure about God's voice, He wants to be heard!

The writer of Hebrews said that in the past God spoke through the prophets and in various ways, but now He speaks through His Son. In other words, if you want to know what God is saying, check out what Jesus said. God will speak to you in a way that will be consistent with His Word.

Respond

I believe God loves to speak to us. The question is: Will we hear Him? Will we follow His instruction when He speaks to us through His Word or His messenger? Take a moment right now to be still and listen to God. Remember how awesome He is to do all the things He does and still listen to you. Then after you hear from Him, submit your will to Him and follow His instruction.

Remember

God's voice can come through loud and clear if we will be sensitive to listen.

Determination

Read

As the time approached for him to be taken up to heaven, Jesus resolutely set out for Jerusalem. — Luke 9:51.

Reflect

My senior year I was supposed to win my conference cross country meet. I had won every race up to that one. But I proved the pollsters wrong and came in sixth. Why? Because I was slower than five other guys — it doesn't take a genius to figure that out. But there was another reason. I focused on the idea of winning the conference meet and rebelled against training on the hills that I would face that day. The same thing is true in our spiritual lives. We love the idea of being committed but lack the discipline it takes to follow through on the commitment.

Jesus "resolutely set out for Jerusalem." Jerusalem was the final destination, for it was there He would hang on the cross and pay sin's price for you and me. That was His focus from the very beginning, and He never turned away from it. Even though He faced several obstacles designed to distract Him from His destination, He had resolved to go to the cross. He had disciplined Himself to go to the hill called Calvary. His determination resulted in our salvation. Because He was determined to go to the cross, we have the opportunity to spend eternity with Him.

Respond

To what are you resolutely committed? What is your Jerusalem? Are you in love with the idea of being committed, or are you in love with the One who deserves your commitment? Your Jerusalem is the place where you reach the climax of God's will for you. The process may be long, but if you resolutely set your heart on it, God will strengthen you all the way.

Remember

Determination is often the single element that separates the mediocre from the excellent.

Confidence in Your Prayers

Read

Dear friends, if our hearts do not condemn us, we have confidence before God and receive from him anything we ask, because we obey his commands. — 1 John 3:21-22.

Reflect

"Dad, I've cleaned my room, done my homework, and fed the dog. Now can I go out and play?" Sound familiar? Children who want to be in the good graces of their parents obey them. And usually they are rewarded for it. Jesus said our heavenly Father also desires to give us good gifts. (See Matthew 7:11.) The problem is that many don't have confidence in their praying.

When you are confident toward God, you will have boldness in your prayers. But what gives confidence? Look closely at how John answers that question in this verse, "...because we obey his commands." Obedience gives confidence in praying. The psalmist wrote, "If I regard iniquity in my heart, the Lord will not hear me" (Psalm 66:18 KJV). Therefore, if you have unconfessed sin in your life, God will not answer your prayer. You can have no confidence in your prayers until you have confessed and repented. God will not trust you with an answer to your prayer if you disregard His will in your life.

Respond

Do you bathe every day? I mean, do you bathe spiritually every day? Do you wash your hands before eating or when they get dirty? Do you go to God in prayer and confess to Him your sins so you can be clean before Him? 1 John 1:9 KJV says, "If we confess our sins, He is faithful and just to forgive us our sins and cleanse us from all unrighteousness." Then you can have confidence before Him as you pray! If you have no confidence in your praying, take some time right now to confess and repent. Take a bath in 1 John 1:9 and let God restore your confidence as you trust Him today.

Remember

God doesn't care if the vessel He uses has been chipped or cracked, just so it is clean.

PUSH THE CLEAR BUTTON

READ

"The older brother became angry and refused to go in. So his father went out and pleaded with him. But he answered his father, 'Look! All these years I've been slaving for you and never disobeyed your orders. Yet you never gave me even a young goat so I could celebrate with my friends.'" — LUKE 15:28-29.

REFLECT

Our brains are much like computers. We store information that we can clear or recall whenever we want. The problem we have in working with our cerebral cortex computer is that usually we push the recall button more than the clear button. The result is painful memories, video displays in our conscious thoughts of mistreatment and old feelings of unforgiveness and revenge. Therefore, the difficulty in forgiving others is often found in our unwillingness to push the clear button in our minds and move on. Pushing the clear button is often difficult. But pushing the recall button can be devastating.

The story Jesus told of the prodigal son illustrates well that we all have difficulty trying to forgive, especially when it appears we didn't do anything wrong. The older brother may have had every right to feel mistreated, and he allowed those feelings to keep him from being able to forgive his father and brother.

Feelings often keep us from forgiving. When memories of what people have done to us are stirred, we experience the same feelings all over again. Why can't we love ourselves enough to press the clear button and rid ourselves of the pain? Simply because we choose not to! Part of forgiveness is choosing not to remember.

RESPOND

When thoughts of being wronged assault you, push the clear button and refuse to come under the control of an unforgiving attitude. God uses His clear button when you confess your sin to Him, and He expects you to be like Him and do the same. Take some time to praise and thank Him for His forgiveness. Then ask Him to help you to be forgiving today.

REMEMBER

Choose to forgive and forget and your feelings will eventually fall in line.

Doing Something Significant

Read

"You are the salt of the earth. But if the salt loses its saltiness, how can it be made salty again? It is no longer good for anything, except to be thrown out and trampled by men." — Matthew 5:13.

Reflect

Houses in the Middle East often have flat roofs. If you watched any of Desert Storm on television, you probably saw guns on the flat roofs of buildings. In fact, the roof was and is an active place for social functions in the Middle East. They throw parties on the roof, they dance on the roof, and yes, they shoot from the roof. Because the roof sees so much activity, it can begin to wear and often needs repair. So "gypsum," a tar-like substance, is used to fill the cracks. In order to get the bitter gypsum to coagulate properly, it is often mixed with salt. Jesus said in this verse that Christians who get mixed with the wrong ingredients, like bitterness or complacency, become weak and are just like that salt. They are only good to be trampled on by the world.

Respond

One of the most significant things you can do in life is to point someone to Jesus. What attracted *you* to Him? Whom did you watch who made you think, "If that's what God is all about, I need Him." That person probably was not an "undercover" Christian. They most likely identified with Jesus and were not ashamed, because of what He had done in their life. They probably were full of joy even though their life had challenges just like yours does. Do you know why you were attracted to them? Because they were salty. They had flavor to their life, and you knew you needed what they had — something found only through a relationship with Jesus. You make a significant impact today as you have social contact with the world. Pray today that as people without God look at you they will develop a thirst for God. Pray you'll have the opportunity to share with them some of what God has done for you.

Remember

When Jesus fills your life, He draws others to you so you can tell them about Him.

Giant Steps for God

Read

"Be strong and courageous...for the Lord your God will be with you wherever you go." — Joshua 1:9.

Reflect

Years ago an experiment was done to test the power of peer pressure. Groups of nine students were shown cards with a single line on the left side and three lines on the right side. They were to determine which line on the right was equal in length to the single line on the left. The first eight students had been told ahead of time to select a line which was clearly wrong. The test was to determine if the ninth student would select the wrong line as well. The result: almost 40% of the subjects participating voted with the majority, making the choice that was obviously wrong. They lacked the courage to take a stand against the majority to do what was right.

Going against popular opinion is never easy. Even when you are right, you don't like to be alone. But down through history there is recorded documentation that tells us of times when the majority was dead wrong. For example, when the twelve spies came back from spying out the promised land, ten reported that there were giants in the land, that they shouldn't go in. The other two, Joshua and Caleb, reported, "Yes, there are giants, but God will take responsibility for them. We must go." They were not too popular for standing up for what was right, but they were also the only two spies who God allowed into the promised land later. God rewarded their stand for Him.

Respond

Do you need to take a stand today? Has God challenged you to change or to move in a certain direction but you are intimidated by your peers? Spend some time right now praising and thanking Him for His faithfulness. Ask Him to strengthen and encourage you to walk in obedience to Him today.

Remember

When you stand for God, all of heaven is on your side.

Money, Money, Money

Read

For the love of money is a root of all kinds of evil. Some people, eager for money, have wandered from the faith and pierced themselves with many griefs. — 1 Timothy 6:10.

Reflect

A rich man who knew he was going to die called in a priest, a rabbi, and a Baptist preacher to make a last request of them. He told them he had always heard, "You can't take it with you," but he was going to try. He gave each of them $50,000 cash and asked them to throw it in his casket before he was buried. Not long after the conversation, the rich man died, and as his friends passed by his casket, each tossed in an envelope. When they were leaving the cemetery, the priest stopped the others and said, "I must make a confession. I used part of the money to help our orphanage, but I tossed in about $20,000 of the cash." The rabbi then confessed that he had used a portion of the money to repair the synagogue, but that he too had tossed in $20,000 cash. The Baptist preacher shook his head and said he was ashamed of both of them. He said, "This man trusted us, so I wrote him out a check for the whole amount." The story brings home a very good point. YOU CAN'T TAKE IT WITH YOU!

Paul did not say *money* was the root of all evil, but the *love* of money. Money is a powerful thing in our lives, but it is just a thing. If we love the thing rather than the One who provides the thing, we are headed for all kinds of evil. The love for money has made grown men and women act tremendously childish and cruel.

Respond

How much are you motivated by money? Your answer to that question will say a lot about how much money influences you. Spend some time right now praising and thanking God for the blessings that have come your way with the money He has provided for you. Ask Him to forgive you for the times you allowed yourself to be controlled by money.

Remember

Money is merely a tool God gives you to build His kingdom.

The Last Word

Read

When Joseph's brothers saw that their father was dead, they said, "What if Joseph holds a grudge against us and pays us back for all the wrongs we did to him!"...But Joseph said to them, "Do not be afraid...I will provide for you and your children." And he reassured them and spoke kindly to them. — GENESIS 50:15, 19-21.

Reflect

Are you one who always has to have the last word? That's the way Joseph's brothers were. They thought they had the last word when they sold him into slavery, but it didn't turn out that way. Through a series of events, Joseph became the second most powerful man in Egypt. And the saying, "What goes around comes around," came to pass in the lives of Joseph and his brothers. The brothers were in great need, and the only one who could help them was the little brother they had mistreated years before. Fortunately for them, he was a man whose life was dominated by the love of God, and the love that God produced in him carried no grudges. 1 Corinthians 13:5 says, "It (love) keeps no record of wrong." Is that the type of love you want produced in your life?

Respond

How do you respond when you have been mistreated? Do you look for opportunity to retaliate? Do you pout? Do you try to gain sympathy from others so you will feel your actions are justified? None of these responses are motivated by God's love. So how can you become a more loving person and abandon the temptation to carry a grudge? Just stop for a moment and think how much God has forgiven you. That should be reason enough not to carry a grudge! If you are carrying a grudge, remember what Jesus carried on your behalf and nailed to the cross. Take some time now to ask Him to forgive you for the times you have carried a grudge instead of exercising His love toward others.

Remember

God is the One who ultimately has the last word, so leave your grudge behind.

Pleasing Your Neighbor

Read

Each of us should please his neighbor for his good, to build him up. For even Christ did not please himself. — Romans 15:2-3.

Reflect

Who's your neighbor? Your neighbor could be the person who lives in the house or apartment next to you. Your neighbor could be your co-worker, a friend, or a relative. If you're married and have children, your neighbor could be your mate or your child.

How do you think you can enhance your neighbor's self-esteem? The scripture above says to do things to please your neighbor for *their* own good. Sometimes this means giving a "love gift." By that I mean doing something you may not feel like doing. It may not be something you like to do, but when you do it, your neighbor knows that you are making an effort to please them.

For example, my wife Rhonda loves crafts. A craft show to her is like baseball is to me. Well, this "crafty" person married a guy with no artistic flare at all. I mean zero. I can't even draw a stick man. Therefore, to me a craft show is only valuable if there is a ball game on TV in a nearby store. But when I go to a craft show with her and take an interest in the things she likes, it affirms her worth and validates her interests. And when she goes to things that interest me much more than they interest her just to be with me, what an affirmation!

All of this affirmation stuff is an attitude thing. You love what you decide to love. It tells your neighbor that they are more important to you than your own selfish interests. Affirmation is a step in showing people that because of Jesus, you choose to lift them up rather than put them down.

Respond

Whom do you try to please? Do you affirm others regularly? Are you actively doing things that bless your neighbor? Take some time to be alone with God and praise and thank Him for your life. Ask Him to forgive you for the times you have failed Him. Now, pray today that God will help you honor Him in your relationships. Make Him look good today!

Remember

By affirming your neighbor in a way that is difficult for you, you allow God to love them through you.

His Thoughts of You

Read

"How precious to me are your thoughts, O God! How vast is the sum of them! Were I to count them, they would outnumber the grains of sand." — Psalm 139:17-18.

Reflect

Not long ago I visited a banker friend who had recently become a believer. I went into his office and we talked about some financial things, then I asked him how he was doing in his new relationship with God. He got up, shut the door, and turned to me and said, "Tom, I think about Him all the time."

How many times a day do you think about God? Did you know He thinks of you even when you are not thinking of Him? David says in these verses that you are the object of God's constant attention. He never stops thinking about you. His thoughts of you are overwhelming and constant. Throughout this chapter David talks about God's power. But he notes here that God did not create us and then leave us to go it alone. He is constantly with us. Billions of prayers go up to God daily, yet He focuses on each one individually. Since He is capable of forming us and giving us life, He is also capable of blessing us. If we allow Him to take control of our lives, He will put the pieces of life together.

Respond

David didn't know much about anatomy or prenatal care or psychology, yet he wrote about all of these things in this chapter. How could he do this? He knew God. Those days in the pastures, taking care of sheep, taught him much about the character and capabilities of God, giving him the confidence to face a giant named Goliath and the courage to lead the nation of Israel. Time alone with his Creator, thinking and focusing on Him, made David a man after God's own heart. Right now and throughout the day, realize how much God values you. You can feel significant even in this negative world when you are constantly aware of His presence.

Remember

God is thinking of you right now…and now…and now.

MAKE UP YOUR MIND

READ

But Daniel made up his mind. — DANIEL 1:8 NASB.

REFLECT

Age has nothing to do with making up your mind. A strong-willed two-year-old can "make up his mind" to scream until he gets his way in the grocery store, embarrassing the daylights out of well-adjusted parents. A teenager can "make up his mind" to rebel against authority and all the doctors in the world can't stop the heartache of a parent who did their best. A senior adult can make up their mind they will not go to a family outing and all the persuasiveness of the children can be powerless.

But hold on a minute. The opposite is true too. A young businessman on his way to the top can "make up his mind" not to compromise his standards in order to get ahead and to live an authentic Christian life in the midst of pressure. A young teenager can "make up his mind" not to give in when his peers say, "Everyone is doing it." Anyone can "make up their mind" to make a positive impact in the world.

Making up your mind means you are determined to live by some absolutes. It means to guard a value system, regardless of the cost. "Daniel made up his mind" to follow God and not bow down to the world's pressure. And God honored his obedience — remember the lions' den? (See Daniel 6:16-28.) Daniel's friends, Shadrach, Meshach, and Abednego, made up their minds not to bow down to the idol the king had erected and God honored their obedience — remember the fiery furnace? (See Daniel 3.) When you refuse to compromise godly standards in your life, you get heaven's attention.

RESPOND

Are you living by absolutes? Can you say, "Integrity is of the highest importance to me"? If you have a family, can your teenager say that sex before marriage is absolutely wrong — no exceptions? Make up your mind! Today, model your values to your family, your friends, and your associates at work.

REMEMBER

Make up your mind to follow God's standards.

God Speaks Through His Word

Read

All Scripture is God-breathed and is useful for teaching, rebuking, correcting and training in righteousness. — 2 Timothy 3:16.

Reflect

"When all else fails, read the instructions." How many times have you heard that one? I don't know how many times I've brought something home that needed to be assembled and only read part of the directions to get started. Then I skipped the rest because I thought I was pretty sure how to finish the job. Almost always, I hit a snag and had to go back to read the rest of the instructions.

The same is true in our Christian life. Too many times we start out reading the Bible consistently; then, after finding out all the good stuff (how to miss hell and hit heaven), we lay it aside. We say, "I know how to live this Christian life," but before long we hit a snag. Sadly, many of us don't go back and read the instructions. If we would, we would discover some of the great purposes of God for our lives.

The Bible tells us not only how to be assured of eternal life in heaven, but how to get the most out of life right now. Isn't it logical that the "Giver of Life" would inspire the writing of a book that would teach us how to get the most out of life? God's Word is where He reveals Himself to us. If we want to get to know Him, we must spend time in His Word.

Respond

If your life seems to have hit a snag today, STOP and pick up your Bible. Go back and read some of the instructions. Get your cues from the Director of Life on what He wants to do through your situation. Pray as you read His Word. Ask Him to speak to you and give you listening ears to hear His voice. Then, when you get new directions for today, go out and do them!

Remember

God's instructions (His Word) are designed for you to build a wonderful life.

Taking Time for Kids

Read

These commandments that I give you today are to be upon your hearts. Impress them on your children. Talk about them when you sit at home and when you walk along the road, when you lie down and when you get up. — Deuteronomy 6:6-7.

Reflect

I recently talked with another parent at my son's baseball practice about our boys' progress. He asked me if I worked with my son much on his baseball skills, and I replied, "Not as much as I'd like to." He said, "I know, there just isn't enough time, is there?" The truth is, though, there is enough time and there always has been.

Do you have time to teach truth? If you have a family, your kids are your first priority. But if you are single, are you involved at your church? Are there kids in your neighborhood who are not saved and need a big brother or sister? We're all given the same amount of time each week, and we are the ones who prioritize it. It is important to take time to teach children how to play baseball (especially with today's baseball salaries...), but it is also important to spend time telling them about Jesus and His expectations for their lives.

The Lord told Moses that the time spent wisely with children is spent in repetitive teaching of godly values. The challenge for us is to take advantage of those teachable moments. However, it is vitally important to remember that all the teaching of godly values goes out the window if we don't *model* the principles ourselves.

Respond

So, how's your schedule? Do you find yourself wondering where the time has gone? The trick is controlling your schedule before the time gets away and you look back and see that you robbed your children or the children in your sphere of influence of valuable time. Ask God to help you plan your schedule. Ask Him to give you wisdom to set your priorities so that you have time for the young people in your life.

Remember

We must take time. Seize it. Guard it. Treat it as a valuable and precious jewel.

JANUARY 16

Knowing God Through Experience

Read

God said to Moses, "I AM WHO I AM." This is what you are to say to the Israelites: "I AM has sent me to you." — Exodus 3:14.

Reflect

Too many people shut God out of their daily experiences. They wait for a crisis to hit before they turn to Him. But if they really want to know God, they need to look for Him in every experience of life. He's there, wanting to become real to them.

For years I have studied and intellectually know many of the names given to God in the Scripture. For example, He is my refuge and strength, my defender, my deliverer, my comforter in sorrow, the bread of life, counselor, Savior, and King of kings. But until I *experienced* Him as my deliverer, refuge, and strength, those names were only names that I believed in. I did not understand the true meaning of what it was like to have God *be* those names.

When I messed up and knew what I deserved, He was my righteous judge. When I repented, I experienced Him as my Savior, deliverer, and refuge. When I felt alone, He became my comforter. It's just as He told Moses, "I AM everything you need." And not only is He what I need, He provides what I need as I seek Him. It was through these experiences in my life that God revealed Himself and I discovered more of who He is and how He wants to be more a part of my life.

Respond

As you spend time alone with God today, thank Him and praise Him for His constant efforts to make Himself known to you. Ask Him to forgive you for the times you have not looked for Him in the everyday experiences of your life. Ask Him to help you be a witness to others by helping them see Him work in the routine of their lives. Finally, pray that God would help you to be sensitive to His work in your life today.

Remember

Look for God in everything today.

CONFESSION

READ

If we confess our sins, He is faithful and righteous to forgive us our sins and to cleanse us from all unrighteousness. — 1 JOHN 1:9 NASB.

REFLECT

Question #1: How many sins had you committed at the time Jesus died on the cross? Answer: None. No one but God even thought of us at that point in history. Question #2: When Jesus died on the cross, how many sins of yours did He die for? Answer: All of them. Even the ones you'll commit tomorrow. So if He died for all of them, even those you haven't yet committed, why do you need to confess them? After all, confessing is a work; it's something you do, and you're not saved by works. So why confess?

Are you totally confused? I hope not. Actually, if you have asked Jesus Christ to come into your life, all of your sins have been forgiven. So why do we have to confess them? First of all, Jesus told us to and that's enough right there! But secondly, confession does the same thing in the New Testament days as the law did in the Old Testament days. It shows us how bad we are and how much we need forgiveness. Thirdly, confessing our sins and repenting restores our fellowship with the Father. Confessing our sins should be an immediate thing. As soon as we realize we have sinned, we need to confess that sin and keep the fellowship and communication lines open between us and the Father.

RESPOND

Pray Psalm 139:23-24 back to God and have a cleansing time of confession. There's nothing quite like being clean!

REMEMBER

Confession is like a spiritual looking glass, showing us who we are as God's children.

Power Over the Enemy

Read

The dragon stood in front of the woman who was about to give birth, so that he might devour her child the moment it was born. She gave birth to a son, a male child, who will rule all the nations with an iron scepter. And her child was snatched up to God and to his throne. — Revelation 12:4-5.

Reflect

Our enemy is commonly known as Satan. He was cast out of heaven long ago and took a third of the angels with him. (See Isaiah 14:12-15.) From the beginning Satan has known his outcome. When he deceived Adam and Eve, God told him that the offspring of the woman would crush his head. (See Genesis 3:15.) Since then, Satan has been out to destroy the Messiah, and there has always been a "dragon" standing by waiting to destroy the ancestors of Jesus. When the royal line to Jesus was down to one little boy, Joash, he was hidden for six years by a nurse while all his family was destroyed. (See 2 Kings 11:1-2.) God protected the line from which Jesus would come.

When Jesus finally came on the scene, Satan used King Herod to try to destroy Him, but Jesus' earthly parents were warned to flee to Egypt for protection. Satan thought he had finally won when he used Judas to betray Jesus and hand Him over to be crucified. But what Satan thought was victory, the cross, only turned out to be his ultimate defeat.

Satan still works today to destroy and bring down all those who represent Jesus. But the Good News is, we are already victorious. Satan's doom is destined and his power is limited. God has given us authority over the devil and the power to resist him, and the result will be his total defeat.

Respond

Praise God and thank Him today for protecting you and giving you authority over the enemy through the precious blood of Jesus. Thank Him and praise Him that at the name of Jesus every demon and Satan himself must bow.

Remember

You are not helpless when Satan attacks — all of heaven is supporting you!

What Is God Like?

Read

"Anyone who has seen me has seen the Father." — John 14:9.

Reflect

Whenever one of my children leave the house to go some place where they are going to be in public view, it is not uncommon for me to say: "Remember, your name is Hufty." The reason I say that is because they carry with them something they need to honor: the family name. When people see them, in a sense they see Rhonda and me. How they act reflects on us. We have poured a lot of our lives into our children. They have heard and seen the principles we want them to follow. In the same way, God's Son represented Him. How Jesus talked and acted influenced how people viewed His Father. Therefore, if we have questions about what God is like, we can look at His Son. Jesus reveals who God is.

I'm sure you have seen someone's son or daughter and noticed how they resembled their parents. It's the same way with God's children. Those who are truly His children resemble His character. The Bible tells us some of the attributes of God's children in Galatians 5:22-23. The Scripture is full of references as to how believers are to appear to the world. We are to be full of love, yet not compromising the standards God puts forth in His Word.

Respond

If it weren't for God's Word and His Spirit, we wouldn't know much about God. In His Word we can understand who He is and what a difference He can make in our lives. By His Spirit, we feel His presence and hear His voice leading and guiding us. In light of this, spend some time today in prayer and God's Word. Pray for those you know who need God's Word and Spirit in their lives. Ask God to use you to have an impact on them for Him. Now, go out today and make Him look good!

Remember

If you've given your life to Jesus, your name is Christian!

Forgive and Be Forgiven

Read

Then the master called the servant in, "You wicked servant," he said. "I canceled all that debt of yours because you begged me to. Shouldn't you have had mercy on your fellow servant just as I had on you?" — MATTHEW 18:32-33.

Reflect

Jesus told the story in Matthew 18:23-35 to show how much God has forgiven us. The man in question owed approximately ten million dollars by our standards today. It was hopeless. It would have been impossible for him to make enough money in his lifetime to repay the debt. The compassion of his master was his only chance. His master graciously forgave, or canceled, the debt. But then this man went and found someone who owed him an insignificant amount of money, approximately one dollar. When the second man asked for patience like the first man had had with his creditor, the first man, who had been forgiven so much, had the second man thrown in prison. Perhaps he had the *legal* right to do so, but he did not have the *moral* right.

In the same way, we have been forgiven much through the death of Jesus on the cross. If anyone should be forgiving, it is those who have been forgiven by God.

Respond

As you praise God for His Son, Jesus, who paid the price for your sins, ask Him to forgive you for the times you have been unforgiving toward others. Ask Him to give you a heart of compassion to look at others the way He looks at you. Pray that God will use you today in a special way to show someone who does not know Him what His forgiveness is really like. You may be the only glimpse of God they will see.

Remember

When you forgive, you are expressing the nature and character of your Father God.

Collective Praying

Read

When this had dawned on him, he went to the house of Mary the mother of John, also called Mark, where many people had gathered and were praying. — Acts 12:12.

Reflect

Have you ever gone to the symphony? Since I was raised on a pig farm, we didn't make it to the symphony much when I was young. I remember the first symphony I went to. I felt like a pig farmer at a symphony! There was nothing quite like it. I wasn't as bad as the Beverly Hillbillies, but I was close. And I loved the music. It was so clean and pure, so soothing and crisp. (Not bad lingo for a pig farmer, but I'm more cultured now.) Every instrument contributed to the piece, producing a masterpiece of sound.

Praying collectively is not unlike the symphony. In fact, in Matthew 18:19, Jesus says, "If two of you agree on earth about anything you ask for, it will be done for you." The original Greek word Jesus used for "agree" in that verse is *symphonos,* which is the word from which we get our word "symphony." What Jesus was saying is that our collective praying is like a symphony in heaven. The early church collectively prayed for Peter as he faced death. They presented their symphony of prayer to God, and He miraculously delivered Peter from death. God honors collective prayers because they honor Him.

Respond

Take some time now to praise and thank God for His willingness to listen to our prayers. Ask Him to reveal His will to you as you pray for others, so you may persistently pray His will. Take the opportunities you have this week to join with other Christians in collectively praying for others. Then anticipate that God will speak to you. And by the way, the next time you go to the symphony, think about heaven and say a prayer for someone you know — God will be listening.

Remember

Joining with others in prayer strengthens you and adds power to your prayers.

THE JOY OF A ANOTHER CHANCE

READ

"For this son of mine was dead and is alive again; he was lost and is found. So they began to celebrate." — LUKE 15:24.

REFLECT

Have you ever messed up really badly! I mean, you blew it and thought there would be no recovery? Something has already come to your mind, hasn't it? Do you remember how you felt? Did you feel embarrassed, guilty, ashamed, repentant, and wished you had a second chance? That is exactly how the prodigal son in this story must have felt. He had taken advantage of his father's goodness and then he was taken advantage of by strangers. So where was the hope of a second chance? The strangers he had wasted his money on were gone. All he could think of was his memory of a loving father. He must have seen his father give employees second chances. So the son who was full of pride decided to drop the pride and humble himself when he got to the point of desperation and could not handle his life. That point came in a pigpen.

This verse is taken from the Parable of the Prodigal Son. The word "prodigal" means "wasteful." The youngest son was wasteful of more than his inheritance. He wasted his father's love. But what he came to realize when he humbled himself was the depth of his father's love. His love was so great he could forgive his son for dragging the family name through the pigpen. His forgiveness was always there, just waiting for the son to return.

RESPOND

If you are in the pigpen right now, remember your loving Father is waiting for you to drop your pride and come home. If you are praying for the wayward one to come home, take "I told you so" out of your vocabulary and start preparing for a party! There is nothing like the joy of another chance – unless it's the joy of knowing the Father who gives it to you!

REMEMBER

The porch light is on. The key is under the mat that reads "welcome."

THE PERFECT FATHER

READ

We dealt with each of you as a father deals with his own children, encouraging, comforting and urging you. — 1 THESSALONIANS 2:11-12.

REFLECT

When I was growing up, I knew I had a good father. As a child I couldn't give you a list of criteria of what made him so good, but I knew he was good. This scripture describes him. It describes a selfless person, one who is wise and generous, one who attracts others because of his patient love, one who has balance and a clear understanding of what God is like.

I developed a greater understanding of my heavenly Father's love when I became a father. Notice what godly fathers do, according to Paul in these verses. They have a balance in relating to family members. They balance encouragement and comfort with challenges. They are never satisfied with the status quo. They want their children to experience the very best, sometimes calling them to leave their comfort zone, but encouraging them all the way. And if they fall, the godly father is there to comfort them and pick them up. Godly fathers put the needs of their families ahead of their own. After all, that is what God the Father did.

Godly fathers have a way of drawing family members together. They do it by demonstrating balance. They never get too high or too low. They provide stability and security. They have fun being dads. They encourage their families to stretch. They urge their families to experience new levels of faithfulness to God. They comfort their families when life gets tough. That's the kind of dad I want to be.

RESPOND

Take some time now to appreciate your heavenly Father. Thank and praise Him for His faithfulness. Confess to Him the times you have taken Him for granted. Pray that He will help you today to be all He wants you to be and do all He wants you to do.

REMEMBER

You're heavenly Father will never leave you or forsake you.

Leave Lust in the Dust

Read

"But I tell you that anyone who looks at a woman lustfully has already committed adultery with her in his heart." — Matthew 5:28.

Reflect

The word "looks" in this verse does not mean a casual glance, but a constant stare with the purpose of desiring. It was this kind of look David had toward Bathsheba. He didn't just glance and turn away. He deliberately stared and let his mind run away in fantasy and lust. It was not accidental. It was planned. Jesus describes the man in this verse as intentionally looking at a woman to feed his own sensual appetites.

Even though nobody may see you, God does — and it grieves Him. He knows the devastation it brings. Oswald Chambers says, "There is no heaven with a corner of hell in it." God is serious when it comes to your purity. That is why He is so concerned with the way you think, because the way you think determines the way you behave. Think about it for a minute. What deliberate sin have you committed that you didn't think about first? None!

Sexual purity begins in the mind and heart. One must consciously make a decision that impure thoughts will not be tolerated. God created sex for marriage only, as a type of our relationship with Him. We worship and love no other gods but Him, and our whole life is surrendered to Him. That makes our sexuality as sacred and holy as taking communion and being in God's presence. When we think lustful thoughts, we violate and begin to destroy that which is holy to God and priceless to our mate.

Respond

The lure of lust is all around you today, and you only have a chance of remaining pure if you discipline your mind. You must keep your eyes from wandering and prohibit your thoughts from losing a godly focus. If you commit yourself to following God's plan in what you think, you will walk in purity and freedom. Spend some time asking God for strength to discipline your mind today.

Remember

KEEP YOUR EYES ON JESUS!

Giving Thanks

Read

The rest of mankind that were not killed by theses plagues still did not repent of the work of their hands; they did not stop worshipping demons, and idols of gold, silver, bronze, stone and wood idols that cannot see or hear or walk. — Revelation 9:20.

Reflect

A police officer once stopped a young man in a new sports car one morning. The driver of the sports car said, "Officer, I'm in a hurry." The officer shot back, "Be quiet." The young man said, "But sir, if you'll just listen, I can save you a lot of trouble." Smiling, the officer responded, "Really. Well, maybe I'll let you think about that in jail." Several hours later the officer looked in on his prisoner and said, "Lucky for you that the police chief's daughter's wedding is today. He'll be in a good mood when he gets back."

"Don't count on it officer," the young man replied, "I'm the groom." Some people just won't listen will they? Tragically, that will be true in the end as well. Even with all the warnings, people will still be stubborn and choose hell over heaven. Can you imagine the hardness of heart that will be displayed by unbelievers in the Tribulation? Despite the warnings and sufferings, they will refuse to give their lives to God.

So, how do you avoid hardening your heart? By taking time to give thanks. The great commentator, Matthew Henry, was once robbed on his way home one night. That night he wrote in his diary, "Lord, I thank You that I have not been robbed before. I thank You that even though they took my all it was not much. I thank You that even though they took my purse they did not take my life. I thank You that it was I who was robbed and not I who robbed."

Respond

Being thankful to God softens your heart so that He can speak to you, change you, and lead you into more blessings. Thank God for your daily joys and the grace He gives to you to overcome any circumstance you face. Thanksgiving makes the things that matter to God important to you, reveals His heart, and brings joy to your soul.

Remember

Be thankful for every blessing you encounter today.

THE LORD OUR GOD

READ

Some trust in chariots and some in horses, but we trust in the name of the LORD our God. — PSALM 20:7.

REFLECT

Probably no one was more familiar with the intimidating presence of horses and chariots than the people of Israel. While slaves in Egypt, they saw the chariots of the armies of Egypt regularly. In King David's day, the most dreaded war machine was the chariot. Armed and swift, it could mow men down like grass. But Pharaoh trusted his chariots, and in the end he played the fool. Why do you think he trusted in his own power? He was deceived.

The psalmist says those who trust in horses and chariots have been deceived. I'm sure the psalmist had been told the story of the floating horses and chariots in the Red Sea when God delivered the children of Israel from slavery. That is why he could so confidently write this verse.

The exciting truth is that we serve the same God today. Many intimidating elements come into our lives, but we need not fear them. We can "trust in the name of the Lord our God." Nothing that comes our way intimidates Him. Therefore, when we encounter difficult circumstances, we need to say, "Lord, I know You are not intimidated by my plight, so I'll trust You. You delivered Israel, and You can deliver me."

RESPOND

In what "chariots" are you trusting? When it really gets down to it and the pressure is on, upon what do you rely to stay strong? Don't fall into the trap of being creature confident, which means trusting in yourself or others. Instead, each day practice being Creator confident. The One who created you deserves your trust because He always has your best interests in mind. If you trust anyone but God, you are deceived. Don't play the role of the fool who leaves God out or just decorates his life with God. Let Him *become* your life today.

REMEMBER

Trust only in God.

The Greatest of All

Read

But now abide faith, hope, love, these three, but the greatest of these is love. — 1 Corinthians 13:13 NASB.

Reflect

Many stories are told about Napoleon Bonaparte, because he was one of the greatest leaders of all time. But the account of his invasion of Russia reveals a different side of the great warrior. During this time, confidence in his leadership in France was fading. He was so concerned about his position at home, he left the French army and returned to France with a few other men. Arriving at a river crossing, Napoleon asked the ferryman if he had seen many deserters come that way. The ferryman replied, "No, you are the first."

Napoleon, for all his success and greatness, was still human. God, however, will never desert us. Even when we are unfaithful to Him, He remains faithful to us. His love for us is never-ending. There is not a time you can say, "He doesn't love me," for His love is constant. No wonder the Scripture tells us there is none like Him.

Just think, all the things we will ever possess in our lifetime will someday come to nothing. All we have ever worked for will pass away. But God's love for us will never fade away. How does that make you feel? Does it stir any emotion in you? To know that you will have God's undying love forever should motivate you to love and please Him.

Respond

Take a few moments to thank God for His great love toward you, a love that will never fade away. Ask Him to forgive you for the times you have not demonstrated your love to Him as you should. Then take some time to pray for those who need His love and ask God to reveal Himself to them in a special way. Finally, pray that today you will show God's love to others.

Remember

Desertion is not a character trait of God. He will stay with you and love you forever.

Simple Truth

Read

"Love the Lord your God with all your heart and with all your soul and with all your mind and with all your strength. The second is this: Love your neighbor as yourself." — Mark 12:30-31.

Reflect

Early in my ministry I interviewed for a ministerial position at a church. I asked the interviewer what kind of person the church was looking for. He said, "We want someone who will love God and love people." Thinking he did not understand my question, I decided to rephrase it to find out exactly what the job description was. So I said, "Okay, but what do you want this person to do." He replied, "We want him to love God and love people." I said, "Okay, let me see if I've got this straight. You want someone to come to your church and love God and love people." He said, "You've got it!" That's a pretty simple message, isn't it? So why does it take us so long to get it?

Jesus was asked, "What is the greatest of all the commandments?" Our verse today gives His answer. He said to love God with all your heart, soul, mind, and strength, and then love your neighbor as yourself. Jesus simplified what it means to live life to the fullest. A fulfilling, successful life is not found in big houses, fame, or political power, but in loving God and people. Whether you live in a big house or build big houses for others, loving makes the difference between misery and happiness.

Respond

Are you trying to make life too complicated? Step back for a minute and allow Jesus' words to simplify your life. Love God and love people. Do this and you fulfill all the law. You will please God, you will please yourself, and you will please others. To do this all you need is to have a relationship with God. He will love you so you can love Him back and give Him your whole life. Have you done that? Spend some time with Him in prayer right now.

Remember

Love God and love people.

What's Your Problem?

Read

For all have sinned and fall short of the glory of God. — Romans 3:23.

Reflect

As a fraternity prank, one evening some college students spread some smelly limburger cheese on the upper lip of a fraternity brother while he was sleeping. When the young man woke up he said, "Boy, it stinks in here." He then went out in the hall and smelled the same odor. Trying to get away from the aroma, he went outside. Still haunted by the smell he said, "The whole world stinks."

We sometimes are like that college student. Our problem is right under our nose, yet we look to blame something else, or we try to find somebody with the same problem so we won't feel so bad. The truth is, we all have missed the mark and fallen short of Jesus' character in some area of our life, and we need to straighten it out. Until we do, everything in our lives will "stink."

Too often we try to find comfort in the comparison game. We think if we can find someone who is sinning worse than we are, then our sin is not that bad. Don't believe that lie! One of the most dangerous traps for believers is to fall into the sins of "good people." All sin is disobedience to God and its very nature is to destroy. With Jesus in our hearts, we have a new nature to help us overpower sinful temptations of the flesh.

Respond

Take some time right now to thank and praise God for His wonderful forgiveness from sin. Ask Him to forgive you for the times you have fallen short and sinned. Also, ask Him to help those you know who are living a sinful lifestyle now. Ask Him to show them how sin destroys them and pray for their deliverance. Finally, ask Him to help you remain strong and not give the devil an opportunity to work his way in your life.

Remember

Limburger cheese and sin have one thing in common, they can both be wiped away.

Trusting God's Plan

Read

"So now, go. I am sending you to Pharaoh to bring my people the Israelites out of Egypt." But Moses said to God, "Who am I, that I should go to Pharaoh and bring the Israelites out of Egypt?" And God said, "I will be with you." — Exodus 3:10-12.

Reflect

A children's Sunday School class was given an assignment to draw a picture of God. Some drew pictures of old, white-haired men, while others drew pictures of superheroes. Still others drew rainbows and clouds. But the most intriguing picture came from a girl who showed her drawing of a man and explained, "I didn't know what God looks like, so I just drew a picture of my daddy."

As a father, there is no greater joy than to be able to provide for my wife and children. Whatever they need, I want to be first in line to help them get it. God the Father is no different. Whenever we have a need or inadequacy, God has a provision for it.

God has a plan for your life, and He also has provision for that plan to be fulfilled. Many of our frustrations come when we form our own plan and try to make it happen. We think if we had this job or that position, we would be happy. If it makes us happy, it must be God's plan. But never did God say to Moses, "I want to make you happy." He said, "I want you to deliver my people." The truth is, when we surrender to God's plan for our life, joy and fulfillment are a result of our obedience.

Respond

Are you making and executing your own plan, or do you know you are right in the center of God's will? Are you being continually frustrated or are you seeing victory after victory through the challenges in your life? If you don't know God's plan for you, ask Him! If you aren't following His plan, submit to it. Then thank your heavenly Father that He has a special plan just for you, tailor-made for your gifts, talents, and dreams.

Remember

You are a part of God's plan today. Play your part well.

DIFFICULT PEOPLE

READ

"You have heard that it was said, 'Love your neighbor and hate your enemy.' But I tell you: Love your enemies and pray for those who persecute you." — MATTHEW 5:43-44.

REFLECT

My sister used to say that she thought the only two sane people in the world were herself and me, and she was kind of concerned about me. Have you ever felt that way? Have you ever thought the only one in the world who had it together was yourself, and everyone else was out of touch? Well, stop and look at what Jesus said about those people who have a way of irritating us.

He said that even though they get under our skin, we should love them. And He did not mean with just a word-of-mouth love, but love in action. Since Christian love is not an emotion but an act of our will, Jesus can command us to love those who mistreat us. After all, He loved us when we were His enemies. (See Romans 5:10.)

When we *will* to love difficult people, we take the poison out of their attacks. By blessing them in word and deed, we can turn away their anger. And by praying for them, we will find it easier to love them. Therefore, the question comes down to this: We know Jesus died for them as He died for us, and we know we have only one enemy, Satan, so do we want the best for difficult people or do we want revenge?

Remember when Job lost his children, wealth, and health? His so-called friends came to comfort him, but their comfort became an irritation, because they spent most of their time accusing him of wrongdoing. In the final chapter, before God blesses Job again, Job prays for his friends. Because he does this, God gives him a double blessing.

RESPOND

I'm sure it wasn't easy for Job to pray for those difficult people in his life, yet he did it. That tells me it can be done. Why don't you take time right now to pray for the difficult people in your life? Ask God to help you show them love and seek the best for them.

REMEMBER

Loving difficult people makes them no longer difficult.

Behind Closed Doors

Read

"But when you pray, go into your room, close the door and pray to your Father, who is unseen. Then your Father, who sees what is done in secret, will reward you." — MATTHEW 6:6.

Reflect

Once a young Christian asked a wise old minister what the most important element of spiritual growth was — prayer or Bible study? The wise old minister looked at the young man and replied, "Which is more important to the bird — the right wing or the left?" To grow as an authentic Christian, prayer and Bible study go hand in hand. If we only have one, we'll go around in circles like a bird with just one wing. We will lack balance and not be able to make an impact on others.

The Bible is filled with examples of balanced Christians who made an impact on their world. For example, Paul knew the Word of God backwards and forwards, but he was a consistent prayer warrior. Stephen knew the Word so well that the men of the synagogue could not argue with his wisdom, but he prayed for his executioners as he was being stoned. (See Acts 7:60.) And then, of course, Jesus often prayed early in the morning and spent time in the Word of God as well. (See Mark 1:35.)

Both prayer and God's Word are necessary to make an impact on the world. When the balance of the Word and prayer bring maturity and success into a believer's life, they can influence the people around them.

Respond

This devotional is merely a springboard for you to spend time with God in prayer and Bible study. And the 4 R's are just the beginning of your special time with God. You will find that your day runs smoother and you have less difficulty when you are full of God's Word and walking according to His Spirit. And Matthew 6:6 will become a reality in your life. As you seek God privately, He will bless you and reward you openly, which is one of the greatest witnesses of Jesus to the world.

Remember

Balance in the Christian life is necessary for maturity and success.

Redirecting the Procession

Read

"Remember that you were slaves in Egypt and that the Lord your God brought you out of there with a mighty hand and an outstretched arm. Therefore the Lord your God has commanded you to observe the Sabbath day." — Deuteronomy 5:15.

Reflect

Several years ago a scientist conducted an experiment on a caterpillar called the procession caterpillar. Procession caterpillars crawl along, following the caterpillar in front of them. They have no imagination, no creativity, and are not too intelligent. They just follow the crowd. The scientist took a potted plant and placed several procession caterpillars around the rim of the pot. Inside the pot was a beautiful plant. What did the caterpillars do? They did the same old thing. They inched around the pot following the one in front of them until one by one they all died — just inches from nourishment.

That is the way Christians often behave in our society. They are consumed by routines and busyness, trying to "keep up with the Joneses," and have no idea where they are and what they are doing to themselves. God gave Israel the Sabbath so they would take time to look around and redirect themselves. The Sabbath is a time to come up for air, take a breath from the routine of the week, and get a fix on where you are. Then you can change directions if necessary. One of the ways you break the cycle of monotony in your life is to observe the Sabbath.

Respond

God has given us the Sabbath to evaluate where we are, where He is, and make adjustments accordingly. He wants to protect us from losing sight of His way in a busy world. Have you stopped to take a look at where you are in life? Are you just inches from nourishment but your eyes are looking down, caught in the routine of busyness? Maybe you are missing the Sabbath! How long has it been since you just rested, relaxed, prayed, and studied your Bible after church on Sunday?

Remember

Just because you're moving doesn't mean your going in the right direction.

The Best Message

Read

For I delivered to you as of first importance what I also received, that Christ died for our sins...and that He was buried, and that He was raised on the third day according to the Scriptures. — 1 Corinthians 15:3-4 NASB.

Reflect

"Yes, I will marry you." "It's a healthy baby boy." "Sir, after examining all the applicants, we've decided to give you the job." "The tumor we found is benign." Messages of joy! We all love to hear them. So, think for a minute. What is the best message you ever received?

According to Paul, the best message any of us has ever received is "that Christ died for our sins...and that He was buried, and that He was raised on the third day." In all eternity that is the best message any of us can ever hear! For without the risen Lord redeeming us from our sin problem, we all would be doomed.

Paul said this news is "of first importance." Not only is it important that we receive it, but also that we share it. The resurrection message is a message of celebration and responsibility. Those who have experienced the joy of deliverance from sin's penalty have an obligation to share what Jesus Christ has done in their lives.

Too often we church members fall into the habit of doing "churchy things" and neglect the most important things, such as having a consistent time alone with God and sharing the message of the risen Lord with those who don't know Him. We neglect the things Paul called "of first importance."

Respond

Have you developed the habit of substituting "church things" for your own personal walk with God? If you have, you know how frustrating life can be without stopping to let God take control. Take time to get alone with Him right now. Then guard a time for Him each day. Spend a moment thanking Him for the best message you have ever received — His redemptive love.

Remember

Your work for God should never become a substitute for your walk with God.

The Test of Authenticity

Read

For the word of God is living and active. Sharper than any double-edged sword, it penetrates even to dividing soul and spirit, joints and marrow; it judges the thoughts and attitudes of the heart. — Hebrews 4:12.

Reflect

I'm told that those who are trained to spot counterfeit money are schooled in a most interesting way. They are trained with real money. They spend hours and hours examining the real thing. They look at it, feel it, smell it, crumple it, and listen to it. They scrutinize it to the point that any currency that comes their way that is not authentic will be obvious to them. Their training regiment puts a whole new meaning on the phrase, "Show me the money."

In the same way, we must realize that there are counterfeit teachings today that appear to be authentic but are not. Checking to see whether or not something is from God can be confusing, because it seems as though Satan has a counterfeit for everything God has. So how can we distinguish between the two? To put it in a nutshell, we can ask ourselves this question: Will this teaching, circumstance, or choice I have to make bring honor to Jesus in the past, present, and future — not *can* it bring honor to Him, but *will* it?

Enemies to Jesus Christ are sometimes hard to spot. They often cloak themselves with appealing or eloquent speech to deceive those who are unfamiliar with God's Word. That is why the discipline of reading and studying the Word of God is of the utmost importance. If we are not familiar with the real thing, we are subject to being fooled by a counterfeit.

Respond

God loves you too much to leave you in the dark about the counterfeit traps that Satan sets for you on a daily basis. That's why He gave us the Bible. As you walk in His Word daily, you discover that His Word is a lamp unto your feet and a light unto your path. If you have neglected your time in the Word, repent and start studying!

Remember

Knowing God's Word enables you to recognize the counterfeits of Satan.

Finding Life Through Serving

Read

"He who has found his life shall lose it, and he who has lost his life for My sake shall find it." — MATTHEW 10:39 NASB.

Reflect

Tonight on my way home I passed a car that was broken down on the road. It looked abandoned. About a half-mile up the road my lights shown on a man walking. Putting two and two together, I figured he was the owner of the broken-down car. I thought, "I've got too much to do to get involved with this guy. Hey, its not raining. It's a nice night for a walk. In that you've done it unto the least of these my brothers, you've done it unto me. Okay, Lord. I'll stop." When I picked the man up, I noticed he was old enough to be my father. He said, "Thanks, son, for stopping, I don't know how much farther I could have gone." Nothing on my to do list mattered at that moment.

Every day of our lives brings a group of things marked URGENT. They are the things that have the potential to turn our busyness into barrenness and could bring spiritual and emotional burnout. Therefore, it is necessary for us to be able to distinguish between the URGENT and the IMPORTANT. The world system says, "Look out for Number One; live for yourself." But Jesus says we're not to take our cues from the world, but from Him.

Respond

Are you a servant-minded person? Is serving others a habitual part of your life? True servanthood is not just a habit. It must come from the heart first. If you don't desire to serve others in some area, chances are you don't understand the servanthood of Jesus. He left the glory of heaven to become a servant, and you are reaping the benefits of His servanthood. Lay aside your urgent list for a moment and evaluate what you are doing as a servant. Jesus called us to servanthood so that through losing our lives to Him and His interests, we would find enjoyment and meaning for our lives.

Remember

On your spiritual to do list marked IMPORTANT, you'll always find servanthood.

Security for the Future?

Read

"And if I go and prepare a place for you, I will come back and take you to be with me that you also may be where I am." — John 14:3.

Reflect

All of us need security. We look for it through finances, relationships, popularity, and gaining power. The world system tells us that anyone of those elements can give us security. Yet countless people seek fame, fortune, power, and pleasure only to come up empty, drowning in a sea of insecurity.

The future is a scary thing if you don't have security. What were the disciples to think about their future when Jesus said He was leaving? Obviously their hearts sank. But Jesus gave them a promise and a hope for the future. He said, "I will come back and get you so you can be with Me." You have the same promise. When it seems your situation is hopeless, remember, He is coming back! It's not over.

Because we have the certainty of His death and resurrection, our hope is not in vain. His return is sure. Why? Because truth characterized Jesus' life on earth. Everything He said would happen did happen. Therefore, based on Jesus' track record, our hope is secure. He will return and take us to be with Him. Whether we go to heaven through the valley of the shadow of death or are still alive when He returns, our future is sure because it is based on His Word.

Respond

Heaven is a place of love and joy. It is the place of no sorrow, death, pain, crying, or night. It is the place where there is no need for the sun, for the glory of God illuminates its expanse. It is the dwelling place of God, and your dwelling place if you've committed your life to Him through Jesus Christ. What do you want to be doing when He comes? Take a moment or two to thank Jesus for the promise of His return. Thank Him for the security you have in His love and ask Him to help you serve Him faithfully until the day of His return.

Remember

He's coming back! Guaranteed!

Developing Good Eyesight

Read

"The eye is the lamp of the body. If your eyes are good, your whole body will be full of light." — Matthew 6:22.

Reflect

Several years ago I went to a Royals game with some friends and saw George Brett go six for six. Six times up to bat, six hits — incredible! You can be sure that night he was focused on the ball and seeing it really well. If a baseball player is going to get a hit, he must watch the ball. If he becomes distracted while he is up to bat, he will never get a hit. Good eyesight is focused eyesight.

As Christians, our eyesight must be focused on the things of God. There is an old saying, "Aim at nothing and you'll hit it every time." But the opposite is also true. If you aim at something and focus your energies there, you may be surprised at all you can accomplish.

Focused spiritual eyesight must be developed, because there are so many distractions in the world system to lure us away from the things of God. In order to develop a focused spiritual eyesight we must discipline ourselves to say no to the temptations of the world and yes to the Word of God and the Holy Spirit.

Respond

Aiming to be a godly person may seem like aiming at an invisible target, but Jesus came to earth to make godliness visible. To become more like Jesus, you must spend time with Him, in His Word. You must give Him your undivided attention and your unquestioned obedience all day long. Sometimes you may not feel like obeying Him, but stay focused and obey anyway. Read Proverbs 4:20-27 and let God fill your spiritual vision with insight into His will for you. Where are you headed today? Focus on God and get corrective spiritual lenses!

Remember

Where the eye of your heart is focused, your mouth and feet quickly follow.

God's Plan Is Good

Read

"For I know the plans I have for you," declares the Lord, "plans to prosper you and not to harm you, plans to give you hope and a future." — Jeremiah 29:11.

Reflect

Does it surprise you that God has a wonderful plan for your life? If it does, then there are three things about God's plan for your life that are very encouraging. First, His plan for you is *eternal.* There has never been a time He has not thought about His plan for you. You have always been on His mind and always will be. Secondly, His plan for you is *continual.* In other words, He thinks about it all the time. You can't name a time He is not thinking about His plan for you. He is consumed with what is best for you, even when you are busy with your own plan and you ignore Him. Finally, God's plan for you is *settled.* He knows what He wants for you. When your plan changes, His doesn't.

The reason you need to follow God's plan instead of your plan is that His plan will always bring peace to your life, regardless of what is going on around you. You will discover that your plan will be difficult to sustain. Because you are going your way and not God's, you are without divine help, and it is very easy to grow discouraged and lose hope for the future. On the other hand, God's plan gives you a hope and a future. When you walk in His plan, the Holy Spirit is right there to give you wisdom and strength. So your hope is sustained, and you are always excited about the future.

Isn't it great to know that when you haven't a clue as to what the future holds, you know the One who holds your future?

Respond

In order to experience God in your life, you cannot ignore His plan for you. He will wait on you until you surrender to His will, so don't struggle with it. Make the adjustment. Turn the corner. Ask Him to help you to follow His plan one step at a time.

Remember

You may not know your future, but you know the One who holds your future.

Get Ready to Be Overjoyed

Read

When she recognized Peter's voice, she was so overjoyed she ran back without opening it and exclaimed, "Peter is at the door!" "You're out of your mind," they told her. When she kept insisting that it was so, they said, "It must be his angel." But Peter kept on knocking, and when they opened the door and saw him, they were astonished. — Acts 12:14-16.

Reflect

Have you ever been so overjoyed with an answer to prayer that you didn't know how to act? Answered prayer is like that. Because you are so sincere in seeking God's will, when the answer comes, all you can do is praise Him in amazement – not amazement that He is capable of answering prayer, but amazement that God *chooses* to participate so powerfully in your life.

There is nothing quite like answered prayer. But the response to the answered prayer we look at today is almost comical. While the church was praying for Peter's release from prison, Peter knocked on the door. When the girl answered the door and recognized Peter's voice, she was so excited she forgot to let him in. Peter was miraculously released from prison, but he couldn't get into a prayer meeting!

When the girl told those in the prayer meeting that Peter was at the door, they didn't believe her. Doesn't that sound a lot like us sometimes? I get encouraged when I read a story like this and see that the early church, with all its power, struggled with unbelief. But God is patient, and when we pray His will, He delivers. In this case He delivered Peter.

Respond

Do you need to be delivered? You may not be in a prison like Peter was, but you may be imprisoned by a habit that is not pleasing to God. You may have been imprisoned by it for years, and you know it's God's will that you stop, but you've tried without success. Pray His will. Ask for His strength and encouragement. If you are sincere, you'll see that when you are tempted, God will show you how to resist.

Remember

Celebrate your answered prayers with others and give God the glory collectively.

DON'T JUST HEAR...DO!

READ

But the man who looks intently into the perfect law that gives freedom, and continues to do this, not forgetting what he has heard, but doing it — he will be blessed in what he does. — JAMES 1:25.

REFLECT

When it took three times to call my son for supper because he was preoccupied with Nintendo, something was wrong. He's a good boy, never has been any trouble, and most people would love to have a child like him. So what was the problem? My delivery was loud enough, the message clear enough, the intent pure enough, so why didn't he come? I mean, I was offering him food! It's good and good for him. It wasn't that he didn't hear, it was that he thought it would be okay to obey later. He was wrong!

The same thing is true for the believer who thinks hearing God's Word is enough. God is not so concerned that our hearing is good as much as He is concerned that our hearing produces obedience. James explained that we are not blessed if we just hear God, but if after we hear, we do. It's sad that sometimes we get so preoccupied with the trivial things of life that we think delayed obedience will be acceptable.

The problem with delayed obedience is that precious time is wasted because we're out of God's will. Moreover, if we don't get into the habit of hearing God's Word and doing it, we will get into the habit of hearing God's Word and not taking it seriously. That is a dangerous place to be! Everyone in the Bible who thought lightly of God and His Word eventually perished unless they repented. But those who loved God and trusted Him with their lives by obeying His Word were greatly blessed.

RESPOND

God loves you and He is never too preoccupied for you. Ask Him to help you be still and listen to Him. Pray that He will forgive you for the times when you have failed to be a doer. Then ask Him to keep you from delayed obedience and give you strength to be obedient immediately.

REMEMBER

Delayed obedience is disobedience – a dangerous place to be in — but obedience brings life and peace.

WORTH LOOKING FOR

READ

"Or suppose a woman has ten silver coins and loses one. Does she not light a lamp, sweep the house and search carefully until she finds it?" — LUKE 15:8.

REFLECT

Every sinner is worth looking for. Every repentant heart is worth rejoicing over. Jesus sent a clear message to us through Luke 15: You matter to God! You matter enough that He left His throne in heaven to come and rescue you from the traps of sin. And not only can He rescue you from the penalty of sin, He will ultimately rescue you from the presence of sin when He calls you to heaven where He is. In the meantime, you and I must be like this woman who searches for what is lost, just as Jesus searched for us.

The woman in this story probably lived in a typical Middle Eastern home that had no windows and only dirt floors. This made the search for her coin very difficult. The coin didn't know it was missing, but the coin meant so much to the woman that she did not rest until she found it.

RESPOND

You will probably meet those today who don't know they are lost. They need Jesus. They might not know it is Him they need, but you know that is the case. Can you turn the light on in their dark lives and sweep away the things that hinder the light from shining on them today? Is there some way they can look at you and see that you have been found but they are still lost? Jesus said that if we will lift Him up in our lives, others will be drawn to Him. So, how can you lift Him up before someone who is lost today? Think about that for a minute. Take some time to pray for the one God has put on your heart. Ask Him how to reach that person today.

REMEMBER

Because you are a Big Deal to God, the lost become a Big Deal to you.

Good Friends

Read

"For Demas, having loved this present world, has deserted me." — 2 Timothy 4:10 NASB.

Reflect

Let's call him, Bill. We laughed together, played together, and ministered together. He was the type of friend you could count on. I'd seen him take a stand on things even before I did, and his stand strengthened me. But one day, I saw him fold. He caved into the world system, was duped by the Great Deceiver, and abandoned the faith. What happened? We were no longer a duo. I was left alone.

Friendship is tough because the world system is aggressively working against it. But this should not be a surprise to us. Paul had the same problem, and his friend Demas left the faith at probably the worst time for Paul.

Demas worked by Paul's side through some tough times. He knew the kind of guy Paul was and even stayed with him during his last term in prison. However, at the most inopportune time, Demas left Paul. No, he didn't just leave Paul, he deserted Paul. Worse yet, he deserted Paul because he loved the world system. When the going got tough, Demas said, "I don't need this. I can't take the pressure anymore. I'm going to live it up." Do you see what the world can do to Christian brothers? It can literally make us desert one another.

Respond

What kind of friend are you? When it gets tough to be a friend, do you take the easy way out? Or are you the type of friend who sticks no matter what the pressure? If you are, you're in good company. Jesus is that type of friend to all who follow Him. So praise and thank Him for being your best friend. Next, reflect on times you haven't been the friend you should have been to others and to God. Confess those times to Him. Take time to pray for your friends – even the ones who have hurt you. Pray for six friends and ask God to touch them.

Remember

Good friends are hard to find. Make someone's search easy today.

Pause to Listen to God

Read

"Be still, and know that I am God; I will be exalted among the nations, I will be exalted in the earth." — Psalm 46:10.

Reflect

Today was "one of those days." You know, just when I was about to accomplish something, someone came into my office with "urgent" written all over their face. And this didn't happen just once. It was all day long. What I needed was time alone. Stillness. Quiet. Time to think. I think I now realize, just a little bit, why God put today's verse in the Bible. It's for days like this. He never wants us to get too far away from spending time with Him. When I spend time with Him and gain His perspective, it changes the way I look at all the interruptions that come my way.

Probably you have prayed, "Lord, give me patience and give it to me now!" You feel that way because there is so much "stuff" in your schedule. Some of it is good, some not so good, and some you allow that shouldn't be there at all. Don't you think it's time to slow down, gear down, quiet down, look up, and hear from God? You remember God — the One whose schedule is infinitely busier than yours, yet He has all the time in the world for you. Get to your schedule now, because if you don't, someone else will.

Respond

Don't let what is urgent take you away from what is important today. Make room for some quality time with God. The more you do, the more the irritations in relationships fade away, agitations become smaller, and God appears bigger to you. He wants to talk to you in quiet times when He has your full attention so He can fill your need for patience, self-control, understanding, humility, and a calm attitude. Take some time right now to listen to the thoughts He gives you through His Word.

Remember

If you are too busy to spend time alone with God, you're too busy.

A Reflector Who Helps

Read

As water reflects a face, so a man's heart reflects the man. — Proverbs 27:19.

Reflect

I celebrate every year of marriage to my wonderful wife, Rhonda. What an incredible ride this is! I can't imagine life without her. She is my best friend and my major source of fun. When I gave myself to her, I didn't know all there was to know about me. In fact, I'm still learning. She has helped me understand myself more, and I have done the same for her. She has seen me at my weakest and shown me the depths of her love. She also has celebrated my triumphs and reminded me of how the Lord has blessed us. She has confidence in me when I lack confidence in myself. Her affirmation often keeps me going.

Solomon was right. Man really can't know himself fully without the help of an outside source. Of course, God is the One who defines us most clearly. But there are times when He will bring another person to show us what we are like. Without this human mirror to help us see ourselves, we become victims of our weaknesses or are deceived by our strengths. And through affirmation and approval from those who are close to us, we can become the person we were created to be.

Affirmation is a significant need in all of our lives. When we are affirmed it places value on us and we respond in positive ways. However, when we don't receive affirmation from those closest to us, we can become discouraged and develop a distorted view of our life. That's why God exhorts us again and again to encourage one another with love and truth mixed together.

Respond

Is there any greater affirmation than God sending His Son to die for you? Thank Him and praise Him for this great gift! Then examine your life and praise God for those dear people He has brought into your life to affirm you. Confess to Him the times you needed to affirm someone and didn't do it. Ask Him to help you be an affirming person to all you meet.

Remember

Make the commitment to affirm everyone you rub shoulders with today.

Keeping Clean in a Stained World

Read

"For them I sanctify myself, that they too may be truly sanctified." — John 17:19.

Reflect

One way I know I can get my wife's attention is to start up the washing machine. Washing clothes is just not my gift. (Have you ever heard that one before?) I know nothing about washing clothes. I've demonstrated this over and over again. I have the multicolored clothes to prove it. If the clothes are stained when I wash, no matter how hard I try, they will still be less than clean when I am finished with them.

That is the way it is with sin. The world system is out to stain us, and when it does, there is nothing we can do about it. Sin dirties up our lives in a matter of seconds, but the terrible results can last a lifetime. Here is some of the dirt the world will throw at us: the stain of dishonesty, the stain of rebellion, the stain of sexual promiscuity, and the stain of unfaithfulness. These stains can destroy you. They will dishonor God and take you down in the process.

The wonderful thing about this staining process is that you can be clean. You can be as white as snow! God's grace is a stain remover, and, if you repent and turn to Him, He will purify you. Far more powerful than the heavy-duty detergent my wife uses, Jesus' blood brings forgiveness from sin and cleanses us from all unrighteousness.

Respond

Are you stained by a sin habit? Are you justifying it? Stop. It's slowly destroying you. Maybe you can't see it, but destruction is the very nature of sin. Be honest with yourself and with God. Ask Him to search your heart and reveal to you any unclean part of your life. Why? So you can confess it to Him and receive a cleansing. Turn to Him. He will strengthen you if you will look at your sin, admit it, and quit it.

Remember

No matter how soiled your life is, Jesus is the "stain remover."

Know Him

Read

Moses said to God, "Suppose I go to the Israelites and say to them, 'The God of your fathers has sent me to you,' and they ask me, 'What is his name?' Then what shall I tell them?" God said to Moses, "I AM WHO I AM." — Exodus 3:13-14.

Reflect

I don't know Abraham Lincoln. I have read a lot about him, but I don't know him. Many people feel the same way about God. They've heard of Him, read about Him, and know people who claim to know Him, but they haven't had the experience of knowing Him themselves. God invites all of us to get to know Him. To some it is in a miraculous way, to others it is just a simple invitation in a quiet time of their lives. But God extends to all of us the invitation to know Him intimately.

God personally extended that invitation to Paul on the road to Damascus. Being the "Bible Brain" of his day, Paul knew all *about* God. But He didn't *know* God until He was knocked off his horse by the blinding light of the glory of the Lord. It was then that He saw God like He had never seen Him before. He saw Jesus and instinctively called him Lord. Shortly after, he actually made Jesus his Lord and Savior. His life changed dramatically as a result. (See Acts 9.) God's invitation to us is always a personal one, and when we accept, our lives are never the same.

Respond

Everyone receives an invitation to know God. His invitation might have come to you as you were reading this devotion. Don't let it go. Pursue Him. Let Him become your great I AM by trusting Him with your life. Let God into your life by allowing Him to shape your thoughts and actions. Take some time right now to praise and thank Him for His patience and love. Ask Him to forgive you for the times you have ignored His invitation. And finally, pray that God will help you today to let Him become the Great I AM in your life.

Remember

His invitation to you is always open. RSVP now.

Appreciating Change

Read

Remember, O Lord, your great mercy and love, for they are from of old. — Psalm 25:6.

Reflect

Astronaut Neil Armstrong once had lunch with the famous photographer, Yousuf Karsh and his wife. Armstrong politely questioned the couple about the many different countries they had visited. Mrs. Karsh finally interrupted and said, "But Mr. Armstrong, you've walked on the moon. We want to hear of your travels." The modest astronaut replied, "But that's the only place I've ever been."

Where you've been and what you've learned from where you've been tells a lot about you. There are some places you can't go without being changed, and the moon is probably one of them! Paul was changed on the Damascus road when he met Jesus. Peter was changed in the boat when he saw the power of Jesus. The lame and the blind were changed when Jesus healed them. Jesus can show up in the most surprising places and bring about change in our lives.

The Bible is full of stories about people who experienced significant changes in their lives because of God's intervention. Sometimes it was a change of direction, sometimes it was a change of character, but it was always a change to accomplish God's purpose in their lives. Sometimes the changing process is painful. It is certainly one of the toughest things to face. It goes against our nature to change, but when we allow Jesus to change us, it is always worth it. Only when we change can we grow into the person God desires us to be. And only by growing into the image of Jesus can we accomplish His plan. The bottom line, of course, is that this is the only way we will ever be happy!

Respond

What changes are tugging at your heart today? If you aren't aware of any or haven't thought about it lately, ask God to reveal to you what you need to change. There is never a time when we don't need a little improvement! Then ask Him to help you change and be committed to the future He has for you.

Remember

God is with you to turn the difficulty of change into an adventure.

The Final Authority

Read

Everyone must submit himself to the governing authorities, for there is no authority except that which God has established. The authorities that exist have been established by God. — Romans 13:1.

Reflect

After I got a speeding ticket, I'll never forget telling a state trooper friend of mine how my cruise control must have malfunctioned. He smiled at me and said, "You actually believe that's the first time I've heard that, don't you Tom?" Needless to say, he got a good laugh out of my excuse, but he was not sympathetic. Why? Because on the highway, he is the authority. He enforces the law.

The job of authorities is to give cues as to what is acceptable and what is not. We have a choice as to what or who is going to be our authority in life. Unfortunately, that is a faulty authority. God has established an authority for His followers — His Word. His Word is where we find our answers to life's problems. His Word gives us a godly perspective and principles to navigate us through the storms of life — if we will trust it and follow its instruction. His Word gives us direction on what is acceptable behavior and what is not. His Word even helps us in selecting acceptable associates and companions. By using His Word as our authority, we are protected from many bad decisions that could be based on emotions or lack of facts. His Word is the most reliable authority by which we can govern our lives, yet many of us make excuses for not following it.

Respond

What excuses do you use for not spending time in God's Word? Do you think your excuses are unique? Or would God respond to your excuses by saying, "You actually think I haven't heard that one before?" Is God's Word your final authority in life? Are you taking your cues from the Bible or your own ability to reason? God's Word will not change. It is trustworthy and dependable. Make His Word your boss today.

Remember

God's Word is to be the final authority in your life.

God Is Working — Join Him

Read

"As long as it is day, we must do the work of him who sent me. Night is coming, when no one can work." — JOHN 9:4.

Reflect

God is always at work around you. It is up to you to join Him in His work. If you see God working, don't pass by — join Him. You will be amazed at the things He will accomplish in and around you. The challenge comes when you say, "Well, I don't know if God wants me to get involved here or not. I had better pray about it." Please understand my heart as I say these words: Some things you don't need to stop and pray about. Rather, pray as you obey! If you already know these things are God's will, you just need to do them. I've seen many people hesitate and just be a spectator of what God was doing, never getting in on what He was trying to accomplish. Sadly, many of those people became critics of what God did.

So how can you recognize when God is working? There are some consistent criteria that follow His work. First, when God works, whatever He does will be consistent with Scripture. He will not work outside or contradict His Word. (See 2 Timothy 3:16-17.) Secondly, He will work in a way that opposes the flesh. He does not wish for any person to get credit for what only He can do. (See 1 Corinthians 1:26-30.) Thirdly, the work that God does requires faith from us. (See Hebrews 11:6.) And there are other criteria, such as when God works He draws people to Him, He causes people to seek after Him, He reveals spiritual truth, and He convicts the sinful.

Respond

Using the criteria mentioned above, can you see where God is working around you and how He is working in you? Today, be more sensitive to where He is working and then have the courage to join Him!

Remember

God is at work all around you. Join His team and experience the true joy of life.

Motivated by Love

Read

We love because he first loved us. — 1 John 4:19.

Reflect

In the Old Testament, the Law was "before the eyes" of God's people, but they still sinned. Today the laws of the land are before our eyes, and we still break them. If we have trouble obeying the rules of life, it could be that our eyes are focused on the wrong thing.

The best motivation for obeying God is not His laws but His love. For example, when Peter denied Jesus by saying he didn't know Him, he didn't feel bad because he broke a law. He felt bad because he hurt the One he loved and the One who loved him. Peter loved Jesus because he knew how much Jesus loved him. He knew in all his weaknesses and sin that Jesus really loved him and cared about him. The same is true for you.

The psalmist put it this way, "For your love is ever before me, and I walk continually in your truth" (Psalm 26:3). When your eyes are on God and His love, you are not motivated to do evil, but to do good and walk in truth.

Now answer this question: Are you practicing sin? If so, then God's love is probably not "ever before you" and you are not being motivated by His love. Look to the One who loves you most and stop sinning. Be motivated by His love.

Respond

Praise and thank God for His great love for you — His unconditional love. Then confess those times you have practiced sin. List them on a piece of paper and repent from them. Now pray for those you know who are trapped by sin. Ask God to speak to them. Let His love motivate your prayers for them today.

Remember

There is no power greater than love. Let His love work in your life today.

Do It His Way

Read

Jesus said to them, "My Father is always at his work to this very day, and I, too, am working." — JOHN 5:17.

Reflect

A few years ago I was in the backyard pushing the mower around, trying to make our lawn look nice. My daughter, Mackenzie, who was about five at the time, wanted to help me. Trying not to be negative, and having little time on my hands, I agreed to let her walk in front of me with her hands on the push bar. She pushed with all of her might but I, of course, had to slow down to make room for her between the mower and me. The work went more slowly, but it was okay because she felt like she was helping. Then Mackenzie began to tell me the manner in which I should mow the lawn. At that point I stopped pushing, and guess what, the work stopped. After struggling for a while, she looked back at me and said, "What are you doing?" I said, "I'm waiting for you to do it my way."

Just then it occurred to me how God works with me. There are those times when I think I know a better way to accomplish His work. Only when things come to a screeching halt and I am totally exasperated do I realize that I have left God's will and gotten in a mess. That's when I learn God knows best and that I would not be able to do anything if it wasn't for Him.

God desires for us to do things His way because He knows the end from the beginning. If we insist on going our way, He will let us go our way and struggle, but He will not join us. He wants us to join Him. And when we do, we experience more prosperity and joy than we could have ever experienced on our own.

Respond

What a privilege it is for us to be used of God! Thank Him and praise Him for using you today. Confess to Him the times you have ignored His work or tried to change it out of your own desires. Pray that God show you His plan for you today and then join Him!

Remember

Do things God's way today, and you are sure to be blessed.

Spiritual Guidance

Read

"But when he, the Spirit of truth, comes, he will guide you into all truth. He will not speak on his own; he will speak only what he hears, and he will tell you what is yet to come. He will bring glory to me by taking from what is mine and making it known to you." — John 16:13-14.

Reflect

God wants to do three things in your life: First, He wants to guard you. He is the God of mercy and grace, and He desires to protect you from harm. Secondly, He wants to guide you. He wants to give you direction to accomplish His will. Finally, God wants to govern you. He wants to have control of your life. He can best use you to accomplish His purposes when He has control of your life.

These verses tell how God guides us. He guides us through His Spirit. God has given all believers the gift of His Spirit to reside in us and guide us in His will. And notice the direction in which He guides us — "into all truth." With so much falsehood in the world today, God has given the believer a built-in counselor of truth. The Spirit speaks to our conscience and guides us to truth.

One important factor to remember in regard to God's guidance in our lives is that the Spirit always guides us according to God's Word. If you feel drawn in a direction that is contrary to Scripture, you are not being led by the Spirit. He will never guide us in a contradictory direction from God's Word — the Bible.

Respond

Now would be a good time for you to evaluate the three areas in which God wants to influence your life. Are you allowing His Spirit to guard, guide, and govern your life this week? Have you thought what God can do through you if He were to do these three things in your life? Wherever you are right now, at work or home, close the door, pull the shade, and take a five-minute retreat with the Lord to commit this day to Him.

Remember

Let God guard, guide, and govern your life today.

YOKED WITH JESUS

READ

"Take my yoke upon you and learn from me, for I am gently and humble in heart, and you will find rest for your souls." — MATTHEW 11:29.

REFLECT

Jesus invites us to "learn from" Him, and as an example He paints a beautiful picture of an ox being trained. In those days a farmer trained a young ox by harnessing it next to an older, experienced ox. He yoked them together in such a way that the older ox carried most of the load, because he already knew how to get the work done. The younger ox learned how to plow the field by pulling with the older ox. In this illustration, Jesus was saying, "Hook up with Me, because I've lived this thing you call life, and I know how to do it right."

Doesn't it make sense that the Giver of life would know how to live life? So it makes just as much sense to want to hook up with Him. But how do you hook up with Jesus? Through obedience to His Word — not only listening to His Word, but by putting it into practice in our lives, day in and day out. The concept of the "yoke" is obedience and companionship. Jesus wants to lead us through life as our Lord and friend. As you get to know Him, you will find His gentle commands aren't burdensome at all, but rather a blessing.

RESPOND

It is only through hooking up with Jesus in our daily lives that we get to know Him. He knows how to live this life to the fullest. But have you fully given your life to Him? Have you taken His yoke upon you? Take some time right now to thank and praise God for loving you and wanting relationship with you. Ask Him to forgive you for the times when you've tried to plow His fields independently. Pray for others you know who need to feel the burdenless touch of His yoke. Hook up with Jesus today!

REMEMBER

When you are yoked with Jesus, you see the world and your life very differently.

Wilderness Time

Read

At daybreak Jesus went out to a solitary place. — Luke 4:42.

Reflect

"It is not in the rush and the hurry of activity that a person gains the respect of those around him; it is what he does when he is all alone."

— Chuck Swindoll

Great men and women of God seem always to have significant periods of aloneness with God before He uses them to accomplish great things. David was alone with God as a shepherd years before he fought Goliath. Jesus was alone in the desert wilderness for forty days before He began His public ministry. He also spent many mornings alone with His heavenly Father in prayer, preparing for the events that He would face that day. After his conversion, Paul was alone in Arabia for many years before setting out to become the greatest missionary of the Gospel. The message to us is that there is no substitute for spending extended periods of time alone with God.

If you are too busy to have a time alone with God everyday, you're too busy. It is during that time that you build your relationship with Him and He speaks to you about your life. If you don't spend time with Him, you become vulnerable to the enemy and an easy target for the world system.

Respond

Are you going through a wilderness time? The challenge for us in this hectic world made up of quotas and deadlines is to be still and listen for God to speak to us. So maybe God has put you in a place where you must stop and listen for awhile. Take a few moments right now to praise and thank Him for the plan He has for your life. Confess to Him the times when you went your own way without consulting Him. Pray that His dream will become your dream.

Remember

The wilderness is a great place to hear from God and be refreshed and empowered.

What If I Don't Forgive?

Read

"But if you do not forgive men their sins, your Father will not forgive your sins." — Matthew 6:15.

Reflect

Several years ago in northwestern Missouri, two brothers who owned a store were partners in every sense of the word — until the day one of the brothers left a dollar on the counter. He turned around, and when he turned back, the dollar was gone. He asked his brother if he had picked it up, but the other brother denied it. An argument ensued, followed by more accusations and denials. This led to other suspicions. They got the townspeople to take sides, and eventually the two brothers broke the partnership. They put a line down the middle of the store and competed for business. Some twenty years later, a big car pulled up in front of the store and a wealthy man got out. He walked into the store and asked to speak to both brothers. Unaware of what had happened to the brothers' partnership, the man confessed to stealing the dollar as a little boy. What a price to pay for an unforgiving attitude!

Forgiveness is not an option in the Christian curriculum. In our verse today, Jesus did not say that we earn His forgiveness by forgiving others. He said that if we refuse to forgive, He cannot forgive us and we forfeit fellowship with Him. This means that our prayers are affected, since He will not hear our prayers if we hold unforgiveness in our hearts. (See Psalm 66:18.) Broken fellowship separates us and cripples our effectiveness as Christians. Therefore, forgiving others is imperative.

Respond

God demonstrated His love to us by sending Jesus to die for our sins. His forgiveness is our most precious gift. Are you imitating God and forgiving those who hurt and offend you? Ask Him to forgive you for the times you have been stubborn about forgiving someone, and determine to have a more forgiving attitude today.

Remember

Decide ahead of time to walk in forgiveness, and you will walk with God.

Loving the Law of the Lord

Read

In the future, when your son asks you, "What is the meaning of the stipulations, decrees and laws the Lord our God has commanded you?" tell him: "We were slaves of Pharaoh in Egypt, but the Lord brought us out with a mighty hand." — Deuteronomy 6:20-21.

Reflect

Rules seem to have a bad rap in our culture. We complain they are too binding, too restrictive, and a downright pain. We bend them, stretch them, and break them. We quote little sayings like, "Rules were made to be broken." Why? Because we have the wrong idea about rules, especially God's rules — more popularly known as "His commands."

When God gave Moses the Ten Commandments, he knew that generations would come along who didn't understand their purpose. So when the little ones started asking their parents what these rules were all about, the first thing they were to tell their children was how God rescued His people from slavery in Egypt. The first thing they were told was how much God loved His people.

God's commands were born out of His love. He loves us and doesn't want us to mess up our lives, so He gave us the Ten Commandments to follow. If we follow them, we will not only show our love for Him, but His commands will protect us from harm and bring us success.

The Bible says that God's law is written on every person's heart. (See Romans 2:15.) Therefore, after we are saved and become His child, how much more will we desire to obey His Word?

Respond

Do you see His love and provision in His Word, or do you see restrictions and limitations? A heart filled with love for God will see freedom in God's law, but a heart filled with selfishness will see bondage. God gave you His commands so you might live a fulfilled life and pass it on to your children. He did not give them to hold you back, but to bless you. So ask yourself: Do I love His commands, or do I resent them?

Remember

The key to obeying the law is to love God more than your selfish, carnal desires.

WORSHIP

READ

O Lord, our Lord, how majestic is your name in all the earth! — PSALM 8:1.

REFLECT

It's funny, but the times I fail to worship God are usually after I've just finished writing about worship, talking about it, or reading about it. I've done everything except worship! When I finally realize my shortcoming, I immediately repent and begin to praise and worship Him.

In today's verse we see how the psalmist called on the name of the Lord. When we call someone's name, we are seeking that person's presence and attention. When we worship, we seek the presence and attention of our heavenly Father. We approach Him by giving praise for who He is and thanksgiving for what He does. As we worship Him, we feel His presence and know we are the apple of His eye.

As you grow in knowing God through the experiences of your life, a natural outflow of those experiences is a willingness and a desire to worship Him — not just publicly, but privately as well. Essentially, worship is getting to know God better and giving honor and adoration to Him. This is expressed through many avenues: singing, calling on the name of the Lord, giving to the Lord, sharing His love, and studying His Word. The Bible records how people worshipped publicly and privately. Jesus is recorded to have spent hours in private time alone with God, worshipping Him and seeking His face.

RESPOND

Why don't you take a few moments right now and worship God? Spend some time just praising Him for who He is — your refuge and strength, a present help in time of trouble, and great deliverer. Then thank Him for the times He has been all of those things to you. If you need Him to be any of those things to you right now, call on His name and seek His presence. As you worship, you will feel His presence and know that you have His attention.

REMEMBER

Worship is eternal, so get used to it!

Meet the Challenge of Your Dreams

Read

But when Sanballat the Horonite, Tobiah the Ammonite official and Geshem the Arab heard about it, they mocked and ridiculed us. — Nehemiah 2:19.

Reflect

The Sanballats of today are those who say, "We kind of like things the way they are right now. Why should we change? God has taken care of us so far without making any changes, so why start now? Let's just maintain." If you have ever caught yourself thinking like that, change your mind now, because you are in danger of losing God's hand on your life. Remember, he is looking for those who want to move with Him and accomplish His dreams. If you get sidetracked by the opposition, you ignore God.

If you've received a word from God and you have prayed and planned, you will be opposed. "You're out of your mind." "You'll never be able to do it." "You don't really believe that you can make this happen!" Words of discouragement. They seem to follow those who are progressive, so you are in good company. They followed Moses. They followed David. They followed Jesus. They followed Paul.

Those who mock usually have no vision and are living advertisements for the status quo, but God moves in spite of them. So when you are tempted to believe them, don't. Focus on the vision God has given you. One of the secrets to Nehemiah's success was his focus. Yes, he heard the opposition, but he kept working on the wall with a determination that could not be swayed.

Respond

First of all, what wall has God called you to build? If you don't know, ask Him right now. If you already know and have experienced ridicule and teasing over it, recommit your life to God and reestablish your determination to do what He's called you to do. Let Him help you focus on His dream for your life.

Remember

If you don't give Satan the time of day, he cannot hinder your momentum.

At Home With God's Word

Read

Let the word of Christ richly dwell within you. — Colossians 3:16 NASB.

Reflect

If I came to your house and knocked on the door, you would probably welcome me by saying something like, "Come in. Make yourself at home." But if I came in and started to move your furniture around to my liking, you probably would tell me to sit down and be quiet!

Many times that's just the way we treat God's Word. We invite Jesus into our lives and tell Him to make Himself at home. But when He starts rearranging our standards and priorities, we put Him in the Sunday corner of our lives and say, "Stay there. I'll call You when I need You."

To let the Word of Christ dwell richly in you is to allow your life to be transformed by the Word. To dwell means "to feel at home," and God's Word feels at home in your life when you are transformed by it. However, many people today cannot honestly say the Word of God dwells richly in them because they don't make reading it, studying it, memorizing it, or applying it a priority in their lives.

Respond

How much time during a day do you allow God to speak to you through His Word? He can speak to you in many ways, but when you know His Word, you can more easily interpret if He is speaking to you through others or through the Holy Spirit. If you want to be transformed in your thoughts and behavior today, take some time to memorize a verse or two of Scripture and look for ways to apply it. God's Word was not given just so we might know Him, but so we might become more like Him by acting upon it. It takes time and effort to develop a habit of practicing His Word, but it is well worth it.

Remember

Let God's Word be the interior decorator and arrange the furniture in your life.

CHOOSE TO LOVE

READ

"Love the Lord your God will all your heart and with all your soul and with all your mind and with all your strength." — MARK 12:30.

REFLECT

For years my wife has prayed this scripture for me. She figured if I loved the Lord with all my heart, soul, mind, and strength, I'd be a pretty good husband. Pretty good plan, isn't it?

Jesus called this the greatest of all the commandments, because if you can get a handle on this one and let it dominate your attitude and actions, then the other commandments are much easier. When you love God with all that is within you (your mind, will, and emotions), you just don't have a desire to lie, steal, or kill. If a temptation comes, your love for God will override it and defeat it. So you see, He made it easy for you.

This type of love-living is strange to the world. The media equates love with sex. It also portrays love as admiration. But these by-products of love are not love. Love is a decision and commitment entered into by the person who chooses to love. God chose to love you. He looked down and saw you with all your faults and said, "I choose to love." There is nothing you can do that will stop that choice. When you get a revelation of this basic truth, everything else in your Christian life falls into place.

RESPOND

The question is: Do you love God? Have you chosen to love Him or have you chosen to take advantage of His love? Do you continue your sinful habits and count on Him to love you and forgive you even though you willingly disobey Him? If you do, you are taking advantage of His love. But if you are following His desires, you have been changed by His love. And there is no other love relationship like that. Take some time now to let the Holy Spirit show you God's love and how you can return His love today.

REMEMBER

God chose to love you, so choose to love Him in thought, word, and deed today.

Deep Interests, Deep Friendships

Read

"You are My friends, if you do what I command you." —John 15:14 NASB.

Reflect

Some of my favorite people are St. Louis Cardinals' fans. We can talk for hours about the Cardinals and accomplish nothing, but we'll enjoy every minute of it. Other favorite groups of mine include Kansas City Chiefs' fans and Mizzou fans. Whenever we get together, we'll be busy for a while because we have some serious things to talk about!

It is obvious that you grow closer to the people with whom you share the most interests. I can grow somewhat close to some people on a shallow level, because I share shallow interests with them, such as sports. (Although, to some it's not too shallow!) However, I will grow extremely close to those with whom I share deep interests, such as love for God and dedication to His purposes. That's what real friendships are made of — deep common commitments.

Then there is our friendship with Jesus Himself. Too many of us just share shallow interests with Him. We love, but not to the degree we know He wants us to. We give to the point that it relieves our guilt, but not to the point that He is pleased. We need to draw closer to Him and allow His interests to become ours. Then our friendship with the most important person in our life will grow very deep.

Respond

Ask yourself if you have a shallow or a deep friendship with Jesus. Are your greatest concerns His greatest concerns? Is your heart knitted together with His in things that need to be accomplished in your life? There is nothing He would like better than to be your close friend. He wants you to share His deepest interests with you. And when you do, you'll find a friend much better than a Cardinals' fan! Did I say that?!

Remember

Jesus wants to share His interests with you.

God Always Has a Plan

Read

Then Joshua son of Nun secretly sent two spies from Shittim. "Go, look over the land," he said, "especially Jericho." — Joshua 2:1.

Reflect

My son is a planner. He's fourteen and works with the DayTimer planner system. I should have known this was coming because when he was only three and his mom and I would tuck him into bed, before we would leave his room he would ask, "what are we having for breakfast?" We would answer that question and then he would ask, "then what are we going to do?" We would fill him in on some of the plans for the following day, and then he would ask, "What are we going to do after that?" Finally we would say, "Go to sleep Zac." He would usually reply, "I just need to know." Knowing the plan made him feel comfortable. Truthfully, knowing the plan makes all of us feel a little more secure. In fact, God expects us to plan.

Joshua needed a plan when he faced one of the biggest challenges of his life. He was to lead millions of people into a place they had never been before, and if need be, fight to take the land. So he picked two trusted men to spy out the land. Then, when he had the facts, He would devise a plan. In the end, the Captain of the Host showed up and gave him God's plan. Then Joshua had both the facts and God's view.

Respond

Does that last paragraph describe you? When you face a challenge, do you seek all the facts, then pray and ask God for His plan? Take some time to praise and thank God for His plan for you, and thank Him for His plan for you *today.* Ask Him to forgive the times you have ignored Him and made your own plan. Pray for those you know who need God to help them through the challenges they may be facing. Finally, ask God to use you to carry out His plan today.

Remember

God has placed you where you are, at this time, to accomplish His plan through you.

Ocean of Love

Read

"For God so loved the world that he gave his one and only Son, that whoever believes in him shall not perish but have eternal life." — JOHN 3:16.

Reflect

Have you ever had the chance to sit on a beach and watch the activities around you? Several years ago, I wrote these words as I sat on a beach in San Diego.

> "The sights and sounds I am experiencing right now include crashing waves, endless water, and children playing. Children playing? How ironic. In one setting to see the Pacific Ocean, one of God's most massive creations, and children, one of His most fragile creations, side by side."

That reminds me of the story of the lady who felt a little seasick as she stood on the edge of the ship. One of the officers came up to her and asked, "Ma'am, are you okay?" She replied as she looked at all the water, "It's so big!" the officer then said, "Yes, and that is just the top of it."

God's love is just like that ocean. It reaches to depths that we will never fully know, yet is shallow enough for children to enjoy. It is more magnificent than our finite minds can comprehend, yet it is for us — our eternal salvation, healing, and hope.

Respond

How deep have you gone into the ocean of God's love? Have you been able to tread in the depths of His love to the point that your devotion to Him is unmatched by any other thing in your life? Do you enjoy swimming in the depths of His love, or would you rather play near the shore and wade in the elementary level of the Christian life? How would you rate your spiritual maturity? Are you a baby, a child, an adolescent, or an adult? Pray today that God will increase your maturity through devotion to Him. Then dive out into the depths of His love. Exercise your faith!

Remember

God's love for you is inexhaustible.

Where Is the Church?

Read

Now you are the body of Christ, and each one of you is a part of it. — 1 Corinthians 12:27.

Respond

I will never forget when my daughter came home from school and told us this wonderful story. During recess she had sat with a friend of hers underneath a tree on the playground and talked with her about becoming a Christian. I can't tell you how thrilled Rhonda and I were to hear her tell how she lead that little girl in a prayer of commitment to Jesus. The work of Almighty God's church took place on a playground!

Along with feelings of pride, I had thoughts like, "This is what the church is all about." Stop and think about it. Generally speaking, it's a very natural process for an eight-year-old to reach another eight-year-old. It's very natural for a teenager to reach another teenager. And it is very natural for adults to reach other adults. When the church is working properly, everyone has a part to play.

The trouble is, we all have a lot of things going on each day. We don't even have one recess planned! We have deadlines to meet, proposals to present, meetings to attend or even direct. But if we stop for a second, we might be able to reach out and make a difference for eternity in someone's life — right in the midst of our busy lives.

Respond

Thank God for bringing someone into your life who cared enough to share the love of Jesus with you. Pray that God will guide your thoughts today as you rub shoulders with those around you, that you will be sensitive to their need for Jesus. And the next time you drive by a playground and see a couple of kids sitting under a tree with their heads bowed, remember, there might be some church work going on there!

Remember

God will continually give you doors of opportunity to reach the lost if you will let Him use you.

Weak Spots

Read
"If you love Me, you will obey what I command." — John 14:15.

Reflect
Popcorn is my weakness. I only eat it until it's all gone. In fact as I write these words of devotion, there's a full bowl of it within reaching distance. The truth is that we all have weak spots. We would like to say that we always love the Lord and keep His commandments. But as soon as we do, Satan accuses us of times when our love for God was so weak that we acted as if we had never heard of God, much less have Him as our first love.

But here is some encouraging news. Even though your love for Him has appeared weak from time to time, His love for you has remained strong. When Peter denied Jesus three times, Jesus continued to love him even to the point of making him the spokesman for the early church. When Paul persecuted the church and killed Christians, Jesus still loved him even to the point of making a special appearance to him and redirecting his life.

The real tragedy comes when we are blind to our weak spots. The Pharisees were oblivious to theirs. They thought they loved God, but they demonstrated just the opposite. They couldn't see themselves as God saw them. They only looked at themselves from the perspective of how others viewed them.

Respond
Do you have any weak spots that hinder your obedience? Forget about your position at church and how people at church see you. Does God see a consistent pattern of obedience in your life? Do you spend time with Him to let Him evaluate your life, or is your time with Him an inconsistent or stale routine? Allow God to show you your weak spots. Admit them to Him and repent. Then determine to be what He wants you to be today. (Excuse me, I need to go throw away some popcorn.)

Remember
Weaknesses are merely springboards to new levels of obedience to God.

Camp Out and Prepare

Read

Early in the morning Joshua and all the Israelites...went to the Jordan. —JOSHUA 3:1.

Reflect

I am not a camper. For me roughing it is a Holiday Inn without a Holidome. But in this verse the children of Israel were camped out before they went into the Promised Land. In fact, they camped three days before making a move. Why? They were in a time of preparation. They may have sent spies to check out the land, and they probably prayed a lot. However, they didn't camp out so they could cop out. They were committed to go, but they were going prepared.

I have seen many people act foolishly when they were going through a transition. They made no preparation, sought no counsel, made no definite plans, and in the end, fell on their faces. After they fell, many of them became disillusioned and blamed God; while others just faded away in embarrassment. How sad! That was not God's plan. They had felt God nudge them in a direction, but they didn't wait for Him and endure that crucial time of preparation.

It takes faith to wait on God. Faith is not a step into the darkness; it is a step into the light, knowing God is trustworthy. Faith means you pray, trust, and obey. It doesn't always mean to immediately "go for it." Sometimes it means "wait for it," or better still, "wait for God." It's important to get His wisdom, to not move forward until He gives you peace to do so.

Respond

Have you come to the moment in your life when God is waiting for you to make some plans based on His guidance? Don't rush into action without His definite direction. Wait for Him to give you the go-ahead sign, and in the meantime, prepare yourself. It may be you need to pray more, or maybe you need more education. Get godly counsel and listen to it. But most of all, seek God with all your heart and let Him guide you.

Remember

God's plan is always awesome, which is why you need Him to prepare you.

CHANGED BY LOVE

READ

I want to know Christ and the power of his resurrection and the fellowship of sharing in his sufferings, becoming like him in his death, and so, somehow, to attain to the resurrection from the dead. — PHILIPPIANS 3:10-11.

REFLECT

My wife, Rhonda, has changed and continues to change my life. She has a transforming power over me. She took the raw materials of this goofy farm boy and turned me into a more refined goofy farm boy. Some of the little things I used to do I no longer do because she has shown me a better way. But these changes only come about as I allow myself to get close to her. In fact, most of the time I don't even realize I'm changing. All I know is that I enjoy being with her, and as the years go by, I like myself more.

Getting to know Jesus and trusting His transforming power is a similar experience — but far more powerful. When you allow yourself to get close to Him, He'll change you from the inside out, healing the roots of things that have hurt you and hindered you all your life. He will take the influence of the past away by giving you a better way — the way of His love. As the years go by, you will know what it is to love yourself — not selfishly — but as a reflection of His love.

And Jesus Christ's transforming power is continual. The closer you get to Him, the more you'll change to become more like Him. However, I should warn you that the opposite is also true: the more you neglect Him and ignore His will, the less you will change and the less you will like yourself.

RESPOND

Take a moment or two now to get close to Jesus. Thank and praise God for His transforming power in your life. Ask Him to forgive you for the times you have failed to stay close, and repent of any sin you've been practicing. Allow Him to cleanse you so your fellowship with Him can be restored. Now don't lose that closeness throughout your day!

REMEMBER

When you get close to Jesus, He will change you into the person you want to be.

Your Place in the Church

Read

Now to each one the manifestation of the Spirit is given for the common good. — 1 Corinthians 12:7.

Reflect

What if you got up this morning and looked in the mirror only to see your big toe hanging out of your eye socket? How's that for an eye-opener? Ugh! Your whole day is messed up now. Not even the darkest sunglasses will hide this freakish thing. People will say to you, "There's something different about you today." Okay, had enough? Me too.

How absurd to consider a toe hanging out your eye socket. Yet in the body of Christ it sometimes happens. Those who serve well as an eye in the body of Christ can see hurting people and have an instinct to know what to do. But when they don't take that responsibility, somebody else often does — someone who is not an eye and is really a big toe. So the big toe is not giving balance to a small group or providing energy to go door-to-door sharing the faith because he is distracted into acting as an eye.

God gave all of us gifts to serve Him in a way that would be productive and accomplish His purposes. When we refuse to use those gifts, the body becomes a freak and very unattractive to those who observe us. It is so important that each one of us find out what our place in the Church is and then fulfill it.

Respond

So today's question is: Are you serving God through the local church with the gifts He has given you? If not, why? Is it because you don't know what they are? Well, what is it that you like to do and what can you do? Make a list of those things and then ask yourself, how can I do this? Be creative and start with what you have right now. It may be God will develop a whole new ministry of the church through you!

Remember

God made you as a unique individual to accomplish special things.

The Map to Life

Read

All Scripture is God-breathed and is useful for teaching, rebuking, correcting and training in righteousness, so that the man of God may be thoroughly equipped for every good work. — 2 Timothy 3:16-17.

Reflect

Do you like to use a map when you travel, or are you the kind of person who just likes to get the general instructions to the destination and then head in that direction? Some people like to have a map with specific instructions and others have the "just circle until you find it" philosophy. I'm afraid I'm guilty of the latter philosophy. Maybe I'm lazy, maybe I'm in a hurry, maybe I want to take the scenic view, or maybe I'm living in the pseudo-macho world that thinks, "I don't need no stinking directions." Whatever it may be, it causes great frustration to my family members when I go on a directionless quest!

Tragically there are many believers who live their Christian life without using the map God has provided, the Bible. Maybe they're lazy, or maybe they are too busy. Maybe they've been distracted by the scenic view of this world system. Or even worse, maybe they are believing a pseudo truth that says, "If you live fast enough or work hard enough you don't need no stinking directions to be successful and fulfilled."

Our map, the Bible, comes from the very heart of God. If you want to know what He thinks, you will find it in His Word. It will tell you what does and does not please Him. And the map accomplishes four essential things in our lives: gives general guidance, locates and eliminates sin, trains us to think like God, helps us to discern the traps of Satan.

Respond

What role is the Bible playing in your life today? Have you been too lazy, too busy or too distracted by the world system to gain God's insight into your life? Be smart. Stop at the first filling station and get directions!

Remember

The direction you take today will determine your destination tomorrow.

Sharing the Gold

Read

I press on to take hold of that for which Christ Jesus took hold of me. — Philippians 3:12.

Reflect

John Marshall was one of the luckiest men in the world in January 1848, not to mention one of the richest. He discovered gold on John Sutter's land in northern California and tipped off what now is known as "The Gold Rush of 1849." Word spread and prospectors came from all over the world with a dream to "get rich."

The tragic part of this story is that John Sutter's land was overrun and destroyed by gold seekers. His cattle were stolen and he was driven into bankruptcy. John Marshall later died a penniless alcoholic. Although these prospectors had access to tremendous riches, none of them were able to truly enjoy them. Why? Because instead of having a giving motive, they had a greedy motive.

Many believers are in the same situation. Philippians 4:19 tells us we have access to all the riches in Christ Jesus, but we seldom enjoy it simply because we don't share it with others. The truth is, we have struck gold in having a personal relationship with Jesus. We need to let others know, so they can have the opportunity to strike the gold of knowing Him as well. If we lift Him up in our lives, He will draw people to us, so we can share the gold of God's love and eternal life.

Respond

I'm sure you were elated to find Jesus. Do you remember who shared Him with you and how you came to know Him? Were there people who went out on a limb to share the Gospel with you, who sacrificed their own comfort zone to reach out to you? Now that you have acquired the gold, are you willing to share it? Pray right now for God to bring hungry hearts to you today so that you can share Jesus with them. Be willing to do whatever it takes!

Remember

You have a gold mine in your relationship with God, and it is meant to be shared.

THE FATHER'S VOICE

READ

"My sheep listen to my voice; I know them, and they follow Me." — JOHN 10:27.

REFLECT

When I was a boy playing baseball, I could block out all the crowd noise except for one voice — my father's. It seemed as though his voice, along with his advice, always carried more weight than any other's. In my mind today I can still hear his voice. "THINK," he would say whenever I was pitching and in a jam. Step by step I would go over the instructions he had given me in private. When I put into action what he had told me, it brought great results.

For the believer, the voice of God should stand out above the crowd. God speaks to us through His Word and gives us instruction that He expects us to follow. When we do, we find that it brings good results. He also speaks to us by His Spirit, which is often a still, small voice, not a loud yell. That's why it is so important to be listening to Him throughout our day. Jesus used the example of the sheep hearing the shepherd to illustrate the attentiveness we need to acquire for God's voice.

My dad's voice was so distinct to me because I spent so much time with him. The same will hold true if we spend a good deal of time alone with God in prayer and studying His Word. This is how we come to know His voice in the first place and continue to recognize His voice as we mature.

RESPOND

Is your heavenly Father's voice distinct to you? How much time do you spend with Him? Are you familiar enough with His Word to know what He wants you to do in situations that come your way? Is your prayer time consistent and do you take time to listen? Set your heart to listen to God speak to you regardless of the distractions around you today.

REMEMBER

Your heavenly Father is speaking. Are you listening?

Our Life Transformer

Read

Therefore, if anyone is in Christ, he is a new creation; the old has gone, the new has come! — 2 Corinthians 5:17.

Reflect

I remember when my son was a preschooler and the toy of the day was called a "transformer." If you remember your Saturday morning television, you can recall that these toys received lots of commercial air time. They were robots, but not your normal, run of the mill, everyday robot. With a twist of the arm, a pull of the neck, and a yank on the leg, BOOM, your robot became an off-road vehicle.

Do you remember that catchy jingle for this incredible toy? "Transformer! More than meets the eye. Transformer! Robots in disguise." As I think about that toy and those commercials, I can't help but stand in awe that I have been transformed by Jesus Christ. Because of His work on the cross for you and me, our lives are transformed.

Jesus died that we might live with Him in heaven, but also that we might live for Him now in His strength. He died that we might experience the new creation and all that it means. When we accepted Jesus as Lord and Savior, we experienced a new relationship with Him, but also a new relationship with the world around us. We no longer look at things the way we used to. "The old has gone, the new has come!" *There is more to us than meets the eye.* We have been miraculously rescued and delivered from the destiny of the world system. Conforming to the world is no longer satisfying, because we have been transformed by Jesus Christ.

Respond

Are you looking at things differently since you made your commitment to Jesus Christ? Take some time right now to praise and thank God for His work in your life. Confess to Him the times you have fallen back into your old ways of thinking and allow Him to transform you even more into His image. Finally, make a commitment to follow Him closer today than ever before.

Remember

Knowing Jesus personally means you've been transformed by the Supreme Transformer.

Mourning the Right Things

Read

When I heard these things, I sat down and wept. For some days I mourned and fasted and prayed before the God of heaven. — Nehemiah 1:4.

Reflect

What hurts you bad enough to make you cry? What makes your heart sad to the point of tears? For Nehemiah, it was the news that God's once beautiful city was in ruins. The earthly representation of God's majesty was in disgrace, which made God look like a disgrace, and Nehemiah mourned over the situation. Because Nehemiah's heart was knit to the Lord's, when God hurt, so did Nehemiah. And Nehemiah didn't try to hide his emotion. He felt this news was worth weeping about. In his sadness, he determined to change the situation, and after prayer and fasting he put his faith into action.

Where are the strong men of our day who cry over the evils of this generation? It takes a strong man of great conviction to shed tears over moral decay. Too few are concerned about the subtle slide of morals and integrity that is so common in our day. If it doesn't make us weep, it should make us sick. May God help us to see the world as He does.

Many today cry selfishly over things they can't have. When things don't work out the way they planned, they grieve over their hard times. God is so gracious to have patience with us when we don't share His perspective. But He is also wanting us to take a stand for Him and leave our selfishness behind. He wants us to mourn over things that hurt the kingdom and dishonor Him.

Respond

What are the kinds of things you grieve over? Ask God to give you a heart that grieves over the things that make Him mourn. Then thank and praise God for His consistent love. Isn't it wonderful that He offers us Himself so personally? Pray for His thoughts to dominate your time.

Remember

Sorrow over the things that grieve God produces a drive to please and honor Him.

SAME-OL', SAME-OL'...

READ

"And when you pray, do not keep on babbling like pagans, for they think they will be heard because of their many words." — MATTHEW 6:7.

REFLECT

"Okay, here we go again." I wonder if God ever says that when we start praying to Him. If the truth be known, we are all tempted to fall into the "same-ol" cliches in our praying. Jesus called these "vain repetitions" (Matthew 6:7 KJV). When we fall back into these "same-ol" cliches, I wonder if God yawns and says, "Enough already. Let's hear something from your heart."

I'll never forget teaching a group of teenage boys how to pray conversationally with God. I instructed them that when we pray, we talk just as if Jesus is right here with us, because He is. I also told them that when you have a conversation, you don't usually go around in a circle, you just talk. So, the first boy started, "Lord, I'd really like to punch Julie's lights out. I know that's not right, but if she starts mouthing me again Lord, You better stop me." I was holding my breath, I was laughing so hard. And it didn't stop there, they went on for about an hour. It was the best prayer time they had ever had. Why? Because they were being themselves in prayer. No fancy words, just being real with God. That's what He wants, you know.

RESPOND

Now it's your turn. Set aside everything that would distract you and focus on the One who loves you more than anyone else ever will. Praise Him in your own words and tell Him how great and awesome you think He is. Don't stop yet. Pray for those you know who need some help making Jesus Lord of their lives — in your own words. Doesn't that feel good? Well, it should, because you've just given heaven something to talk about.

REMEMBER

God is real, and He wants you to be real too.

The Rabble

Read

The rabble with them began to crave other food, and again the Israelites started wailing and said, "If only we had meat to eat! We remember the fish we ate in Egypt at no cost — also the cucumbers, melons, leeks, onions and garlic. But now we have lost our appetite; we never see anything but this manna!" — NUMBERS 11:4-6.

Reflect

When you decide to walk a godly life, be prepared for opposition. Moses faced a group of people the Bible describes as "the rabble." The rabble consists of people who oppose godly living. They are generally characterized by complaining and pettiness. The rabble make the Lord angry because they attempt to discourage those who are called to lead. In Numbers they opposed God and His chosen leader, Moses. Moses had even come to the point of asking God to take him home. He was that depressed (v. 10). But God stood with Moses and the vision they mutually shared for the people — God is so good!

When you determine in your heart and mind that you will live a godly life, you become the target of the enemy. But that isn't all. You also become the target of God's special attention. Moses didn't handle every decision the way he should have. But God was patient with Moses because he was consistent in his walk and wanted to see God's vision fulfilled.

Respond

How do you handle discouragement of the rabble when you face it? Moses went straight to God — sometimes complaining, sometimes pleading, but always submissive. Has the enemy targeted you lately for your faithfulness to God's call? If so, why don't you go to God right now, like Moses always did. Take a minute or two to praise and thank Him for His love and protection in your life. Also be sensitive to pray that He will forgive you if you have numbered yourself among the rabble. Ask God to help you follow His leading today — and stick to the vision He has for you!

Remember

When you choose to live a godly life, God's presence will outweigh and overcome any opposition you face.

How is Your Vision?

Read

Where there is no revelation, the people cast off restraint; but blessed is he who keeps the law. — Proverbs 29:18.

Reflect

In 1900 the U.S. Patent Office sent an interesting letter to the President. It went something like this: "Dear Mr. President: It is our suggestion that the U.S. Patent Office be closed, due to the fact that we believe everything that can be invented has been invented." Can you believe that? If that office had been shut down, I probably wouldn't be writing this devotional with the aid of a computer. The person who wrote that letter lacked revelation from God.

The writer of this proverb told us that when we lack revelation, or vision, we are unrestrained. That means without the Lord's revelation, we have no direction, and people with no direction are wanderers in life. They jump from one situation to another without ever making a significant impact on anyone or anything. Visionless people never focus. They swerve all over life's roads, traveling aimlessly, and as a result they never grow — nothing changes for the better.

Mediocrity has become a way of life for many today. If another dares to look beyond the horizon, they could be labeled as fanatical and out of step with the status quo. Yet, people are still awed today by those who have vision. How is yours?

Respond

Just as a football player must get into the huddle to know what the next play is, so we need to huddle up with God in prayer to be sure we're headed in the right direction. Do you need a vision check today? Are you walking in the revelation God has given you for your life, or are you swerving all over the road without a clue? Ask Him to forgive you for the times you have ignored Him when He tried to tell you about your life, and receive some revelation from heaven now.

Remember

Get a vision check from Dr. Jesus and when revelation comes, begin to walk in it.

Strength to Carry On

Read

"Be strong and courageous, and act; do not fear nor be dismayed, for the Lord God, my God, is with you. He will not fail you nor forsake you until all the work for the service of the house of the Lord is finished." — 1 Chronicles 28:20 NASB.

Reflect

When my son won a spelling bee (a trait he did not inherit from his father), I was so proud. But I've always been proud of him, not for what he does, but for who he is. So I seek to help him anyway I can. One of those ways is helping him with his spelling every day. He learns many new words every week because of our teamwork study. And one of the most important elements in our times of study is encouragement. My son needs to hear me say, "I know you can do it."

We all need encouragement, no matter how confident we are in what we are doing. When it was time for young Solomon to take over, his father David handed him the plans of God's temple with the words of encouragement in our devotional today. Solomon was inexperienced and needed all the help he could get. David knew his son would face opposition and that an encouraging word from his father was important. But even more important was how David encouraged Solomon — God "will not fail you nor forsake you."

Respond

Do you need an encouraging word today? We all do. If you don't have an earthly father or mother to encourage you, you have a heavenly Father who has a whole book of encouraging words. Read a chapter of Psalms or Proverbs, then a chapter of the New Testament. Pray and ask God for His understanding and perspective of your situation, and don't allow yourself to be blinded by your own wishes. Then, after your heavenly Father gives you the encouragement you need, ask Him to send you someone else who needs strength to carry on so you can encourage them.

Remember

Encouragement gives you the confidence and strength to do what God has called you to do.

Maturing in the Word

Read

"Like newborn babes, long for the pure milk of the word, that by it you may grow in respect to salvation." — 1 Peter 2:2 NASB.

Reflect

Babies have appetites just like all of us, but sometimes they don't have an appetite for the right food. They often like the wrong things — things that may be tasty, but have no nutritional value. The same is true spiritually. Sometimes we try to substitute other things that have no eternal value in place of God's Word.

When we are born into the family of God, we have an appetite for His Word, which not only gives life and hope, but nourishes us as Christians. But there is a great tragedy in the church today. We often substitute Christian entertainment for the food of God's Word. Christian entertainment is not bad, but it generally won't nourish us or cause us to mature. So a steady diet of God's Word is a must if we are to grow up. His Word contains milk for spiritual babies and meat for those who are more mature.

There is no substitute for Bible study and prayer when it comes to growing spiritually. However, growing spiritually doesn't involve just learning more about the Bible. Growing spiritually means applying what you've learned and putting it into practice in your own life until it becomes a part of your character. If all we do is get understanding, that is no guarantee our life will change.

Respond

How much time do you spend taking in spiritual nourishment from God's Word? If you don't eat a regular, steady diet, you will become spiritually weak and susceptible to sin. Make a habit of coming to His table every day for the pure milk of His Word. After awhile, you'll crave strong meat. Spend some time alone right now with God in the Bible and pray for His understanding. Ask Him to direct you to sources that can enhance your Bible study. Meditate and keep His Word in your heart today, and it will help you to avoid sin. (See Psalm 119:11.)

Remember

You must eat right to stay healthy, naturally and spiritually.

Understanding His Plan

Read

There is a way that seems right to a man, but in the end it leads to death. — Proverbs 14:12.

Reflect

The great architect Christopher Wren designed St. Paul's Cathedral in England. When the city officials saw his plans, they returned them, requiring changes before they would approve the cathedral's construction. When Mr. Wren made the appropriate changes, the officials approved the new plans and gave him the go-ahead. But when Wren built the Cathedral, he trashed his altered plans and went back to his original blueprint. The structure, meant to last centuries, eventually burned down.

Unfortunately, many of us have trashed God's plans for our lives and gone our own way. Like Wren, we think our plans are better and that we know what we want. But that isn't what really counts in life. What really counts is what God wants. God has a blueprint for the church, and we need to seek understanding of it. It is a sin to take God's plans for our lives and trash them because we think our plans are better. The worst thing we can do is ignore God and try to make things happen ourselves. Like Wren's cathedral, things will eventually get hot!

God has a plan for your life that is just as detailed and specific as the plan He gave David for the building of the Temple. When David passed the plan down to his son, Solomon, he said, "The Lord made me understand in writing by His hand upon me, all the details of this pattern" (1 Chronicles 28:19 NASB). How much more will He give you the pattern and plan for your life?

Respond

Do you seek God's plan for your life on a regular basis? Or do you make your own plan and pass it off as the will of God in your life? Take time right now to thank and praise God for the plan He has for your life and make a commitment today to know His will and carry it out.

Remember

If you build your life from God's blueprint, your life will stand as a monument to His glory throughout eternity.

Impossibilities Are God's Specialty

Read

"Here is a boy with five small barley loaves and two small fish, but how far will they go among so many?" — JOHN 6:9.

Reflect

Imagine the scene: Five thousand hungry men on a Tiberian hill, and the only thing they can find to feed them and their families is five barley loaves and two fish. It seemed an impossible situation to the disciples. One of the twelve, Andrew, said the words of our verse today. Now don't get down on Andrew. He was merely reporting the obvious. There was no natural way to satisfy this hungry crowd with what they had. But the thing Andrew didn't stop to realize was *Who* they had.

The feeding of the five thousand was one of the most important miracles of Jesus. It is the only miracle recorded in all four gospels. And it was the only miracle witnessed by multiplied thousands who all benefited from it at the same time. Perhaps the most interesting thing about this miracle is what happened when it was over. Jesus had the disciples pick up the leftovers after everyone had eaten. How much was left over? Twelve full baskets — one for each of his doubting disciples to carry down the mountain.

Sometimes we are a lot like Andrew. We report the obvious natural facts without seeing the obvious supernatural facts: impossibilities are God's specialty. God's plan for our life will always go beyond our natural abilities and strengths. Why? Because He wants us knit together with Him in everything we do, so He makes it impossible to do it without Him.

Respond

I believe God wants to multiply the "small fish" in your life. This could be your talents, your strength, or your finances. He wants you to pray and ask Him to work in your life in a way that is beyond what you see. He is still in the miracle-working business and wants to provide for you so you will know and experience Him more powerfully every day.

Remember

Give whatever you have — no matter how small — to God today. He will do incredible things with it.

Commitment to Vision

Read

Then I heard the voice of the Lord saying, "Whom shall I send? And who will go for us?" And I said, "Here am I. Send me!" He said, "Go and tell this people: Be ever hearing, but never understanding; be ever seeing, but never perceiving..." Then I said, "For how long, O Lord?" And he answered: "Until the cities lie ruined and without inhabitant, until the houses are left deserted and the fields ruined and ravaged." — Isaiah 6:8-9, 11.

Reflect

Isaiah had just experienced a pretty dramatic worship experience when the Lord asked, "Whom shall I send?" Isaiah responded with a willing heart, but like anyone else, he wanted to know what the results from his efforts would be. God let him know that there would be no results, that Israel would lay in ruins even after Isaiah spent his life warning them to turn to God and repent. In essence, God encouraged Isaiah to be more concerned with his faithful obedience than any "ministry results."

When you obey God, He knows you truly love Him. (See John 14:15.) Our greatest joy should be obeying Him. But too often we fall into the trap of getting more excited about results. We forget that God is more interested in our relationship with Him than any results our vision may or may not produce.

Respond

Without God's purpose for you, life is empty. What is your commitment to the vision He has placed in your heart? Have you been frustrated because of a seeming lack of results? Ask Him to forgive you for focusing on results and concentrate on your relationship with Him. Then renew your commitment to obey Him in all things, regardless of results. Have you felt an emptiness in your life, but never identified the problem as a lack of vision? Thank and praise God for His ability to reveal Himself to you and show you what His purpose is for your life.

Remember

When you are totally surrendered to God's will for your life, results are overshadowed by relationship.

IT'S ALL HIS

READ

"But who am I, and who are my people, that we should be able to give as generously as this? Everything comes from you, and we have given you only what comes from your hand." — 1 CHRONICLES 29:14.

REFLECT

My son just loves to spend money. When we try to teach him how to save, he makes excuses to spend. (I wonder where he learned that? Ouch!) In a very noble fashion, he says, "I want to buy you something, Dad." And that's great. But there's just one problem...he has to borrow from me to buy for me. I guess that isn't really a problem. After all, he is trying to show me how much he loves me with what I give him.

The same thing is true in your relationship with God. He gave you everything you have, and you show your gratitude and love to Him when you give it back. David certainly understood what giving was all about. He knew you can never out-give God, because everything you give is God's in the first place. It's all His. So giving to support His plans is a privilege because it reminds us that everything belongs to Him.

In 1 Corinthians 4:7, Paul said, "What do you have that you did not receive?" Good question. The answer? Nothing! Therefore, we can rejoice when we look at God's master plan as an opportunity to take what He has so generously given us and give back to Him.

RESPOND

Take a little time right now to make a list of things that God has given you — things you can see and things you can't. I know this list could be endless, but it will show you on paper how God has blessed you. Now praise and thank Him for those gifts. Ask Him to forgive you for the times you've taken His blessings for granted, and pray to always give in a way that pleases Him.

REMEMBER

You are probably never more like Jesus than when you are giving.

Asking and Missing

Read

"You ask and do not receive, because you ask with wrong motives, so that you may spend it on your pleasures." — James 4:3 NASB.

Reflect

Another translation of this verse says, "You ask and do not receive, because you ask amiss." One little boy who had heard this translation when trying to memorize it once said, "You ask and do not receive, because you ask and miss." He didn't have it worded perfectly, but he couldn't have interpreted it any better.

Our prayers should make an impact on the world, but unfortunately sometimes the world makes more of an impact on our prayers. How? We approach the Lord with our wish list of things the world offers instead of what He wants to see accomplished in the world. Then we justify our requests by saying, "O Lord, if you give me this or that, I could honor you with it." And many times when He blesses us with those things, we don't honor Him with them. The world says, "Get all you can." But God says, "Don't worry about things. As long as your will is surrendered to Mine, I will take care of your needs." (See Matthew 6:33.)

God knows the innermost motives of our requests. If it is something that will bring us glory or something that we will substitute for God later on, we are asking "amiss" for the wrong thing. We need to ask our Father for things that bring glory to Him alone. His purpose and plan is of the utmost importance, and He is constantly searching for those who will pray according to His will.

Respond

If God didn't answer your regularly offered prayer requests, would the work of His kingdom suffer? Would His kingly rule in your life suffer? Check out the motives of every request. It could be that some are impure. God wants to work through you, but He cannot do very much until you really surrender your will to His.

Remember

Test for prayer requests: Will this glorify God? Will it further His kingdom?

An Obedient Heart

Read

...but showing lovingkindness to thousands, to those who love Me and keep My commandments. — Exodus 20:6 NASB.

Reflect

Suppose you told your spouse you loved them every day, but you never did anything to please them. What kind of love is that? It's fake love. It is nothing more than lip service. To say you love someone and then to act coldly and insensitively toward them, even openly dishonoring them, is a lie.

Down through history, the evidence that a person was devoted to someone else was proven through obedience and devotion. In Exodus 20:6, loving God is synonymous with keeping His commandments. Jesus confirmed this truth when He said, "If you love Me, you will keep My commandments" (John 14:15). There is never an assumption in Scripture that comes close to implying love and obedience are not related. They always go together.

God is looking for people who will obey Him, not out of compulsion, but out of pure love. In essence, this verse says that if we hold His commandments in high regard, He will hold us in high regard. God's "lovingkindness to thousands" means that it is endless. You can never exhaust His love for you. No matter what you have done, no matter how immoral your life has been, if you will disavow your allegiance to that type of behavior and pledge your allegiance to God, He will take you in, forgive you, and give you a brand-new life.

Respond

How have you done so far in your spiritual walk this week? Have you proved your love through obedience? The best praise and adoration you can give God is an obedient heart. Make a list of the things in your life in which you have "fudged" on obedience. Then confess those areas and commit yourself to obedience.

Remember

Words that are backed up with action are powerful, life-giving words.

Who Do You Impress?

Read

"Your beauty should not come from outward adornment...Instead, it should be that of your inner self, the unfading beauty of a gentle and quiet spirit, which is of great worth in God's sight." — 1 Peter 3:3-4.

Reflect

She is probably one of the reasons I am a Christian. I knew her best when she was in her 70's and 80's. Whenever I went to her house, I couldn't leave until she prayed with me. In fact, it was not unusual for her to mention someone who wasn't a Christian and say, "Tom, would you pray for them, they haven't made a commitment to Jesus yet." My wife, Rhonda, was deeply impressed by her love for the Lord and her burden for the lost. I remember Rhonda saying, I want to have a burden for unbelievers like she does. Who was it? My grandmother. She influenced many.

Too often in life our priorities get muddled by the influence of the world around us. We tend to put more value on acceptance than integrity. We get distracted by the fads of the day that surround us and major on external beauty instead of internal character. The world says, "It's what is on the outside that counts." But God says the opposite.

Paul said a "gentle and quiet spirit" is what gets God's attention and approval. When we spend too much time trying to impress people whose opinions don't count instead of doing those things that count in the eyes of God, our lives are sadly wasted. However, when we follow the leading of the Holy Spirit and let God's Word rule our hearts and minds, then our outward appearance is like Jesus'. God is pleased and — often to our surprise — our lives are filled with great joy and success.

Respond

Who are you trying to impress today? Are you climbing a ladder that is leading you farther and farther away from God? Are you going as fast as you can with your plans and asking Him to bless you? Or are you taking your cues from God? Stop and take some time to evaluate — it might be time for a change.

Remember

The people who impressed me the most never tried to.

CHANGE

READ

"I tell you the truth, unless you change and become like little children, you will never enter the kingdom of heaven." — MATTHEW 18:3.

REFLECT

Jesus didn't say to become "childish," but to become "like little children." There is a big difference between the two! To become like a child means to take on innocence and dependence — which usually means change. The challenge set before us is to humble ourselves and simply follow God. On the other hand, to become childish means to live independently, always seeking to get our own way.

To change is an act of the will. If a change in behavior is needed in your life, you must find the motivation that impacts your will and promotes change. One motivator is God's Word. Scripture leads us in the right direction, but too often we do not let the power of the written word make the necessary impact. Prayer, when it is sincere, is another method of motivation to bring about change. It has been said that prayer changes *things,* but the truth of the matter is that prayer changes *me.*

When we continually choose not to enact the changes our Bible study and prayer are prompting us to make, we usually end up in a crisis. God does not deal with us about an area of our life for no reason. He knows that we are heading for a fall and is trying to get us to reverse our course before it happens. But when it does happen, He will use it. There is nothing like a crisis to help us change direction! The crisis causes us to let go of our childish behavior and embrace God like a child instead. Thus change occurs.

RESPOND

What do you need to change this week? Do you harbor an attitude that is eating away at you? Is there a sin you just don't want to face? Take some time to become a child — depend on God completely, hear what He has to say, and then obey Him.

REMEMBER

No one likes a childish, selfish brat, but everyone loves a child who is loving and obedient.

Power Over Temptation

Read

The tempter came to him and said, "If you are the Son of God, tell these stones to become bread." — Matthew 4:3.

Reflect

Jesus was tired, hungry, and exhausted. He hadn't eaten in forty days. It was at that weak moment that "the tempter" came to do his thing. Satan always hits us when we are weak and vulnerable. So where was Jesus the weakest? At His power level. Satan said, "If you are who you are, Jesus, show us Your power." Jesus showed him power all right — the power to resist temptation.

Jesus responded to all of Satan's temptations (which were very powerful in themselves) with the greatest power tool we have as believers — the Word of God. His Word overpowers the potency of temptation. Without it, we're easy prey. So we must not only trust God's Word, but we must become so familiar with it that it becomes a vital part of our lives. If we don't, we will be overpowered regularly by temptation and compromise our faith.

When we are overpowered or intimidated by those who represent the world system, the tempter has struck. He has hit us in a vulnerable spot in an effort to make us a powerless Christian. If we try to make strides for the Lord, he will accuse us of sin that has already been forgiven. He will tell us we're not good enough to serve God. We must defeat those lies with the truth of the Word of God.

Respond

Take time now to praise and thank God for His Word, which helps us overcome every temptation. Also take some time to pray for those you know who are going through tough times (it might be you). Pray that God will strengthen and protect them (and you) from the tempter. Then ask God to show you the particular parts of the Word that you need to defeat the lies of the enemy.

Remember

God gives you His Word to prevail over any temptation or lie of the devil.

Taking a Stand

Read

I am not ashamed of the gospel, because it is the power of God for the salvation of everyone who believes. — Romans 1:16.

Reflect

At his school, my son was dubbed "Bright Knight" for a week. One thing the Bright Knight gets to do is bring things such as trophies and pictures — kind of a show and tell. Zac had a poster to fill out that revealed his favorite colors, hobbies, songs, and other trivia. I was just sure that he would write down Christian songs, because that is what he listens to most. When he didn't, Rhonda and I asked him why. He gave some hesitant excuses and then admitted he was a little embarrassed to choose Christian songs in front of the other kids. I was glad he was honest. So, trying to avoid being too pushy, I invited him to do what Jesus would have him do. Evidently, Jesus didn't want Zac to write down the Christian tunes, because he didn't!

The next item up for bid was the picture section. He put some pictures of himself in his backpack. Then, I handed him a picture of his baptism to see if Jesus wanted him to take that to show his class. Without a word, he put it in his backpack along with the others, and I thought by the look on his face that the picture would never see the light of day. But I was wrong. I prayed that Zac would have the courage to be bold that day, and when I got home, he was so excited. "Dad, guess what?" he said joyfully. "Today one of my friends saw the picture of me getting baptized, and he started asking me questions about how he could visit church and get baptized." I told Zac, "Isn't it wonderful that when you take a stand for Jesus, you give Him a chance to stand with you?"

Respond

When we allow the name of Jesus Christ to be glorified in everything we do, we give Him the opportunity to win someone new. Pray today for strength to take a stand for the One who stands for you. Use your platform to make Jesus look good.

Remember

Take a stand today for the One who took an eternal stand for you.

Substitution

Read

He himself bore our sins in his body on the tree, so that we might die to sins and live for righteousness; by his wounds you have been healed. — 1 Peter 2:24.

Reflect

What is your most favorite possession? Think about that for a minute. Now consider how you might respond if someone came along and destroyed that possession. How would you feel? Violated and angry? After all, that person had sinned against you. You would probably expect them to pay for it.

But instead of that person paying for it, what if someone else who had done nothing wrong stepped up and said they would pay for it? You would probably be shocked. Yet that is exactly what Jesus did for you. He stepped up and paid the price for your sin. The penalty you deserved was death, but He died in your place to pay the penalty. Forgiveness for our sin came at a very high price. Jesus, like the sacrificial lamb in the Old Testament, was the substitute on the cross to pay the price for our sin.

Consider God's extravagant love for you to allow His own Son to die in your place. I've known of parents who have allowed their son to go overseas to die for their country. But I know of no father who would allow his son to die for a cruel, evil, hardened criminal. Yet that is what God allowed for you. He watched His Son die on the cross for you.

Respond

For God so loved you personally, that He gave His only begotten Son. Spend some time now praising and thanking God for His love for you. Let Him cleanse you by admitting your sin and asking for His forgiveness. Finally, pray for someone you know who needs to experience that forgiveness. Choose to live your life in a way that others will see that Jesus is your most favorite possession.

Remember

No one proved His love for you like Jesus did.

Remember

Read

"This is my body given for you; do this in remembrance of me." — Luke 22:19.

Reflect

What is the most memorable meal you have ever experienced? Do you remember what was on the menu? Was it the people who were with you that made it special? Or was it the occasion that causes fond memories of the event? The last meal Jesus had on earth was certainly a memorable one for His disciples. The Lord had sent Peter and John to prepare the Passover, keeping the location a secret. When the disciples opened the door, they were greeted by the aroma of freshly baked bread and roasted lamb. As usual, the food was great, but this meal was different. It was a meal that etched a memory in the hearts of Jesus' followers to this day.

When Jesus came into the room, He began the evening's activities by washing the disciples' feet. What a memory — the King of kings washing your feet! But it was most memorable because of the announcement Jesus made at the table. It began, "I have eagerly desired to eat this Passover with you before I suffer." That statement surely stuck in their memory as it quieted the room.

I wonder how the bread tasted that night for those followers of Jesus. I wonder if they lost their appetites after His words. I wonder if they whispered to each other about the announcement. I also wonder if they had any idea what would happen in the next twenty-four hours. One thing was certain. They remembered.

Respond

How well do you remember Jesus' Passover sacrifice? Oh, I know you weren't there. But in a sense you were. Maybe not physically, but positionally you were there. You were there at the cross where the price was paid for your sins. Do you remember when you first felt forgiven by God? Do you remember your sorrow at the news of His death for you? You were there. We all were. Take some time to remember and thank Jesus for bearing your sin upon that cross.

Remember

When you say, "pass the bread," at dinner, let it remind you that you were there.

THE FINAL WALK

READ

When he had finished praying, Jesus left with his disciples and crossed the Kidron Valley. On the other side there was an olive grove, and he and his disciples went into it. — JOHN 18:1.

REFLECT

After Jesus finished his last meal and sang his last song (possibly Psalms 113-118) in the upper room with His disciples, He walked through the streets of Jerusalem, out the city gate, down across the Brook Kidron, and up into the Garden of Gethsemane.

I wonder what they talked about as they crossed the Brook Kidron. The Brook was the carrier of the blood of animal sacrifices from the Temple. Perhaps Jesus paused at the blood-tinted water and thought, "Tomorrow my blood will be flowing here, the final sacrifice for sin." If He did stop and ponder this, what a moment that must have been.

The writer of Hebrews tells us that without the shedding of blood there is no remission of sins. However, you and I need not shed any blood for the remission of our sins, for the blood has already been shed by our Savior. The sacred hymn writer, William Cowper, penned it this way:

There is a fountain, filled with blood
Drawn from Immanuel's veins.
And sinners plunged beneath that flood
Loose all their guilty stains.

RESPOND

Have you been stained by guilt and sin? Are you struggling with sinful habits that seem to control you? It is for those sins Jesus died. Spend some time with Him right now. Praise and thank Him for the willingness to take that last walk, suffer the incredible pain, and freely sacrifice His life for you. Allow Him to cleanse you and restore your fellowship with Him.

REMEMBER

When you see blood, you see life. Jesus' blood provides eternal life for all who will accept its cleansing.

Do You Really Believe?

Read

And as the women were terrified and bowed their faces to the ground, the men said to them, "Why do you seek the living One among the dead? He is not here, but He has risen." — LUKE 24:5-6 NASB.

Reflect

"Why do you seek the living One among the dead?" was a good question. But Peter and John and the women were not seeking the living, they were seeking the dead among the dead. Even though Jesus had told them that He would be raised from the dead, they didn't believe it. (See Luke 24:11.) And that is exactly how a lot of people treat the Word of God. They hear it over and over, but somehow, it has no effect on their lives.

Jesus told the disciples on many occasions that He was going to Jerusalem to suffer and die, but that he would be raised on the third day. However, they could never accept that until it was all over. How ironic that the first unbelievers of the resurrection were the disciples themselves! We call Thomas the doubter, but they all doubted until they saw Jesus after His resurrection from the grave.

Jesus' resurrection is the basis of our faith and salvation. (See Romans 10:9,10.) This historic event is set in time as the point where all mankind turns to believe and be reconciled to God — or not. Jesus is the only religious leader whose body cannot be found, and His life fulfills all the prophecies of the first coming of the Messiah. In short, God has done everything He could do to show us the way to be saved and that His Word is completely trustworthy.

Respond

Do you believe God's Word? Oh, you might say, "I believe it from cover to cover." But does it affect your life in a transforming way? If you truly believe it, you will act on what you believe. Put yourself in the place of those who visited the empty tomb. Let your thoughts be expressed in praise to your God, who conquered death and will give you that same blessing.

Remember

You serve a risen Savior — the foundation of your faith.

Faith to Please God

Read
And without faith it is impossible to please God, because anyone who comes to him must believe that he exists and that he rewards those who earnestly seek Him. — HEBREWS 11:6.

Reflect
Those who go on faith never go alone. Exercising faith always gets the Lord's attention. His Word tells us it is impossible to please Him without faith. Therefore, the opposite is also true: it is possible to please Him *with* faith. When we step out from under our earthly safety net and begin to trust God for our livelihood, it doesn't go unnoticed from heaven's perspective. In fact, all of God's heaven wants to see the exercise of faith rewarded. Exercising faith is simply saying, "I choose to trust God over and above anything I can produce on my own." This doesn't mean we do nothing; then expect God to bail us out. It means we trust God for our provisions and He will honor our faith.

Paul exercised faith and his life was full of miracles. He trusted God to protect and provide for him as he sought to do God's will. He didn't always know how God would come through, but he had all the confidence in the world that He would. And when God made provision for him, Paul was the first to give God glory for His faithfulness.

Respond
How much have you been "faithing" it? Are you trusting in your paycheck to bring you security and significance? Who provided the paycheck? I know, your workplace. But Who gave you that job? It all comes from God. He knows where you're working and how much you're making, because He provided it for you. So take some time to recognize God as the provider and protector of your life. Thank Him for His faithfulness. Take a look at all the things He has given you and learn to be contented with them. In fact, be open to the possibility that He might want you to give some of that stuff away. Ask God to help you live by faith today.

Remember
When we walk by faith, and not by sight, we bring a smile to our Father's face.

The Most Important Book

Read

The heavens declare the glory of God; the skies proclaim the work of his hands. — Psalm 19:1.

Reflect

My kids are into reading, and I couldn't be more thrilled. When I was a child, reading was not my favorite thing to do. I remember once when my school teacher gave the class something to read silently at our desks, I turned my pages in sync with the rest of the class to make them think I was just as fast a reader as they were. Little did I know at the time I was only hurting myself. I was missing the point, and I wasn't learning.

Now I read to comprehend. I want to get all I can get out of it, which brings me to the Bible. Are you getting all you can get out of it? How can it help you? What place should it take in your life? Questions like these, if taken seriously, can lead to a deeper relationship with God than you ever dreamed. His Word, the Bible, reveals who He is and how you can have a living, vital, and ongoing relationship with Him.

Today's verse tells you that just by looking up in the sky you can see how big God is. Many today believe God is like He is portrayed in the movies, as a doting grandfather or a fix-it guy who rushes in to bail them out when they get in trouble. Some people I know have the concept that God is always angry and is just waiting to punish them when they do wrong. But nothing could be further from the truth. God is love. He has instructed us to call Him Father. He is patient and forgiving. He went to the greatest length possible to have a relationship with us by allowing Jesus to be sacrificed to pay the price for our sin. Someone who has done all that for us is worth knowing.

Respond

If it's early morning or night, step outside and look up at the sky to witness His grandeur. Read today's verse again, and thank God for His creation, including you.

Remember

The Bible is God's personal love letter to you.

Effective Prayer

Read

In the morning, there was a great commotion among the soldiers. "What could have happened to Peter?" they asked. — Acts 12:18.

Reflect

Can you picture this scene? The soldiers who were chained to Peter in his prison cell awake to find him gone. I wonder what they said to their superior. "I know he was asleep. I heard him snoring all night! Maybe he greased his wrists and just slid out of the chains...maybe he just went to the bathroom and will be back later...maybe, uh...maybe...". Did they ever stop to think that some people across town might have been praying all night for God to deliver him? I don't think so.

If the soldiers really knew what happened that night, would they have believed it? Had they known they were in the presence of an angel, could they have fathomed it? Probably not. The world will never understand effective prayer. The world's idea of prayer says, "I prayed for it because that's what I wanted." Effective praying says, "I prayed for it because that's what God wanted."

People in the world pray when they have a desperate need or desire, which seldom lines up with God's will for their lives. But real effective prayer seeks to accomplish God's plan for your life. Peter's brothers and sisters in Christ prayed for him to be released from prison because he was innocent. That was in line with God's will, because Peter still had many things to do for the Lord.

Respond

How are you doing in your prayer life? Are you praying what *you* want or what *God* desires? Have you been praying for your deliverance *from* what God has called you to do or in order to *do* what He's called you to do? Would answers to your prayers arrest the attention of the worldly people around you? Take time to pray and seek God's will. And ask God to use you to pray for someone else today, so they can see Him at work in their lives and trust in Him.

Remember

Effective prayer is seeking what God desires for us and what He desires to do through us.

To Know Him

Read

I want to know Christ and the power of his resurrection and the fellowship of sharing in his sufferings, becoming like him in his death. — PHILIPPIANS 3:10.

Reflect

A little girl got a new Bible storybook and with excitement went through its pages circling the word, "God," wherever it appeared on the page. Her mother, wanting to scold the child for defacing the book, sternly asked, "Why are you doing that?" The little girl replied very matter-of-factly, "So I will know where to find God when I need Him."

One of the most practical reasons for getting to know God intimately is that we need Him. God created us with a void in the center of our being that can only be filled with Him. Sometimes we try to fill the void with temporary things like popularity, possessions, pleasure, and position. When those things fail us, which they always do, we find ourselves in need again. It takes eternal life to fill an eternal void, and only Jesus can impart eternal life.

Paul said he wanted to "know Christ and the power of his resurrection." He knew the closer he was to Jesus, the more fulfilled his life would be. Sometimes people get so callused that they refuse to go to God because they don't understand that He will accept them and help them. But He patiently waits for them just like He has for you and me.

Respond

When you get to know God in an intimate relationship, His divine guidance and power always follows. He wants to give you guidance daily. He wants to bless you and do great exploits through you. So take a little time right now to praise and thank God for saving your life and for wanting to direct you along His paths. Show Him today how important having a relationship with Him is to you!

Remember

The God of all creation wants to have a personal relationship with you. What an honor!

Clean the Temple

Read

Now when Asa heard these words...he took courage and removed the abominable idols from all the land of Judah...He then restored the altar of the Lord... — 2 CHRONICLES 15:8 NASB.

Reflect

It takes courage to stand up and say that something is hindering your consistent walk with Jesus Christ. It takes even greater courage for you to say, "I abandon all that robs me of my intimate relationship with Him."

Asa cleaned out the entire nation of Judah. He didn't tolerate one idol. But that was only half the battle. The other half was restoring the altar of the Lord. All men worship something, so when one object of worship is torn down, it doesn't take long for another one to be erected. And before new idols could be erected in Israel, Asa restored the altar of the Lord.

This concept is true in our lives. We are the temple of God. We are His dwelling place. So when we ask Jesus to come into our lives, we are inviting Him to make Himself at home in us, to take over and replace anything that isn't pleasing to Him. Therefore, we must not tolerate even one thing in our life that obstructs His work in and through us. We must remove the obstacles and immediately replace them with our allegiance to Jesus Christ.

Respond

Today you see so many people who worship their jobs. You see some who worship their possessions. Others worship money, and still others just worship themselves. Many of them seem happy, but don't be fooled! Their happiness is temporary and hollow. Only the Lord Jesus can bring true satisfaction into their lives. If you have been struggling with idols of any sort, make your devotion time today a time of tearing down. Like Asa, you must tear down the idols and replace them with total devotion to Jesus — the only One worthy of our all.

Remember

Your body is the temple of the Holy Spirit. Does He feel at home?

LIVING IN HIS PRESENCE

READ

How lovely is your dwelling place, O Lord Almighty! My heart yearns, even faints for the courts of the Lord; my heart and my flesh cry out for the living God. — PSALM 84:1.

REFLECT

Oswald Chambers said: "Unless in the first waking moment of the day you learn to fling the door wide back and let God in, you will work on a wrong level all day, but swing the door wide open and pray to your Father in secret, and every public thing will be stamped with the presence of God."

The presence of God is something most of us want, but there are those who are uneasy in His presence. The words "God is near" can be comforting to the one who has just lost a loved one and is experiencing pain; but the same words can be very threatening to an unbeliever or a believer caught in sin — both under conviction. I was taught as a young believer that no matter what you accomplished in a day, if you ignored God throughout that day and worked in your own strength and thinking, your accomplishments would be in vain. From heaven's point of view, that is true.

God is more interested in our relationship with Him than our ability to accomplish great things. It is God's desire that we experience His presence every day. Jesus consistently pulled away from the crowd to spend time with His Father. He knew that nothing was more important than His relationship with the One who held all the keys to the past, present, and future. He knew that to be effective in carrying out God's work, He had to spend time alone with God daily.

RESPOND

There is no way you can escape God geographically. However, you can get away from Him morally. Are you experiencing His presence daily? Do you stop during your day and develop your relationship with God through prayer? Why don't you take some time right now to spend with Him and experience His presence. Open the door, as Oswald Chambers says.

REMEMBER

God wants to spend the day with you.

Right Decisions

Read
Because those who are led by the Spirit of God are sons of God. — Romans 8:14.

Reflect
When I was young my parents helped me out with my decisions. I thought my dad was full of wisdom, so I took my cues from Him. Whenever I asked, "Dad, what do you think?" he would always give me an answer filled with wisdom and my best interest in mind. As I grew older and left home, I still consulted my dad by phone. Listening to his wisdom and watching his decisions made me a better decision-maker. In the same way, a close relationship with your heavenly Father will help you make better decisions.

There are some basics to making godly decisions. First, we must pray, because God honors those who pray consistently. In Luke 18:1-7 we read the story Jesus told about a lady who persistently sought a judge to help her. The judge said he didn't have to help her, but because of her persistence, he finally helped. In this parable, Jesus taught how the Father is much more willing to help those who are persistent in their prayers.

Second, we must be in the Word. That means we must persistently study God's perspective. He gives guidance through His Word, and His Word is clear. The Father wants His children to know His will, and when we open His Word, God opens His mouth. But to be led by Him, first we must listen to Him.

Third, to make godly decisions, we must commit ourselves to doing the known will of God. If we don't do what we already know God's will to be, why should He reveal any more to us? If we can't be trusted with what God's Word and the Holy Spirit have already told us to do, why should He give us more direction?

Respond
Thank God for His guidance in today's crazy, confusing world! Ask Him to help you do the disciplines it takes to be led by His Spirit. Finally, pray that God will guide you in all of today's decisions.

Remember
Good decisions are made when godly counsel is sought.

Cooperating with God

Read

The Lord is with you when you are with Him. And if you seek Him, He will let you find Him; but if you forsake Him, He will forsake you." — 2 Chronicles 15:2 NASB.

Reflect

One time I was watching *Sesame Street* with my kids, Zac and Mac, and the word for the day was cooperation. We sang about cooperation with the characters on TV, were given examples of it, and we talked about it. The goal was to teach children what it means to cooperate, not only through singing and speaking, but through demonstration as well. I began to think, *Oh, that the children of God could learn the same thing — not only to cooperate with one another, but even more, to cooperate with God.* When we don't cooperate with God, it is evidenced in our relationships with others.

The prophet Azariah gave his King Asa some sound advice in our verse for today: "The Lord is with you when you are with Him." Now we think the Lord is always with us, and that is true. His presence certainly is. But His blessing is only with us when we are cooperating with Him and consistently seeking to obey His will. God blesses the obedient when they "are with Him." (See Luke 15:11-32.) Asa's cooperation with God cleansed the nation of Judah by destroying all idols. And we know, because of God's desire of faithfulness, that He blessed him.

Respond

Have you been cooperating with God in your prayer life? Do you consult Him about all your involvements? He wants to be intimately involved in the details of your life, and He longs for your cooperation so He can accomplish great things through you. If you're struggling with your cooperation level, ask God to forgive you and start again. You may even want to tune in to Sesame Street sometime! Become a child and learn cooperation...cooperation with God!

Remember

Cooperation means working together. (I learned that on Sesame Street!) Cooperation with God makes great things happen.

Mature in the Word

Read

For you are still fleshly. For since there is jealousy and strife among you, are you not fleshly, and are you not walking like mere men? — 1 Corinthians 3:3 NASB.

Reflect

She came to me wanting to lead a Bible study in her home. But I knew her maturity level wasn't to that point yet. Nice lady, but still childish in a lot of areas in her life. As I talked with her I prayed, "Lord, give me wisdom, she doesn't have the maturity to do this." I asked her to get involved in another Bible study as a helper, and that we would talk about her beginning one at a later date.

You don't have to be around a Christian very long to tell how mature they are. You can tell by their spiritual diet. I could tell this woman wasn't spending much time in God's Word because she didn't have much patience or show much love. If she was spending time in the Word regularly, she would have been growing more rapidly. So I encouraged her to start helping at another Bible study, to grow in God's Word.

Are you still growing in the Word? Are you looking deeper into the doctrines of our faith and applying them to your daily life? One who claims the name of Jesus Christ should never be satisfied with not spending time in the Word. If you know the joy of studying the Scriptures and have been away from it for a while, you feel frustrated in your prayer life and in your walk with God in general. You probably aren't witnessing as often, and your attitude toward people has taken a subtle downslide. That is why walking with Him in the Word is so vital. It affects your spiritual well-being, which affects your relationships and your ability to succeed.

Respond

Have you been consistent in studying God's Word? Does that describe you? Ask God to help you establish a regular time to spend in Bible study. It may be that you need a partner to help you. Ask God to provide just the right one. Believe me, He wants you to study and read His Word every day.

Remember

Maturity is demonstrated by the ability to apply godly principles to every area of life.

Only One Way

Read

But as many as received Him, to them He gave the right to become children of God, even to those who believe in His name. — JOHN 1:12 NASB.

Reflect

A couple of decades ago, Minnesota Viking defensive lineman Jim Marshall collected a fumble and ran it into the end zone for a touchdown. There was only one problem — he ran the wrong way and scored six points for the other team. I suppose he could have argued that it was pretty narrow-minded of the rules and referees to restrict a team to running in only one direction, but the rules were established to provide enjoyment and prevent chaos during the game. The rules had to be enforced, and Marshall was embarrassed.

The same principle is true in our spiritual walk. If we want to enter into God's heaven, we must be born again. There just isn't any other way. We must receive Jesus as our personal Savior and Lord. The Scripture isn't narrow-minded, it is simply the truth as God established it.

Many people today believe that if they live a good life, they will be able to enter into heaven. But that's not true. They're running in the wrong direction with a man-made philosophy that leads many astray. If we could enter heaven by being good, then why would Jesus have had to die? Our salvation came at a great price: the death of God's only Son. He died so we could be born into His family by accepting and receiving Him into our lives. If we play by His rules, we will win in the end.

Respond

If you've never truly asked Jesus Christ into your life, to be the Lord and Master of your life, now would be a great time to do that. Ask Him to come to forgive you of your sins. When a person is sincere, they are born into the family of God at the instant they ask. Perhaps you know Him personally already but you have some friends who are thinking they can get to heaven by just being good. Take some time right now and pray for them. Get them turned around and running in the right direction.

Remember

God made the way to Him very simple and very clear: receive Jesus Christ as Lord and Savior.

We Are Stressed, But...

Read

We are hard pressed on every side, but not crushed; perplexed, but not in despair; persecuted, but not abandoned; struck down, but not destroyed. — 2 Corinthians 4:8-9.

Reflect

Think about some of the things Paul was going through when he wrote this verse. His integrity was being challenged by many troublemakers in Corinth. Since he had changed his itinerary, they said he wasn't trustworthy. They also accused him of being a false apostle and of mishandling funds. He and the authenticity of his ministry were both being challenged. And these were just the things going on in Corinth!

Paul was persecuted throughout his ministry. He was abused physically, mentally, and emotionally, but he didn't let any of that affect his attitude of service to Jesus Christ. Paul had narrowed life down to simple terms: a person was either for God or against God. There was good and there was bad. What he recognized as bad he tried to avoid. But what was good, he embraced. Simple.

The *New Century Version* of these verses says, "There's trouble all around us, but we are not defeated, we do not know what to do, but we do not give up." This has actually become a song around our home. There are times when we just don't know what to do, but one thing we do know — we're not giving up! God will make a way when there is no way. We just need to stick close to God and press on.

Respond

How is your stress level today? Is anxiety bubbling on the inside of you? Is your physical body tense and your temper short? Remember that your condition is no surprise to God. He is still with you. His attitude toward you hasn't changed. Take time right now to praise and thank Him for His love — and relax in His care. Decide to depend on Him for all your needs today.

Remember

When you are pressed on every side, don't give up. God hasn't!

Crisis Praying

Read

Then Asa called to the Lord his God, and said, "Lord, there is no one besides Thee to help in the battle between the powerful and those who have no strength; so help us, O Lord our God, for we trust in Thee, and in Thy name have come against this multitude." — 2 Chronicles 14:11 NASB.

Reflect

When my eight-year-old daughter, Mackenzie, lay on the ground in the backyard screaming in pain, I knew we had a crisis on our hands. She had fallen from the swing set and broken her arm at the elbow. I'll never forget Rhonda's prayer in the emergency room. "Lord, if she needs surgery, I pray you will select the doctor for us and that he will make sure her arm is perfect again." The doctor came in and introduced himself, showed us the X-ray, and said, "She needs to have surgery, and it needs to be perfect." Coincidence? No, just the God of all creation giving comfort in a crisis through a few little words. You should see Mackenzie's arm today. It's perfect.

Crisis praying isn't difficult if you've prayed and obeyed all along. Because prayer and communication with God is a natural and everyday experience, when trouble strikes you just slide right into God's lap and talk to Him. Notice how Asa began his crisis prayer. Asa's walk with the Lord was consistent, so just like all his prayers, he began with the acknowledgment of who God is: "There is no one like You." When you are in continuous communion with God, your crises become smaller and your victories larger.

Respond

If you're not facing a crisis today, continue with your consistent prayer life so you will be so in tune with God that no crisis can ever leave you dismayed. If you are facing a crisis today, who are you trusting? Yourself? Other people? Don't trust anyone but God and those you recognize He is using to minister to you!

Remember

Time spent alone with God in prayer is powerful time – for now and for later.

The Love of Money

Read

The love of money is a root of all kinds of evil. — 1 Timothy 6:10

Reflect

The next time you get a chance, take a good look at a one-dollar bill. When you do, you will see a picture on the back of an eagle with outstretched wings. Now, do you want to know what that really means? Okay, I'll tell you. It means he's ready to fly out of your wallet. I'm sure you thought that illustration was going to have a much deeper meaning. But hey, there is a truth here. In Proverbs 23:5, Solomon, who was the richest man in the world, pictured riches as growing wings and flying away. And Paul says, the love of money can lead us to all kinds of evil.

One of the dangers of money is that the more we have, the more we often want — because our hunger for money is elastic. No matter how much we have, it isn't enough. In the end, no amount of money and riches can satisfy. In Ecclesiastes 5:8, Solomon also said those who love money will experience oppression, dissatisfaction, and anxiety — three deadly poisons that result from misplaced love. And Solomon should have known. He had more money than anyone, and it still couldn't buy him the happiness he sought.

Respond

One of Paul's antidotes for overcoming the tendency to fall in love with money is to "do good, to be rich in good deeds, and to be generous and willing to share" (1 Timothy 6:18). I invite you to use this scripture today as your prayer. But first, thank God that His love will never grow wings and fly away. Make yourself available as a lavish giver while you ask Him to protect you from the corruption of lusting for money. Dedicate your finances totally to the work of the Lord. Pray for Him to show you where you can be generous today.

Remember

Since all wealth belongs to God, He knows how you should use it to bring the best results for His kingdom and your life.

Completely His

Read

For the eyes of the Lord move to and fro throughout the earth that He may strongly support those whose heart is completely His." — 2 Chronicles 16:9 NASB.

Reflect

When I was seven years old my dad bought me a seven-year-old mare named Molly. Molly was mine. She responded to everything I commanded her to do, until the day Dad brought another horse home. Suddenly, Molly wouldn't listen to me anymore. In fact, she threw me off her back. What happened? I thought she was completely mine, but she got distracted by the other horse, forgot about me, and hurt me.

We also sometimes get distracted and hurt our heavenly Father. To further my Molly analogy, notice what today's verse *doesn't* say: "The eyes of the Lord run to and fro throughout the earth that He may strongly support those whose heart is divided between Him and their selfish interests." No. You'll never find that verse in the Bible. God is constantly looking for those "whose heart is completely His!"

Think about Peter. You would think that after listening and following Jesus for three years, he would be completely His. But after Jesus was taken by the authorities, Peter followed from a distance, tried to blend in with the world, and denied Jesus three times, confirming once and for all that he wasn't completely His. (See Luke 22:54-60.) What can we learn from this? First, it is possible to be very earnest and still have the power of the flesh dominating our lives. And second, only Jesus can deliver us from the power of self.

Respond

Can you relate to Peter's uncommitted actions? If so, you might not completely belong to Jesus. Take some time right now to recommit your life to Him, and praise Him for His commitment to you. Ask God to forgive you for any "Petered out" actions you may have taken in the past. Finally, make a strong decision to be totally devoted to Jesus and seek to glorify His name today.

Remember

Look out for distractions. Belong completely to Jesus.

Power in the Garden

Read

"You will not surely die," the serpent said to the woman. "For God knows that when you eat of it your eyes will be opened, and you will be like God, knowing good and evil." — Genesis 3:4-5.

Reflect

One of the lies of the world system is that power brings satisfaction, significance, and security to one's life. When the serpent tempted Eve to eat from the tree that God had forbidden, he told her, "You will be like God." In other words, he led Eve to believe she would have power she had never known. The serpent tried to make God look bad by accusing Him of selfishness. "He is keeping this power from you, Eve!" The woman was seduced into questioning the Word of God and, as a result, destroyed the power of God in her life.

When Adam and Eve ate of the tree, they challenged the power of God's Word and were immediately separated from Him. For the first time shame, fear, and loneliness entered into the world. The promise that they would be like God was a lie. And, interestingly enough, the serpent was nowhere to be found after Adam and Eve ate the forbidden fruit.

It's easy to see now that the serpent's deception for power didn't bring satisfaction, significance, or security. In fact, it brought the exact opposite. God's rules are for our protection, and His power is demonstrated best when we are totally dependent on Him. In fact, when we act independently from God's guidance and leadership, we refuse the opportunity for His power to work in our lives.

Respond

God told Paul that His power was perfected in human weakness. (See 2 Corinthians 12:9.) So if you're feeling weak, just simply relax, take a deep breath, and become totally dependent upon and surrendered to Him. You have God's guarantee that He will replace your weakness with His strength — and that's real power!

Remember

True power is found in complete surrender to the Lord Jesus Christ.

Decisions That Make Sense

Read

Jesus answered him, "It is also written: Do not put the Lord your God to the test." — MATTHEW 4:7.

Reflect

I had a couple of married friends that had a lot of difficulty making decisions. The wife made decisions based on emotions, or how she *felt* about things. The husband, on the other hand, made all his decisions through the logic of his thought processes. She was emotional; he was analytical. Well, one day the husband came home to find a person in his house that looked like they just came off the street. He looked homeless and dirty. "Where did this guy come from? he asked. "I just felt sorry for him," his wife replied, "and thought I'd let him stay with us for awhile, until he gets back on his feet." Obviously this made no sense whatsoever to the husband. So a lot of discussion had to take place between them. In the end, they gave him some money and sent him on his way.

Too often I'm afraid we make decisions based on what we want or what we feel compelled to do by outside sources instead of the Holy Spirit on the inside of us. Never consulting God about what He wants in a situation is what Jesus meant when He taught against "putting God to the test." Was this homeless man sent by God to this couple for ministry or was he sent by Satan to do them harm? Only God knows, so we must consult Him always, regardless of what our emotions or our logic says.

Respond

Divine guidance is available to you if you'll accept it. Emotions are good, and so is logic. But God wants to give you direction through His Word and by His Spirit, even in the smallest details of your life. When He does, you will find that the restlessness you once knew is replaced by security and satisfaction. Spend some time alone with God right now and ask Him to help you make decisions that are in line with His will.

Remember

Let God be your chief consultant on every decision you make.

Attitude Is Everything

Read

"You intended to harm me, but God intended it for good to accomplish what is now being done, the saving of many lives." — Genesis 50:20.

Reflect

When the going gets tough, what really matters is not what happens *to* us, but what happens *in* us, because what happens in us will surely come out. And when it does, it reveals who we really are. Tough times will make us bitter or better. I know several people who have gone through bad times who felt closest to God at those very times. I've known others who have gone through similar trials and distanced themselves from or became angry at God. What was the difference? Attitude.

Of all the people in the Old Testament, Joseph had one of the best attitudes. His brothers sold him. His boss's wife framed him and he was thrown into prison. Yet through it all he kept an attitude that was pleasing to God. He knew that God had a plan. He didn't know the whole plan, but as he stayed faithful each day, God rewarded him for his faithfulness. Joseph was eventually paroled and promoted to the position of prime minister of Egypt. And at the end of the book of Genesis, Joseph tells of his troubles to his brothers, "You meant it to harm me, but God had a different plan." God's attitude was revealed in Joseph's life.

Respond

Are you experiencing tough times? If you're not right now, chances are you will. But don't despair, they won't last forever and God will be with you in the midst of them. He wants you to depend on Him now. He wants you to take on His attitude. Take a moment to consider Joseph's life again and read Romans 8:28. See if this doesn't help your outlook. Now, let God dominate your attitude toward others and life in general today. Go out and make Him look good to others because of your excellent attitude.

Remember

Determine to choose a godly attitude, no matter what, and God will work mightily through you.

Substitutes for God

Read

"Why did the Lord bring defeat upon us today before the Philistines? Let us bring the ark of the Lord's covenant from Shiloh, so that it may go with us and save us from the hand of our enemies." — 1 Samuel 4:3.

Reflect

Have you been down the cereal aisle in the grocery store lately? Options. Our world is full of them. Unfortunately, many Christians see the options the world offers and substitute them for God. The ark represented God's presence among His people, but it was never intended to replace Him. The Israelites turned the Ark of the Covenant into a substitute for God in a day when His presence was neither honored nor sought in Israel. They took it with them only so it would save them from their enemies.

Sometimes we substitute ourselves for God because we want control of our lives. "Nobody has the right to tell *me* what to do," we proclaim. Or we substitute "stuff" for Him. You know, the stuff our friends have and we don't. There are a multitude of possible substitutes for God: people, money, popularity, pleasure, and others.

A substitute takes the place of what or who is supposed to be there. When we substitute something for God, we put something in His place. God's place — the place He desires to occupy more than any other — is right in the center of our hearts. So when we substitute money for God, money sits on the throne of our heart and kicks God out. Pretty ugly picture, isn't it?

Respond

Have you been substituting anything or anyone for God in your life? To grow closer to God, you must get rid of all the substitutes you use to fill the "God-shaped" void in your life. Ask Him to forgive you for the times you have substituted other things in His place, and kick everyone and everything off the throne of your heart but Him.

Remember

There is *no substitute* for the precious presence of God in your life.

DON'T CUT SCHOOL

READ

"Blessed are those who hunger and thirst for righteousness, for they will be filled." — MATTHEW 5:6.

REFLECT

As a kid, did you ever want to stay home from school? If you have kids in school, or if you're currently in school, you know what I'm talking about. My kids have promised the world to my wife and me if we would let them skip one day. But, of course, we make them go to school anyway. How do they feel about school when they come home? They're filled with story after story. Do they like school? Yes, they love it. So what's the problem? Nine out of ten times, its simply a matter of their flesh trying to get them to do the wrong thing. They want to do something less disciplined during the week; like watch TV or fly a kite.

Have you ever seen a believer who didn't grow spiritually? Nine out of ten times, the problem is simply a matter of discipline. In a matter of seconds, you can tell how they feel about themselves and about God. "I know I'm supposed to study my Bible and pray, but I'm really tired and need to sleep another hour."

Growing spiritually is something every believer knows they need to do, but some have stopped growing because they chose to stay home from school. They can deceive themselves and say, "I don't need this," or "I'll get what I need in church on Sunday." But the truth is, "Believers' School" is never out. And the choice is always ours to attend or cut class. If we choose to go and are attentive in class, a strange thing occurs. Self-discipline comes easier and going to school is no longer work, but pleasure.

RESPOND

Self-discipline is one of the fruits of the Spirit (see Galatians 5:22). So God has already imparted that character trait to you. Now you simply have to exercise it; it's a choice. So choose to hunger and thirst after righteousness. Choose to study God's Word and pray for revelation. Your Teacher will be pleased — and you will probably get an "A" for the day!

REMEMBER

Decide to have a great day in "school" today — so you can have a great day.

Channel of Love

Read

Dear friends, since God so loved us, we also ought to love one another. No one has ever seen God; but if we love each other, God lives in us and his love is made complete in us. — 1 John 4:11-12.

Reflect

The story is told of a Salvation Army worker who found a poor homeless woman alone on the street and invited her to come inside to the chapel for help. But the woman refused to move. The worker assured the woman of her motivation as she explained God's love. "God loves you and Jesus died for you," she said. Still, the woman wouldn't even acknowledge the worker. Then the Salvation Army worker did something unusual. She leaned over and kissed the woman on the cheek and took her into her arms. As she did, the woman began to weep. The worker then led her carefully into the chapel, where she ultimately received Jesus. Later the homeless woman said, "You *told* me that God loved me, but it didn't mean anything until you *showed* me that God loved me."

When God lives in you, the only way you can truly show it is through your actions toward others. When you begin to see people as Jesus sees them, you will view others as you were before Jesus came into your life. You will learn to ask yourself, "If they are good enough for Jesus, aren't they good enough for me?" Is that the attitude you have toward those in need?

Respond

Take some time right now to praise and thank God for loving you when you were at your worst. Ask Him to forgive the times you have ignored those who needed His love. Pray that He will help you to be a channel of His love today to those He brings into your life.

Remember

God designed you to be a channel of His love.

In His Time

Read

"Martha therefore said to Jesus, 'Lord if You had been here, my brother would not have died." — John 11:21 NASB.

Reflect

Many times we are like the sisters of Lazarus. We think if the Lord would just hurry and answer our prayers, we wouldn't have to experience all the stress that's in our lives. But we fail to see Jesus' perspective and realize His timing is always right. Even though His friend Lazarus was dead, Jesus wasn't late. When you read the Scriptures you understand that He was "late" on purpose. And his purpose was accomplished: "that they may believe."

As we grow closer to Jesus, we find this is always true. His purposes will always be accomplished on His timetable, not ours. Many times that calls for patience on our part. Habakkuk cried out to God about injustices in the land, and it seemed God was ignoring him. However, nothing could have been further from the truth. (See Habakkuk 2:3.) As we believe our heavenly Father, the same is true for us.

We must develop the ability to view things from God's perspective. When we gain His perspective, it helps our patience to grow. If you think God is delaying an answer to one of your prayers, stop and ask these questions:

1. What is God trying to do by not answering according to my timetable?
2. What adjustments do I need to make in order to hear God speak?
3. What would it take to accomplish God's goal in this circumstance?
4. Am I praying for His will but expecting mine?

Respond

The raising of Lazarus brought God glory that only He could initially understand. Others understood it later. So thank God for His perfect timetable and ask Him to forgive you when you've tried to "force" His hand. Pray for patience to wait an believe He always has things in hand.

Remember

God makes all things beautiful in His time. Trust Him.

My Day Off

Read

By the seventh day God had finished the work he had been doing; so on the seventh day he rested from all his work. — Genesis 2:2.

Reflect

I love my day off. It's a time to build memories. There was one day when I got some rest. God knew I needed a day of rest. Then there was another time that was even more awesome. Zac and I were throwing passes around on the field at Arrowhead Stadium. I turned into a kid again. My eyes focused on the ball and my imagination sprung to life as 80,000 fans screamed for my touchdown success. But then I dropped the ball and all of a sudden I was glad the stands were empty. I picked up the ball and I started throwing to Zac again. Then he dropped the ball too. But we continued.

Zac and I got better. We moved the ball down the field. I remembered thinking, *Thank you Lord. Gosh, this is fun.* Then, out of no where, it was time to go. "One more dad?" Zac asked. "Go for the end zone son!" I shouted while waving him down. He's almost there. I throw. It looks good...a perfect spiral. He turns to look, reaches out, the ball is there, his feet cross the goal line — and the ball enters his hands. TOUCHDOWN AT ARROWHEAD!!! my imagination rings out. The crowd goes wild for both of us! What a catch! What a thrill! What a night!

When Zac and I played on NFL turf that day, I was reminded of the "serious fun" of life. I know I've dropped the ball many times in my life. I will never forget the moment of that experience. Building memories on your day off, should be a priority. If you don't take a day, you're too busy.

Respond

Take a good hard look at your life today. Are you taking some time to be with friends and family when you're not rushing around. If you're too busy, ask God to show you how to adjust your schedule — and maybe you need to ask Him to teach you how to enjoy a day off.

Remember

Even God took a day off!

Hello Jacob

Read

He chose our inheritance for us, the pride of Jacob, whom he loved. — Psalm 47:4.

Reflect

Do you remember who Jacob was? He was Issac's son, the one who stole the birthright from his brother and then lied to his father about it. The name Jacob means trickster, conniver, manipulator, and cheater. I'm not sure that many of us would want him as a member of our family. But God...well...look at what the last part of today's verse says, "...Jacob, whom He loved."

This statement should be a great encouragement to you and me. Countless times in the Old Testament, God identified Himself as the God of Jacob, that is, the God of a trickster and a cheat. But that's the kind of God we serve. He wants our love so much that He is willing to love us at our worst. And of course, when Jacob finally surrendered his will to God, God turned him into a leader. Under God's influence, Jacob did not remain a trickster and a cheat.

Also, isn't it good to know that God has already made provision and plans for us because He loves us? "He chooses our inheritance..." We've all had times when our name could have been Jacob, so we can take great comfort in the fact that God chooses to love us and provide an inheritance for us. And when we receive His love, we are changed to be more like Him, just like Jacob was. Amazing!

Respond

Thank God for His love, that He loves you in spite of your shortcomings, and that He has provided everything you will ever need through Jesus Christ. Ask Him to forgive you for the times you have acted like Jacob. Pray that He will strengthen you to share His unconditional love with those you come in contact with today.

Remember

When you begin to lose heart, become discouraged, and think you'll never get it right, remember Jacob.

POWER TO SPARE

READ

And God is able to make all grace abound to you, so that in all things at all times, having all the you need, you will abound in every good work. — 2 CORINTHIANS 9:8.

REFLECT

On March 5, 1979, an amazing demonstration of power and energy was displayed. Scientists recorded one of the most incredible bursts of energy in the universe. One description of the event read, "The burst of gamma radiation picked up by satellites lasted only one-tenth of a second. However, in that brief instant, it emitted as much energy as the sun does in three thousand years. If the sun had burst out the same amount of energy, the earth and everything in it would have been vaporized instantly."

Isn't it interesting that about the time we think we have learned so much about the universe, something like this happens and we see how much we don't know? To this day scientists and scholars are still trying to figure out what God did on the first day of creation. This is no discredit to them, but it says a lot about the Creator.

It's easy to notice God's creative power in the universe. But Paul said that God wants to release His power in our lives. Can you intellectually grasp that truth? If you can, how will that change the way you pray? How will that change the way you see yourself? Should knowing that God can do "exceedingly abundantly more than all you think or ask" change your life? (See Ephesians 3:20.) The answer is yes! The challenge for us is to grab hold of the truth of God's power in our lives and start depending on it.

RESPOND

God can do anything in the world around us and whatever He wills in us. Therefore, it is our duty as believers to yield to Him and allow His power to work in us. In your devotional time today, allow God to work in your life. Praise Him for His power. In Jesus name, invite Him to take control of your thoughts, motives, and actions today.

REMEMBER

There is nothing God can't do, because He has power to spare.

Simple Caring

Read

Cast all your anxiety on him because he cares for you. — 1 Peter 5:7.

Reflect

I missed my flight home, so I had to take an alternate route and change airlines. Frustrated at the delay, but thankful I was able to catch another plane, I sat down in my seat. I did not want to talk to anyone. I'd been talking all weekend to parents and kids, and I just wanted to be quiet. I pulled out my Bible and opened it — only to repel anyone who wanted to talk.

A man sat next to me and cordially said hello. For more than half the flight He was quiet, but after the beverage service was completed he started talking. He was on his way home from visiting his daughter in Texas. Then he asked, "Tom, I noticed you have a Bible. Do you pray?" I said, "Sure, why do you ask?" He answered, "Well, I was wondering if you would pray for my daughter. I just got finished visiting her in prison." I said, "Oh, I'm sorry to hear that." Then he continued, "You see, Tom," his voice beginning to break, "about six months ago she shot and killed my wife. I still love her, but she's got a long way to go, so if you could pray for her, I'd really appreciate it."

At that moment, this man didn't care how much theology I knew or if I had written any books. All he wanted to know was, *Did I care enough to pray?* I told him I would, and we bowed our heads together.

Respond

People are hurting all around you, but most of the time they don't tell you. Deep inside they are crying out, "Does anybody care?" And only God hears. But here's the good news: God can tell you! Are you listening to Him today? Spend some time praying for those you have been around who may have never asked, but who could use your prayers. Then tell them you prayed for them when you see them next.

Remember

People will never care how much you know until they know how much you care.

The Art of Communication

Read

A word aptly spoken is like apples of gold in settings of silver. — Proverbs 25:11.

Reflect

A couple of years ago, as we took our son Zac to school one morning, Rhonda asked me if I would stop and get a can of Coke. I grunted, not wanting to get into a long conversation because the sports report was coming up on the radio. When we came to the quick stop, I stopped, ran in, bought a can of Coke, and took it back to the car. Rhonda grabbed it and began to put it away fast. I remember thinking, *Boy, she must be thirsty!* But I didn't say anything because I wanted to listen to the sports. As we drove along she offered a drink to everyone in the car. It was like she was on a mission to empty that can of Coke.

We were almost to the school when Rhonda cried, "STOP THE CAR!" I thought, *Oh no, she must be sick,* but I didn't say anything because the sports report was on the radio. I stopped. She handed me the empty Coke can and said, "Get out and smash it." Even though I was frustrated that I was about to miss last night's scores of my favorite team, I got out of the car and started to smash it. She said, "No, don't you smash it. Let Zac smash it." That was it. I couldn't handle it anymore. Sports or no sports I had to know. I asked, "What's this all about?" She said, "Zac had an assignment to bring a smashed aluminum can to school today to celebrate Earth Day."

Good communication is a wonderful thing when you use it. It takes work. It requires mental effort to focus on one thing at a time. And it's not just talking, but listening, gesturing, and responding as well.

Respond

Are all your words spent by the end of the day? Do you find yourself responding to those you love with grunts, or even worse, silence? Guess what? God is never too tired to communicate with you. As you spend time with Him today, thank Him for being such a good communicator. Pray that He will help you to communicate His love more effectively.

Remember

Your words taste better when they are seasoned with love.

ALL!

READ

And Noah did all that the Lord commanded Him. — GENESIS 7:5.

REFLECT

Whenever my "to do" list covers more than one page in my planner, I know I'm not going to be able to get it "all" done. I can shift some things to the next day and try to delegate other tasks, but when the day is over, I still don't have everything checked off. However, when I think I'm busy or I've got it bad, I stop and think about Noah. His "to do" list was massive — and it would change the world.

Think how big that little word, "all" is in this verse. Consider "all" that Noah did. He built an ark that was 450 feet long when no one had ever heard of water falling from the sky. He gathered a male and female of every type of animal and put them in the ark. Think of the energy that took. Think of the details — not to mention the mess that the animals made. Once the rain came, Noah and his family lived in the ark for one year, not seeing land for eight months.

Then there was the ridicule Noah endured from all the people who thought he was crazy. Still, he consistently warned his neighbors of the judgment to come and preached the Word of God to them. He begged them to repent, turn to God, and save themselves from total destruction. Although only his three sons and their wives received the message, Noah walked with God and he did "all" the Lord commanded him to do. Now that's faith.

RESPOND

Is your "to do" list filled with world-changing items? Has God put the things on your "to do" list, or is it all your idea? Are you doing all God's commanding you to do today? You can. Just submit "all" of your will to "all" of His — and then give Him your "all."

REMEMBER

When God asks for "all" on His "to do" list, He gives you the wisdom and strength to do it.

Family Chores

Read

"It was he who gave some to be apostles, some to be prophets, some to be evangelists, and some to be pastors and teachers, to prepare God's people for works of service." — Ephesians 4:11-12.

Reflect

One of my jobs in my family is to take out the trash. It's not glamorous. In fact, it stinks. But if I don't do it, the whole place will stink. Other family members have different roles, and things seem to work out okay. But when one of the jobs isn't done, it slows us all down.

The same thing is true in the Church. God designed the Church in such a way that each one of us has a role to play. We are to use the gifts He has given us to carry out His will in the earth. In the verse above, Paul said that God gave the Church some people who have the gift to proclaim the good news, some who share their faith well, some who care for others effectively, and some who teach so others can understand. If those people don't do their jobs, it slows down the work of God — and that stinks.

Too often when you do not use your gift, the job isn't done, or someone else will try to do your job, and they are not effective because God has not gifted them for that job. They need to do what God has called them to do, and you need to do what God has gifted you to do.

Respond

You know you are using what God has given you effectively when He is honored by your efforts. Is that happening in your life? Do you have a sense in your heart that God is pleased with the role you have in His family? Take a little time right now and praise God for giving you a spiritual gift. Ask Him to help you use it in the family of God in a way that will make Him look good. Now take some time to pray for your church. Pray that God will use its members to draw more people to Him.

Remember

The Church is a beautiful place when we're all doing our job.

THE CROWN OF LIFE

READ

Blessed is the man who perseveres under trial, because when he has stood the test, he will receive the crown of life that God has promised to those who love him. — JAMES 1:12.

REFLECT

If you were drowning in a pool, you probably wouldn't be too concerned about tomorrow's schedule. If you were in a burning house, you probably wouldn't be checking your appointment book to see what was happening tomorrow. Why? Because when bad times come, we sense a strong need to focus on the present. But there is one truth we must remember when we go through hard times: they don't last forever. This truth is difficult to focus on when you feel like everything is falling apart and no one cares, but that doesn't make it any less true.

Just like rainy weather affects your moods, difficult times can affect your attitude. Disagreeable weather has a way of wearing you down, and so do disagreeable circumstances. But just as a runner must run until he gets his "second wind," those enduring difficult times must continue on until they rise above the bad time and reach a higher level of living in Christ.

James says a crown of life waits for those who persevere under pressure. Those who complain in troubled circumstances drain their own energy, but those who "rejoice in the Lord always" (see Philippians 3:1) — even in the bad times — find it easier to keep going and believing. You must seek God and trust Him in the middle of bad times for the good times to come.

RESPOND

Today in your prayer time, praise and thank Jesus for His perseverance when dying on the cross. Confess to Him the times you've given up. Ask Him to help you and those who are dear to you endure unpleasant times with His mindset until you get that second spiritual wind to make it through to the end.

REMEMBER

Earn the crown of life today by persevering through any difficulty that comes your way.

You Can Control It

Read

My dear brothers, take note of this: Everyone should be quick to listen, slow to speak, and slow to become angry. — JAMES 1:19.

Reflect

Have you ever lost it? I mean, have you ever had a big argument with someone and really vented your anger? You know, when you weren't only telling them how you felt, but communicating it "loudly" and "clearly." And then the phone rang, and you answered it in your regular non-angry telephone voice. Why? Because you chose to control your anger. So many just say, "I just have a bad temper." But it can be controlled if you *choose* to control it.

Some couples control their anger and save their big disagreements for restaurants. When they know they are going to have a conflict that will lend itself to heightened emotions, they head out for a restaurant and whisper their anger across the table. They force themselves into a situation where they must control their temper.

The challenge for many of us is that we choose not to control our anger. This is why James says we need to be slow to become angry. This calls for thought-out responses and disciplined emotions. In fact, a good recipe for controlling the emotion of anger is to practice the first two disciplines James mentions in today's verse. First, we must be quick to hear. That means be a good listener. Second, we are to be slow to speak. In other words, don't fly off the handle. After we've listened carefully to the other person, we must think through what we need to say and control our anger.

Respond

Anger has destroyed many relationships just because it couldn't be controlled. What is your anger level today? One way to defuse anger is to be thankful. So take some time right now and think of the things in which God has graciously blessed you and thank Him for them. Next, admit to Him the times you haven't controlled your anger. Finally, give your emotions to Him today and ask Him to help you honor Him in all you do.

Remember

There is only one letter difference between anger and danger. Choose to control your anger.

Skeletons in the Closet?

Read

But one thing I do: forgetting what is behind and straining toward what is ahead... — Philippians 3:13.

Reflect

So you have some skeletons in the closet of your life that are robbing you of joy? You're not alone. Let me list a few who were in the same boat.

Abraham worshipped idols but was later called the "friend of God."

Joseph had a prison record but later became Prime Minister of Egypt.

Moses was a murderer, but became Israel's leader.

Rahab was a prostitute in the streets of Jericho and made it into the lineage of Jesus Christ.

Jonah and Mark were both runaway missionaries, but they were later used by God to minister to many.

Peter denied the Lord and cursed, but became the leader of the early church.

Paul persecuted and murdered Christians, but he later became the greatest missionary of the cross.

The truth is, we all have skeletons in our closets. So Jesus died to make us new and seal the closet door. Those who say they don't have any skeletons, or even a closet, are worse than all of us combined who do.

Respond

When you accepted Jesus Christ, you were forgiven of your past to live new and free life. So if any of those old man bones are rattling in your closet, spend some time with God right now and choose to forget the past. Quit beating yourself up over past failures. Like Paul, forget those things which lay behind and press on to the goal which lies ahead. If Paul would have allowed his past to direct his present and future, he may have never left Damascus. Moses would have stayed with his sheep. Peter would have returned to his boats. The same is true for us. God wants to use you like He has used others in the past, who left their past, in the past. So leave it; He has.

Remember

You must leave the past in the past to be useful today and in the future.

He Can Handle It

Read

"Where, O death, is your victory? Where, O death, is your sting?" — 1 Corinthians 15:55.

Reflect

I remember going to a man's funeral and thinking he was the kind of guy who could handle anything. He was probably in his early sixties and had a great reputation in his town. He was poised, stable, a "rock-type" guy. Lots of friends showed up at his funeral and said nice things about him, all which I knew were true. He left a nice family and a solid business. But he died. And I was reminded that there is one thing no one can handle: death. That's why he needed Jesus. He's the only One who can handle death. When we have Jesus in our lives, death has no sting. The grave has no victory.

Sin was what brought man under the power of death. It was Adam's sin that brought about his death and ultimately ours. But where sin abounded, God's grace abounded even more, because while we were sinners Christ died for us. Those of us who have been justified by His blood will be saved from God's wrath through Jesus.

Are you the type who can handle just about anything? Independent? Self-sufficient? Self-reliant? That is admirable, but not scriptural, because believers are to be totally dependent on God. We are to allow Him to handle the things in life that we can't.

Respond

Are you willing to become dependent on God? Does that thought scare you? Spend some time right now praising and thanking God for taking the sting out of death in your life. Confess to Him the times you have ignored what He wanted and relied on yourself without consulting Him. Decide that you will live your life depending on Him to protect and provide for you. Let Him take on the things that you can't handle — and rest in His love and care.

Remember

There is no sting in death for those who will never die.

COUNSEL

READ

"Where there is no guidance, the people fall, but in abundance of counselors there is victory." — PROVERBS 11:14 NASB.

REFLECT

One vital step in making godly decisions and stay in God's will is to get the counsel of others, those who are wise, godly people. These might be your parents, pastors, or Christian friends you know can hear from God. The following scriptures give encouragement to seek the counsel of others.

Proverbs 11:14 — God gives you safety through the counsel of others.

Proverbs 15:22 — God gives you security through the counsel of others.

Proverbs 27:9 — God gives you satisfaction through the counsel of others.

God will give you direction through the counsel of others. Moses received direction from his father-in-law, Jethro (see Exodus 18). God can use your parents to guide you even when they are old (see Proverbs 23:22). And what if these wise, godly people don't have any expertise in the area in which you have to make a decision? Consult them anyway. Give them the facts and ask them what their impressions are and what they believe the Holy Spirit is saying to them.

RESPOND

As you pray today, ask God to direct you to godly people for advice. Ask Him to give them wisdom and ask for wisdom for yourself. As you seek Him, you should notice a consistency in what you hear from God through His Word and what others tell you. That is one way He affirms His will to you. One caution: Be open enough to listen but do not receive anything contrary to God's Word. God will never guide you in any direction that is not consistent with His Word.

REMEMBER

When your way becomes uncertain, seek out a wise, godly counselor.

Picking Your Pattern

Read

Hezekiah was twenty-five years old when he became king, and he reigned in Jerusalem twenty-nine years...He did what was right in the eyes of the Lord, just as his father David had done. — 2 Chronicles 29:1-2.

Reflect

How well do you know your family tree? You probably know your parents, your grandparents, maybe even your great-grandparents. Of all those ancestors you know, think of the one you would want to be most like. What made you choose the one you selected? Strength of character? Success? Money?

Hezekiah's father, Ahaz, was very wicked. He shut up the temple of the Lord and promoted the worship of other gods. He even sacrificed some of his own sons. But when Hezekiah became king, he rejected what Ahaz left behind. In fact, he went all the way back to King David to chose David's pattern for ruling the nation of Israel. It is interesting to note that the of writer of 2 Chronicles even refers to Hezekiah's father as being "David." And when Hezekiah called for the people to return to God, the nation experienced a fresh encounter with God's presence and national blessing.

All of us choose whom we will pattern our lives after. We observe people every day and draw conclusions as to whether or not they live a life worth following. Hezekiah looked back in his family tree and found a godly example of leadership to follow. But God may have provided spiritual parents and grandparents as your pattern.

Respond

Who are you patterning your Christian life after? If there is no one in your natural family, is there someone in the Scriptures or in your church you look to as a model? Take a moment today to praise and thank God for the family tree and examples He has given you in His Word and in His church. Then ask God to strengthen *you* as an example for others to follow.

Remember

Many things in life come without choices, but you can pick your mentors.

Managing God's Affairs

Read

"But seek first his kingdom and his righteousness, and all these things will be given to you as well." — MATTHEW 6:33.

Reflect

One day I was in the grocery store buying four or five different items at the deli. After about the fourth item, the lady waiting on me said, "Boy, you must have come in here hungry or the cupboard is bare." Slightly embarrassed because I was about to order six more things, I admitted that both were true. And even worse, I hadn't started shopping for the things I had gone into the store to buy in the first place.

Being God's manager is a lot like going shopping. First, you need a list of priorities — a list of what is important. Allowing love for anything other than Jesus to invade your attitudes leads to a selfish set of priorities. As you decide with God what is important, you eliminate a lot of things that can sidetrack you. Second, don't shop while you are hungry! You'll buy things that temporarily satisfy your appetite but don't nourish the body. Hunger for the wrong things often robs you of getting things that count and last. Dieting on the wrong things can also make you weak and ineffective in the kingdom work for which you were called.

The beautiful thing about putting God first in your life is the promise that He will take care of all the other necessities that perhaps we would worry about. He has given us His Word that He will take care of the rest if we will put Him and His desires for our lives first.

Respond

What have you been shopping for as God's manager? Are you letting Him set your priorities? Are you letting Him satisfy your appetite before you make your purchases? Pray and ask Him for guidance in all areas of your life. Seek God first, as the Scripture says, and trust Him to provide all your needs.

Remember

Put God first in everything: your family, your church, your job — even your recreation.

Don't Look Back

Read

Still another said, "I will follow you, Lord; but first let me go back and say good-by to my family." Jesus replied, "No one who puts his hand to the plow and looks back is fit for service in the kingdom of God. — Luke 9:61-62.

Reflect

I remember when my brother went to college for his freshman year. Even though he was the big brother who picked on me (not that I didn't deserve it), I cried when he left. I thought, "Why does he have to go so far away to school?" It was about five hours from home, and there were schools closer and just as good. But my tears made little difference, probably because I was a little brother. He knew that was where He was supposed to go to college, and my crying about it didn't help make his decision easier.

In today's verse Jesus told a would-be disciple not to go home before committing to follow Him. Why? Because He knew what would happen if the man went home. Jesus knew there would probably be a party, and at the party cousins and friends would probably say to him, "You're going where? To do what? For how long?" Because Jesus sensed a lack of commitment, He cautioned the young man not to go back, because there were influences that would make him back down from his commitment to follow Him. Jesus knew the man's friends and family would not understand.

Looking back is unacceptable when it comes to commitment. The children of Israel looked back to Egypt when they said, "At least we had food back there." Lot's wife looked back when they left the wicked city of Sodom before it was destroyed, and she didn't live to see another thing. The lesson learned is that when God calls you out of one place and into another — don't look back!

Respond

Is God asking you to take a step up in your walk with Him which would require you to move out of your comfort zone? Just do it — and don't look back! Ask God to give you discernment of the wrong influences. Let His wisdom guide you to the influences that support the principles of commitment and service He is calling you to walk in today.

Remember

Avoid those who will try to talk you out of following Jesus.

Be Stable

Read

"Then we will no longer be infants, tossed back and forth by the waves, and blown here and there by every wind of teaching and by the cunning and craftiness of men in their deceitful scheming." — Ephesians 4:14.

Reflect

When I was young, I started running around with a certain crowd whose ideas didn't fit my family's. In fact, if they had lived in my house under our family rules, they would have had to change their behavior, language, and general attitude. But the concern wasn't that they might move in with me. I knew that wouldn't happen. The question was: Would I bring their ideas into my house, with my family? Or even worse, would I become like them and abandon the stable family I loved?

The church is to be a stable family, but it is challenged from the outside too. In fact, some people on the outside may even come in and try to spread their false ideas. However, a stable church is the church that takes its cues from God and Him alone. Those cues are in His Word and revealed by His Spirit. Like me, they will either convert the invader or separate themselves from them to protect the purity of their congregation.

Whenever the family of God moves away from His directives, it becomes unstable and less attractive to the hurting world. More important, because God cannot bless them, they have nothing to give those who are hurting and full of need.

Respond

Has your thinking been challenged by those outside the family of God? Do you find yourself thinking like them? It won't happen all of a sudden, but gradually. So be careful! Guard your heart and don't accept anyone's thinking patterns but God's! Get into God's Word and renew your mind to think like Him. He knows what life is about. There is nothing new to Him. Praise Him for the stability He provides for those who seek to serve Him. Ask Him to help you become a stabilizing member in His family, the Church.

Remember

No garden is suddenly overcome by weeds, no church suddenly splits, no family suddenly falls apart, and no believer suddenly stops believing.

The Money Trap

Read

For the love of money is the root of all sorts of evil, and some by longing for it have wandered away from the faith, and pierced themselves with many a pang. — 1 Timothy 6:10 NASB.

Reflect

Americans these days seem to have the false idea that to gain affluence is to gain value as a person and peace of mind. Too often we think that having more money than others places us above them or makes us smarter. And we believe peace is something that is obtained by acquiring more. We think if we can just have this or that, then we'll be happy.

But this is a trap. Money can't ultimately bring about these goals. In fact, money can be a snare that is camouflaged with many empty promises. This verse is trying to tell us that those who want to get rich can't rest because the desire for money — instead of the desire for God — fills their minds. Therefore, Paul adds, they will experience some unexpected traps along the way of their empty pursuit. A great example of this was Howard Hughes. He was extremely wealthy, yet he died a miserable man.

The result of seeking riches is to wander spiritually and encounter personal grief. But the result of seeking first the kingdom of God is to have all your needs met (see Matthew 6:33). You can still have lots of money and love and serve God. In fact, it's a joy to be blessed financially and be able to give generously to the work of the Lord.

Respond

What do you really love most in life? You demonstrate what you love most by how you spend your time, talents, and money. Take a look at your checkbook. What does it reveal about what you love? If God's ledger looks a little light, ask Him to deliver you from the trappings of the love for money and the things it buys and commit your heart to seek Him first.

Remember

Use your money to build God's kingdom, not yours.

LEAVE YOUR SIN

READ

Jesus straightened up and asked her, "Woman, where are they? Has no one condemned you?" "No one, sir," she said. "Then neither do I condemn you," Jesus declared. "Go now and leave your life of sin." — JOHN 8:10-11.

REFLECT

Jesus removes man's heart of stone and replaces it with His loving presence. If you don't believe it, take time to read the story of a woman who was caught in adultery. (See John 8:1-11.) Jesus delivered this woman from her executioners and invited her to start a new life. The hard-hearted Jews who caught her intended to trap Jesus. If He told them not to stone her, He would disobey the law of Moses. If he said to stone her, the Jewish leaders could claim that Jesus was no better than them.

What did Jesus do? After they presented the woman and her sin before Him, He started writing in the ground. No one really knows what He wrote. It could have been a reminder to them that the very law they referred to was written by the finger of God. He could have even been writing out each of the accuser's sins. Whatever the case, Jesus then upheld the law of Moses and showed His compassion in one sentence. "He who is without sin among you, let him be the first to throw a stone at her."

Only one was qualified to cast a stone at the adulteress that day, and He was Jesus. But instead of exercising the judgment of a person, He took the opportunity to show the woman God's condemnation of sin and His compassion for sinners. After He forgave her, He invited her to leave her life of sin.

RESPOND

That is exactly what God is saying to you today. "Leave the sinful habits that keep you from serving Me and give your life totally to Me." Confess any sin in your life right now, take Jesus' hand of forgiveness, and walk with Him throughout your day.

REMEMBER

God's love is what gives you the strength to leave your sin and walk with Him.

Don't Forget God

Read

"Each of you is to take up a stone on his shoulder, according to the number of tribes of Israelites, to serve as a sign among you. In the future, when your children ask you, 'What do these stones mean?' ...Tell them these stones are to be a memorial to the people of Israel forever." — JOSHUA 4:5-7.

Reflect

The Israelites were at the point of going into the land God had promised them, but first they had to cross the Jordan River. So God instructed Joshua to have the priests carry the Ark of the Covenant into the river. And when their feet touched the water, the river parted. Then the priests stood in the middle of the river bottom as the nation of Israel crossed over. What a scene!

All Israel stood gazing as twelve select men descended the West Bank of the Jordan and reverently walked out to where the ark was resting on the shoulders of the priests. Each pried a large stone from the bottom of the Jordan River, then marched back up to Gilgal, placing the stones in a rude, humble heap. Not much of a monument, considering the great display of God's power they had just witnessed. But it was to commemorate God's deliverance. Not only that, in the coming months when the Israelites would engage in battle, if any were to flee, these stones would cry out as a reminder to them that they were abandoning the God who had delivered them.

Respond

What reminders have you placed in your life to keep you from forgetting God and all He has done for you? Do you have any stones of remembrance that alert you to the fact that God has been real in your life? If not, write some down today. Spend a moment or two praising and thanking Him for His power to deliver you. Confess to Him the times you have forgotten Him. And ask Him to help you be a reminder to others of His love and grace.

Remember

Memorials remind us that God was working in the past and He is still working today.

Staying True to Yourself

Read

"Now they found an Egyptian in the field and brought him to David...Then David said to him, 'Will you bring me down to this band?'" — 1 Samuel 30:11, 15 NASB.

Reflect

As David and his men chased the enemy who had kidnapped their families, they came upon a half-dead Egyptian. They stopped, revived him, and found out that he knew all about the enemy. He helped David and his men conquer the enemy. What does this say to us?

In the midst of a crisis we need to remain true to our beliefs, to who we are in Christ. Even though they were busy pursuing the enemy and anxious to get their families back, David stopped the campaign to help this one who was in trouble. David was a shepherd at heart, so he could not in good conscience leave this man to die. Because he was true to himself, God made what seemed to be an insignificant act the key to victory.

Many times in a crisis we tend to run — and we run over people in the process. We get busy trying to deal with the things that are causing our stress and miss the little things that God may be using to speak the answer to us. Basically, all we are talking about here is resting in God and trusting Him even when a crisis hits. If we will do that, and remain true to who we are as believers, then God can bless us and deliver us.

Respond

Do you wait on God in a crisis, or do you try to make things happen yourself? Wait on God today. Spend time praising and thanking Him for His faithfulness and ask Him to speak to you. Be true to yourself, to who you are in Christ, at all times. And trust God without reservation and doubt. He was faithful to David, and He will be faithful to you.

Remember

Be who God created you to be, especially in a crisis, and you will walk in His blessings and see His deliverance.

Godly Confrontation

Read

And let us consider how we may spur one another on toward love and good deeds. — Hebrews 10:24.

Reflect

When I was compelled to confront a friend about some improper behavior that was affecting family and friends, I didn't want to do it. I put it off for weeks. I was afraid. I wanted to sweep it all under the rug. But I knew God was prodding me. So I confronted my friend in love and with total confidentiality. I was rejected and crushed. A week went by with no response. A month. Two months. About three months later, my friend stopped me and said, "Thanks. You were right." It was worth it.

If you like confrontation, probably something is wrong with you! One reason we don't like confrontation is that we are afraid of rejection. Initially, that may be the case. However, when confrontation is presented with the other party's best interest in mind and in a spirit of love, it can positively transform a life.

Some people respond well to confrontation. King David was confronted by the prophet Nathan about adultery, and because he knew in his heart that Nathan was right and he had grieved God, he responded positively. Was it pleasant? Not at all. Was it worth it? Absolutely.

It's important to remember that before confrontation occurs, you must be sure your heart is right, that this is God's idea and not yours. If it is yours, you may purge yourself of a lot of resentment or anger and lose a friend, and no fruit comes of it in either of your lives. So go in love and with God's wisdom and blessing.

Respond

Do you need to be confronted? Do you need to deal with some things in your life that would be an embarrassment to God? Do you need to confront someone about Jesus Christ? Has the groundwork been laid, but you have not confronted that person to ask them to make a decision? Seek God's direction right now, and then do what He tells you to do.

Remember

Effective confrontation is done in love and with the other party's best interest in mind. Ask God for wisdom, and follow His lead.

A Head and Heart Thing

Read

That if you confess with your mouth, "Jesus is Lord," and believe in your heart that God raised him from the dead, you will be saved. For it is with your heart that you believe and are justified, and it is with your mouth that you confess and are saved. — Romans 10:9-10.

Reflect

Have you ever been to a basketball or football game and watched a team get destroyed because of their attitude? They knew all the plays. They had the game plan in their minds, but they didn't have the heart to pull it off. I have seen games where there was no way a certain team should have lost. Their statistics proved they were much better than their opposition. So what was the problem? No heart and bad attitudes. It can happen in the game of life as well as in the spiritual realm. People have the head knowledge about what Jesus came and did for them on the cross. They show up for the game — go to church — but somehow they miss the heart thing. They miss the change that takes place when He takes over.

During Jesus' day many religious leaders focused on works to be approved by God. When Jesus came on the scene, it was His objective to change things. He didn't focus on all of the *negative* commands the Pharisees felt were the litmus test to being accepted by God. He focused on the *positive* act of developing a personal relationship with God the Father through faith in the Son.

Respond

You don't have to work to gain a relationship with God. You don't have to look a certain way or do a certain number of good deeds to get to heaven. You just simply believe and give your heart to Him. Thank Him and praise Him now for making it so simple to have a relationship with Him. Ask Him to help you make it simple to others.

Remember

Head knowledge is nothing without a heart relationship.

How Do We Really Change?

Read

God made him who had no sin to be sin for us, so that in him we might become the righteousness of God. — 2 Corinthians 5:21.

Reflect

Some people will never change. But some will change when they have enough information to see that change is in their best interest. Some will change when they hurt enough. Some will change when they receive so much that they are compelled to change. People seldom change because someone is trying to change them. There have been many marriages that went down the tubes because there was a false assumption on one party's behalf that, "I can change them."

A beautiful illustration of change is found in the book of Philemon. This short book is almost like a postcard that the apostle Paul wrote on behalf of his friend Onesimus. Onesimus was a slave who had stolen from his master, Philemon, and then had run away to Rome. In Rome, he became a Christian. He then returned to Philemon with a letter from Paul which explained that Onesimus was now a brother in the faith and was changed, that Philemon could be reconciled to him.

The truth is, God is the only One who can really change anybody. He changes people from the inside out — when they allow Him to. He has a way of melting our stubborn, hard heart so a transformation can take place on the inside of us. The Holy Spirit moves on our hearts just like He moved over the earth in Genesis 1:2, bringing life back to what was cold and dark.

Respond

Thank God for His mercy and grace in changing your life. Confess to Him the times you have been unwilling to change and become more like Jesus, and allow the Holy Spirit to work in your heart. Finally, pray for those you know who need to be reconciled to God and those who need to change. Release the Holy Spirit in Jesus' name to do a work of change in them today.

Remember

God can change the lives of those who irritate you today!

Don't Deceive Yourself!

Read

Do not merely listen to the word, and so deceive yourselves. Do what it says. — James 1:22.

Reflect

When I was a small boy I remember playing outside of our country church after services and hearing my dad call me to come to the car so we could go home. I continued to play with my friends. After a minute or two I faintly recall hearing him again, "Tom, come on. We're leaving." I continued to play with my friends. The third time, my dad raised his voice (discipline by decibel) and said, "LESLIE THOMAS HUFTY GET OVER HERE NOW. WE'RE LEAVING." It was at that point that I scampered over to him. Before I got in the car he asked me, "Son, did you hear me call you the first two times?" I replied, "Yes sir." He said, "Then why didn't you come?" I said, "Because daddy, you didn't use your loud voice."

Every time my father spoke, his objective was the same: obedience. And when God speaks to us, His objective is no different. I believe sometimes we deceive ourselves into thinking, "This isn't important right now." Maybe it's because God doesn't speak again and again, getting louder and louder, like many parents do. He speaks just a time or two and then leaves His Word with us.

Today's scripture reminds us that we had better do more than listen. We had better obey what God says, because obedience to God's Word brings His will to pass in the earth. Only through our obedience can God reach the lost and disciple nations. God's Word has been affecting people's lives for centuries and it will continue to do so. Our responsibility is to be "doers of the Word," and not just hearers.

Respond

Is God speaking to you today? Are you waiting for the loud disciplinary voice before you obey, or are you just not listening at all? God is speaking to you about your life, so take time to listen — and then obey.

Remember

God wants to speak to you today, so listen for His voice and then obey His Word.

All The Right Moves

Read

No one will be able to stand against you all the days of your life. As I was with Moses, so I will be with you; I will never leave you nor forsake you. — Joshua 1:5.

Reflect

I'm not a roller coaster guy. Now, don't get me wrong, I love to watch them. But being a spectator is as close as I ever want to be. I'll never forget when my son was younger and wanted to ride the Timber Wolf at World's of Fun in Kansas City. The giant roller coaster had just been constructed, the lines were always long, and the hype was heard daily. The more Zac looked at the roller coaster and contemplated his ride, the more nervous he became. The sheer size of it was intimidating. There was only one thing that would ease his nerves. He needed someone he had confidence in to go with him.

Zac looked at me, remembered my horror stories, then turned to his mom. "Mom will you go with me?" He said. "I'd love to," she responded, and off to the long line they went. As I waited at the exit, praising God quietly that my wife loves roller coasters, I saw them coming out, smiling from ear to ear. Zac was saying, "What a rush!!! It was great!!!" Why was it such a good experience? Because his mom was with him.

Like Zac, Joshua could not have taken Moses' place and led the children of Israel into the Promised Land without God being with him. Knowing God was with him at every turn made the difference in Joshua's confidence and his ability to enjoy the journey.

Respond

God is with you too. At every turn of life, watching every move, protecting and guiding, He is there. Take some time right now to thank and praise Him for His presence in your life, for His guidance and comfort as you ride the roller coaster ride of life. It's great when He is by your side.

Remember

You can have all the confidence you need for today, because the Lord is by your side.

Be First to Serve

Read

The Son of Man did not come to be served, but to serve..." — MATTHEW 20:28.

Reflect

Have you ever had the opportunity to work with ten or twelve second graders? If you have, you know when you ask them to form a straight line, nine of them will usually clamor to be first. In so doing, they illustrate what society has taught them, that coming in first is what's most important. The disciples in Jesus' day weren't unlike second graders. They argued over who would sit closest to Jesus. So they too were accustomed to the habits of their peers.

Jesus, however, teaches that first doesn't mean first when it comes to living a life that pleases God. In fact, if you want to be great, He says you must be a servant. If you want to be first in the eyes of God, you must put others ahead of yourself. This philosophy goes against the grain of what society teaches to be successful. Yet in God's eyes, success isn't based on how many people you boss, but on how many you serve.

A servant will reach out to touch someone who can do absolutely nothing for them in return. Jesus didn't say, "I came to serve when I felt like it." He said, "I came to serve." Our attitude as believers should be no different. If we truly want to be like Jesus, we should look for every opportunity to help people.

Respond

Who can you serve today who can do nothing for you in return? Spend some time thanking God for His faithful service to you. Thank Him for listening to your prayers, and for protecting and providing for you. Ask Him to forgive you for the times you haven't been a servant to those around you. Also ask Him to give you the wisdom needed to serve others the way He would. Then go out and be last!

Remember

If you want to get God's attention today, serve someone.

Surrendered

Read

Therefore, I urge you, brothers, in view of God's mercy, to offer your bodies as living sacrifices, holy and pleasing to God — this is your spiritual act of worship. — Romans 12:1.

Reflect

Henry kept a list of all the people he could whip. He even boasted of his list, and as a result it made him feel very confident about himself. Then one day a big guy in town came up to Henry and said, "Hey, is my name on that list?" Henry looked and replied, "Yes it is, right here," showing the man. "Right. I don't think you can whip me," the big guy challenged. "Well O.K. then," Henry sheepishly said, "I'll just scratch your name off the list."

We're often like Henry. We try to bluff our way through life, trusting in our own ingenuity, craftiness, or ability to con someone. We trust in our personality, talent, goodness, and reputation. We have no trouble trusting God with our eternity, but we have great difficulty trusting Him with our daily lives. And this type of behavior simply says God is not trustworthy.

Surrender is not a word that fits into our vocabulary very well. After all, we are a part of "the land of the free and home of the brave." We surrender to no one. But Paul says in light of the mercy God has demonstrated toward us, we must by all means surrender to Him, because He is trustworthy.

Respond

If your life is a mess right now and you can't understand what's going on, let me assure you that God IS trustworthy. He isn't surprised by your predicament. Spend some time now with the Lord adoring Him for His continual presence and concern for you. Ask Him to strengthen the trust level of you and others you know who are currently struggling in a life storm. The storm raging in your life has been calmed by Him many times before. Just realize He is in your lifeboat again and turn to Him.

Remember

When you surrender to Jesus, you win.

The Harvest Is Ripe

Read

Then another angel came out of the temple and called in a loud voice to him who was sitting on the cloud, "Take your sickle and reap, because the time to reap has come, for the harvest of the earth is ripe." — Revelation 14:15.

Reflect

His name was Tim. A pastor friend and I met him in a hospital waiting room. As I visited with an area pastor, Tim came in and got on the telephone. His language was foul, and it was obvious he was upset. After he finished his conversation on the phone, he sat down with a tremendous sigh. We engaged Tim in a conversation only to learn this twenty-something young man was facing the decision of taking his mother off a respirator. His father had died just four months earlier. He made statements like: "I don't know which way to turn," and "What's God trying to do in all this?" After about forty-five minutes of conversation, my pastor friend asked Tim if he would like to have a personal relationship with Jesus Christ. Tim not only said he did, but within minutes he was giving his life to Jesus. We all stood and embraced each other in that waiting room and prayed together.

There are "Tims" all around us asking the same questions: "Where is God?" and "What's He trying to do in all I'm going through?" The message for us here is a simple formula we need to remember every day when we get out of bed.

Willing Witness + Seeking Soul = Divine Encounter

Respond

Where do you fit in this equation? Are you a willing witness? Would you like to have a divine encounter? Spend time with God right now and ask Him to help you be the willing witness He has called you to be. Pray that He would lead you to a seeking soul today.

Remember

If you will be a willing witness, God is preparing a divine encounter for you today.

Love in Action

Read

I am not commanding you, but I want to test the sincerity of your love by comparing it with the earnestness of others. — 2 Corinthians 8:8.

Reflect

Several years ago, I ran across the following letter a boyfriend wrote to his girlfriend to express how much he missed her:

> Dear Beth,
>
> Thoughts of you are dancing throughout the portals of my mind. As I think of you, I get goosebumps from the bottom of my feet to the top of my head, and my earnest desire to be with you is causing all kinds of palpitations within me. I will assure you, my dearest sweetheart, that there is nothing, absolutely nothing, that will keep me from coming to you soon. Mount Everest becomes but a little hill that I am willing to take the challenge to climb if that, in fact, was the thing that kept me from you. The Pacific Ocean becomes but a small pool, because the knowledge that you would be on the other side is all I would need to know to tread water for as long as it would take, because if you are on the other side, it's worth the journey. The Sahara Desert becomes like an Alaskan freeze, knowing that you're on the other side waiting for me. If there are no oases out there, I will make them. If I cannot make them, I am willing to become dehydrated, in my pursuit for you. What I am simply trying to say to you, my little chipmunk, is that I love you, and my desire and passion to be with you is burning within me.
>
> In love, Ralph.
>
> P. S. I will see you Friday night if it doesn't rain.

Ralph's talk sounded good, but when it came to proving them, his words didn't mean anything. Words are cheap if they're not backed up by action.

Respond

Ask God to show you if you have spoken words of love and then not acted upon them. Pray for a heart of compassion that demonstrates God's love to others today.

Remember

Unless your love is put into action, all you are is a lot of talk.

ULTIMATE LOVE

READ

But from everlasting to everlasting the Lord's love is with those who fear him. — PSALM 103:17.

REFLECT

When I accidentally dropped my wife's antique jar on the kitchen floor, it shattered into a million pieces. I remember that my daughter was just learning to walk, and how I needed to pick up every sliver of glass so she would not cut her feet. Rhonda and I went to great lengths to clean that floor. We vacuumed, mopped, and as a final resort I went over every inch of that kitchen with my bare hand to detect any piece of glass I missed. Once I ran my hand across a sliver of glass. I felt it, looked at my hand, and saw the blood surface. I remembered thinking, I'm glad its my blood and not my baby's. I can stand seeing my blood, but seeing the blood of my child tears me up inside. It struck me that it was the same for our heavenly Father when He saw the blood of His Son, Jesus, shed for you and me.

If there is anything you need to know through this passage of scripture today, it is this: You are secure in God's love. Nothing you can feel or do will stop Him from loving you. His love is the ultimate love — from everlasting to everlasting.

All of us have been rejected by another person at one time or another. Maybe someone promised us that they would always love us, and then to our surprise, one day they told us their love had grown cold or that they had found someone else. But we can be assured that that will never happen between us and God. His love for us will never cease. It is from everlasting (before time) to everlasting (for eternity).

RESPOND

When you pray today, spend some time thanking God for His unceasing, unconditional love. Ask Him to heal your scars caused by rejection and conditional love and replace the hurt with His overflowing love.

REMEMBER

God loved you before you were born and He will love you throughout eternity. Today, you are loved with the ultimate love.

R·E·S·P·E·C·T

READ

Submit to one another out of reverence for Christ. — EPHESIANS 5:21.

REFLECT

Respect is a big deal to God. Throughout Scripture, He drives home the point that we are to show Him respect. The reason is simple, God knows that where there is no respect, there will be no relationship.

Think what your home would be like if there was no respect shown for your family members. If you don't respect someone, you will eventually stop trusting them. If you stop trusting them, you will eventually stop loving them. I've seen many relationships die because somewhere along the line there developed a disrespect that went unchecked.

Pop singer, Aretha Franklin, made the word "respect" popular in the seventies. Her hit song told listeners that respect is what is needed in relationships. The apostle Paul had brought this point out centuries earlier when he wrote to the church in Ephesus about husband and wife relationships: If a husband does not respect his wife, the relationship is in trouble. But the opposite is also true. If the wife has no respect for her husband, the relationship will suffer.

The truth is, you're not going to want to get close to someone you do not respect. Nor will they want to get close to you if you do not respect them. Our reverence and respect for God draws us to Him and Him to us. We bring honor to Him by the way we live if we show respect for Him in our daily lives. Likewise, it is equally important that we show respect for other people. If we do that, our relationships will be good ones.

RESPOND

Take some time to pray about your respect for God. Ask Him to show you the areas of your life where you are not showing Him reverence. Then ask Him to show you the people in your life to whom you need to show more respect. Pray for His love and compassion to flow through you to them today.

REMEMBER

Show some respect today and see if it doesn't enhance all your relationships.

Purity Is Not Obsolete

Read

It is God's will that you should be sanctified; that you should avoid sexual immorality; that each one of you should learn to control his own body in a way that is holy and honorable, not in passionate lust like the heathen, who do not know God. — 1 Thessalonians 4:3-5.

Reflect

Each year America sees a rise in the number of cases of AIDS and other sexually transmitted diseases. It sure doesn't sound like the "safe sex" campaign is working. And why should that surprise us? There is no such thing as "safe sex."

Sex is in the news, and we're faced with it in some way every day. We need to submit our sexual desires, like everything else, to the authority of God, who made them and therefore knows how they can be used positively.

Many people today think that God's will about sex is a mystery, but Paul spells it out clearly in this verse. Sexual immorality has no place in the life of a Christian, no matter how many TV shows and movies glamorize it. Our sexual desires are to be under control and reserved only for marriage.

The challenge is that many people think even though they have lustful thoughts, they have control over their bodies. But in reality, their sexual drives are controlling them. If they do not stop these immoral fantasies, they will eventually begin to act them out. Inward sin always works its way out. The only way to protect ourselves from sexual sin is to be honest with ourselves when we are tempted and run straight to God, or we will fall into unacceptable, ungodly behavior patterns. We need God's help and support to overcome any temptation.

Respond

Reaffirm with God right now that your body is His temple and you have the mind of Christ. Thank Him for His strength to overcome any temptation that comes your way today and commit yourself to live a pure life.

Remember

A life of purity is a life of security.

It is No Longer I

Read

I have been crucified with Christ and I no longer live, but Christ lives in me. — Galatians 2:20.

Reflect

I love the story about the great theologian Augustine. One day after his conversion to Christ he was passing by one of the bars he used to frequently patronize. As he walked down the sidewalk, a prostitute approached him, a lady of the evening with whom he was all too familiar. She was smiling, assuming Augustine had returned after his little phase of religion. As he drew nearer, Augustine kept his eyes focused straight ahead and never looked at her as she brushed his shoulder. After he passed her, she stopped and called his name, "Augustine" she said, "Don't you recognize who you just walked by? It is me." Augustine stopped, turned to her and said, "Yes, but it is no longer me."

Augustine experienced the life-changing principle that when you give your life to Jesus, it is no longer you who lives, but Jesus who lives in you. He comes into your life not to take second or third place, He comes in to take over! Throughout history God has turned drunks into disciples and sinners into saints. And His life-transforming power is still at work today.

Respond

Have you had the same kind of experience Augustine had? When the past failures brush through your life do you keep your focus straight in resistance to the temptations? Take some time today to praise and thank God that you are no longer walking in darkness, and that He is there for you when you face temptation. Ask Him to cleanse you for the times you have submitted to the temptations and ignored Him. Pray that God would place a hedge of protection around you so you may be a stronger witness for Him.

Remember

Jesus died on the cross not to be a part of your life, but to become your life.

A Right to Be Angry?

Read

But the Lord replied, "Have you any right to be angry?" — Jonah 4:4.

Reflect

My high school basketball coach expressed his anger in a unique way. During a game, an empty chair was always positioned to his right. No player, statistician, or assistant coach was allowed to sit in that chair. Why? Because that was his "hitting chair." Every time he became upset with a player or referee, he yelled and hit the chair with his right hand.

God spoke the words of today's scripture to Jonah, whom He commanded to go and preach to the evil city of Nineveh. At first he ran away. But after a three-day "submarine cruise," God convinced him to obey. What was Jonah's message? Repent or God will destroy you in forty days. And what was the good news? They repented. The bad news was that Jonah became angry at God because he spared the people of Nineveh. He was angry about the wrong thing, and God told him, "You have no right to be angry."

In his anger, Jonah went outside the city to pout. So God provided a vine to give him shade. Jonah was pleased with the shade, but the next day the vine died and he was left in the scorching heat again. Once again he pouted. God told him he had no right to pout, because he was only concerned about his own comfort.

Respond

None of us have a right to be angry when it comes to doing God's will. So ask the Lord's forgiveness today for the times you haven't been concerned about the things He is concerned about. Thank Him for His patience toward you. Pray for those you know who have a negative attitude that contributes to their anger. Then pray that God will use you today to do His will — cheerfully and thankfully.

Remember

If you need to get angry, get angry at Satan, he's the real enemy!

Leaving and Receiving

Read

And everyone who has left houses or brothers or sisters or father or mother or children or farms for My name's sake, shall receive many times as much, and shall inherit eternal life. — MATTHEW 19:29 NASB.

Reflect

The Hufty family hasn't moved much. In fact, my son was fourteen before he knew ministers moved. When we did sense the direction of the Lord to move, it was to move closer to Rhonda's and my parents. I thought, *Lord, I've already left the farm and family, so now, do we really go back?* It was like God was saying to us, "You've already left, and you were willing to go farther, but now I'm calling you back home to be with the family that raised you. Make an impact where I put you, no matter where it is."

To be a consistent follower of Jesus Christ there must be a "leaving." We must all leave things behind that were once the most important things in our lives and replace them with Jesus. Now don't think this verse says that to be a real Christian you are to disregard your family and possessions. In fact, it is telling us the opposite. God gave you your family and possessions, and He expects you to be a good steward of them. However, those gifts are never to come before the Giver.

Our society promotes the idea that to find satisfaction we must constantly pursue something else that we don't have. But the Bible offers us the exact opposite conclusion. It teaches us to leave and give, because contentment never comes from obtaining externals — NEVER!

Respond

When God tells you to leave someone or some place, He has your best interest in mind. When you leave according to His direction, you receive His blessings. In your devotional time today, ask Him to help you accomplish what would please Him today. Ask Him to help you "leave" the emptiness of striving for power, position, and things and receive the joy and contentment found in intimately knowing Him.

Remember

To follow Jesus fully, you must leave the old things and embrace Him.

Are You Lost?

Read

In all your ways acknowledge him, and he will make your paths straight. — Proverbs 3:6.

Reflect

I learned how to follow directions from my dad. One night when I was a boy, we were out "coon hunting." I'll never forget that night. Stars filled the pitch black sky of a beautiful, peaceful night. But it stopped being peaceful when dad said, "I think I'm lost." When he said that, the beauty and peace of the night were immediately replaced with fear and panic. My brother and I had racing hearts and imagined crazy things — like what was going to eat us — but dad stayed calm and looked to the sky. He located the north star and said we needed to walk that way. As we followed him, we could hear him mumble. "This sure doesn't feel right." But he kept following the star, and we came out of the woods. There was peace and relief.

God has a definite direction for our lives. He wants to guide us in His ways. But some of us trust our feelings too much. We go in one direction because it feels good, and we just get deeper and deeper in the woods. This is why the writer of Proverbs says we need to be praying about the direction we are going all the time. We get into trouble when we try to impose our feelings on God's directive. He is the star we must follow, no matter how it feels.

Respond

Have you been following God's direction for your life? Are you seeking Him and praying more today than you were two years ago? Or have you been wandering around in life's woods, fearfully lost? God reveals His direction through His Word and prayer. If you're struggling right now with God's direction, get His map — the Bible — and take a look. Then get on your knees and look up. Find His star and follow it.

Remember

Don't trust your feelings, trust the Father.

The Kingdom of Forgiveness

Read

"Therefore, the kingdom of heaven is like a king who wanted to settle accounts with his servants." — Matthew 18:23.

Reflect

Relationships are a big deal to God — so big that He allowed His only Son to be sacrificed so we could have a relationship with Him. The kingdom of heaven is the kingdom of right relationships. And since it takes forgiveness to have right relationships, it could be called the kingdom of forgiveness. Jesus made it clear in Matthew 18:21-35 that if we want to have anything to do with His kingdom, we must be forgivers.

The truth is, there are many downsides to unforgiveness. If we refuse to forgive, we become hypocritical. And the strongest language Jesus ever used was against those who were hypocritical in their religion. (See Matthew 23:13-36.) In practical terms, what this means is that our Christian life becomes a lie. We accept God's forgiveness for our sin, but refuse to offer forgiveness to someone else.

Another downside of unforgiveness is the inner stress we experience because we refuse to forgive. The misery that an unforgiving spirit produces is tremendous. It often results in tormenting thoughts and agonizing unrest. In fact, unforgiveness affects every part of life. It is a poison that kills inner strength and contentment — and can even destroy the physical body.

Respond

I'm sure you know people who are going through inner agony because they have refused to forgive. Pray for them today. Pray that they will release the bitterness that has caused their inner torture. Then take time to pray for yourself. Ask God to be the King of all your relationships. The more you allow Him to rule, the more you will understand the kingdom of heaven and the more forgiving you will become.

Remember

Be a solid citizen of God's kingdom: forgive others as God has forgiven you.

Make a Difference Today

Read

"Get yourself ready! Stand up and say to them whatever I command you. Do not be terrified by them, or I will terrify you before them." — Jeremiah 1:17.

Reflect

Hollywood has inspired all of us who love the underdog. If the five Rocky movies weren't enough, the Karate Kid flicks would make you think the little guy always wins. But unfortunately, real life isn't always this way. Sometimes the little guy loses and feels real pain. And the pain never goes away in the two hours it takes to sit through a movie.

Jeremiah knew what pain was. God gave him a message to proclaim, but there was just one catch...no one would listen. There would be no converts, only ridicule and rejection. Everybody Jeremiah told refused the message. So, why go? Because of the One who sent him. Jeremiah knew that the One who sent him was worth every rejection.

Then there would be One who would share a message like him. Jesus would cry over the people who rejected Him just like Jeremiah. But Jesus would take it further. He would die for those who rejected Him. Jeremiah was in good company and so are you when you take a stand for Jesus.

Rejecting the message of Jesus is nothing new. People today often won't listen unless they hurt bad enough. So, what are we to do? Like Jeremiah, we are to be faithful and refuse to worry about who listens, because our job is simply to do the will of Him who sends us.

Respond

Have you ever been rejected? What did you do? Did you blend into the woodwork, or did you take your stand? Spend some time during today's devotional praising and thanking God for being on your side as an obedient believer. Declare your trust in Him, so you can stand strong. Then go out and take a stronger stand today than you did yesterday.

Remember

Keep sharing your faith, because you can make a difference. In heaven you'll be surprised who was paying attention.

Don't Put It Off!

Read

Then Agrippa said to Paul, "Do you think that in such a short time you can persuade me to be a Christian?" — Acts 26:28.

Reflect

I saw a sign not long ago that said, "Never put off to tomorrow what you can do the day after tomorrow." Procrastination puts things off until sometimes it's too late. And the worst procrastination is to put God off. Agrippa was one who did this. Paul told King Agrippa the story of how he became a Christian. With great detail and convincing truths, he led up to a final question: "King Agrippa, do you believe the prophets? I know you do." But Agrippa refused to answer Paul, saying he needed more time.

No one really knows for sure if Agrippa ever became a Christian, but I think it is doubtful. Still, he heard the message. There are a lot of Agrippas out there in our world today who are close to accepting Jesus Christ but keep putting off their decision for one reason or another. For some, the stumbling block is their intellect. Like Agrippa, they are well educated and have influential positions. They are full of philosophical and scientific questions that cause doubts about the "viability" of God.

Paul knew Agrippa was an intellectual, so in his presentation he tried to answer every possible question the king might have had. Paul also knew this would be his last shot at Agrippa, so he communicated clearly the message that had changed his life. Sadly, Agrippa refused. Was it pride?

Respond

Do you know people who need more time before they make their commitment to Jesus Christ? Have they been needing more time for years? It is the biggest decision in life, and it should be thought through. But it shouldn't be put off. There may be those who know the Bible is true, but they have been deceived into thinking they can rebel one more day. Pray that you will be able to communicate clearly to them today. Let them think it over, but encourage them not to put it off. Because that one more day may be their last.

Remember

Time is ticking away. Don't put God off.

Coming Home

Read

"In my Father's house are many rooms; ...I am going there to prepare a place for you.... I will come back and take you to be with me that you also may be were I am." — JOHN 14:2-3.

Reflect

I'll never forget when my eight year old daughter Mackenzie and I arrived home from our trip to Denver. We got up early and were excited about all the things we had to share with Rhonda and Zac when we got home. We were scheduled to sit in different rows in the overbooked flight, and Mackenzie was uneasy about not sitting next to me. But once again, the Lord came through. The one passenger on the flight who didn't show up was in the seat assigned next to me. So when the door shut for the flight to begin, I called Mackenzie back to sit next to me. God still amazes me. He cares about the little things in our lives, and over and over again He gives us rest and peace when He senses we are uneasy.

When we arrived home it was great. There's nothing quite like coming home. Only God and I really know how I felt when I saw Rhonda. When we hugged, I didn't want to let go. Each day I get a little better glimpse of what "becoming one" is all about. We all went out to a restaurant for a feast and shared all the things that happened while we were apart. There was never a break in the conversation. Coming home has never been better. But someday, it will be.

While we're here, God will continue to care about our window seats and all the little things in our lives. But when we come home, our hearts will jump at the sight of each other. We'll feast and talk, and talk, and talk. And Jesus will sit at the head of the table, making sure our plates are full.

Respond

Spend some time alone with your Father now, and thank Him for the way He takes care of the little things while you are here on earth. Then praise Him for the homecoming awaiting you.

Remember

There is a homecoming on God's calendar — it could be today!

Oh You of Liddell Faith

Read

"Remember the Sabbath day, to keep it holy." — Exodus 20:8 NASB.

Reflect

"Chariots of Fire" was one of the most refreshing movies of the 1980's, not because it was about running or because it was true, but because it was about a Christian who stood up for his principles. How refreshing it was to see an Academy Award winning motion picture that didn't glorify drugs, sex, or dirty language!

The plot of the film centered around the Olympic champion, Eric Liddell, who refused to run his Olympic event on Sunday. As a Christian, Sunday was his Sabbath. But Liddell was unaware of his scheduled Sunday heat until he arrived in Paris. When he announced to his coach that he wouldn't run because of his Christian principles, it caused quite a stir. Such a stir, in fact, that Liddell was brought before the Olympic officials and the Prince of Wales to get him to change his mind. But Eric stood firm in his conviction, and the Lord opened the door to allow him to run in another event.

After Liddell left the meeting, the movie portrayed one official saying to another "I thought the lad had beaten us." To which the other replied, "He did have us beaten, and thank God he did…the lad, as you call him, is a true man of principle and a true athlete. His speed is a mere extension of his life, its force. We sought to sever his running from himself." What a great story — and it's true!

Respond

If you were in Eric Liddell's shoes, what would you have done? Would you have sacrificed your own personal glory to stand firm on your scriptural beliefs? Could your Christian principles be bought with an Olympic medal? Eric Liddell knew that God's laws are valuable for no other reason than that they are His. When we obey them, we glorify Him regardless of the opposition. Eric Liddell isn't remembered in history as much for the race he won, as the principles he kept. What better way to be remembered! Will you be remembered as one who honors God with unwavering faith?

Remember

God honors those who honor Him.

Cinderella's Ugly Sisters

Read

And the Lord had regard for Abel and for his offering; but for Cain and his offering He had no regard. So Cain became very angry and his countenance fell. — Genesis 4:4b-5 NASB.

Reflect

Can you remember what made Cinderella's sisters ugly? Jealousy! Why do you think the story of Cinderella has stuck around so long? It's still a big draw in video stores today not because it's a fairy tale, but because it's true! The story of Cinderella is true in the sense that jealousy is here to stay.

Jealousy is nothing new to human nature. Consider these examples:

Cain and Abel. Genesis 4
Joseph and his brothers. Genesis 37
Saul's jealousy of David. 1 Samuel 18
Herod's jealous of a baby king. Matthew 2
The Disciples. Matthew 20:20-28

All through the Bible are examples of unchecked jealousy causing setbacks, failures, and even murder. Simply defined, jealousy is when you think someone is superior because they make you feel inferior. Because we're human, not one of us is immune to jealousy. So the way to conquer jealousy is to realize who we are in the eyes of God. We are the ones He sent His Son to die for. WE are a precious prize to Him, and whatever position we gain before men, it can't measure up to the position we hold with Him.

Respond

Are you jealous today? Are you feeling a little inferior? Has your "countenance fallen," like Cains? That's jealousy. STOP! Nothing was ever gained by being jealous. In fact, much has been lost by the trap of jealousy. In your time alone with God today, pray and let Him remind you of your tremendous value to Him. Thank Him for your deliverance from sins like jealousy. Ask Him to guard your heart from jealousy today. Now, rejoice!

Remember

Jealousy never wins the glass slipper.

Proof to Believe

Read

But God demonstrates his own love for us in this while we were still sinners, Christ died for us. — Romans 5:8.

Reflect

Let's define the word "believe." It means to be convinced something is true according to an authority. For example, when you go to the doctor to get a shot of penicillin, you believe you got a shot of penicillin by the authority of the doctor who gave you the shot of penicillin. He believes you are getting a shot of penicillin by the authority of the pharmaceutical label on the bottle that says it's penicillin. Even the name you bear, you believe to be your name by the authority of your parents who tell you it is your name. We believe in so many things today because of some authority.

For the Christian, the Bible is the final authority. It tells us that "while we were still sinners Christ died for us." It tells us when we "confess with our mouth Jesus is Lord and believe in our heart that God raised Him from the dead we will be saved." (See Romans 10:9-10.) When we believe these facts, we take a giant step in understanding what salvation is all about.

God's love for us is more than just a lot of talk. He "demonstrated" His love to us. He did not just send us a letter or a book that said, "I love you." He expressed it by giving the greatest and most sacrificial gift possible — His Son. If this doesn't prove to us that God deeply loves us, nothing will.

Respond

Allow me to be blunt for a minute. If you have not given your life to Jesus Christ, you are lost and you probably don't even know it. He has made it simple. Just believe in your heart that God raised Jesus from the dead and confess with your mouth that He is your Lord. When you pray this and mean it, He will come into your life (Revelation 3:20). If you are sure of your salvation, begin to pray for those you know who need to receive Jesus.

Remember

You are a big deal to God, so make Him a big deal in your life today.

God is Bigger Than Your Sin

Read

...that ye may know what is the hope of his calling,... And what is the exceeding greatness of his power to us-ward who believe, according to the working of his mighty power. — Ephesians 1:18-19 KJV.

Reflect

Have you ever received a gift you didn't deserve from someone? Remember how you felt? You wanted to pay them back or do something for them, but there was nothing you could really do. So you sat there and accepted it. This is exactly how we must receive God's love. He communicates His love for us through His words and actions. We can't do anything to deserve it, much less pay Him back for it, but He still gives it. The gift is new life, bought and paid for with Jesus' death on the cross.

Many people today don't feel like God could ever love them. They think they have sinned too much or done something "so bad" that God just couldn't forgive them. If you're one of those people, let me assure you that He does love you. In fact, there is no end to His love for you. And if you don't believe that He loves you and can forgive absolutely anything you've done, you are placing your sin above His ability to love and forgive.

Don't make the mistake of thinking your messed up life is bigger than God's ability to straighten you out, heal you, and bless you. His power is His love. His love has all the power needed to forgive you, cleanse you, teach you, grow you up into the person God purposed you to be, and give you the ability to do what He's called you to do.

Respond

Are you feeling unloved and useless today? Take a look at Romans 5:8 and realize that He loves you today as much as He loved you before you were born. Just accept it and thank Him for the power of His love to change your life. If you have never received His love, open your heart now and ask Him to make Himself real to you. He desires to do just that. Then tell someone about it, because He wants to touch them too.

Remember

God's love is the power you need to be free — really free.

THE ROARING LION

READ

Then the dragon was enraged at the woman and went off to make war against the rest of her offspring — those who obey God's commandments and hold to the testimony of Jesus. — REVELATION 12:17.

REFLECT

Among the many descriptions of Satan in the Bible, the one I understand best is that of a roaring lion seeking whom he may devour (see 1 Peter 5:8). Peter describes him in this way and then encourages his readers to "Resist him, by standing firm in the faith, because your brothers throughout the world are undergoing the same kind of sufferings" (1 Peter 5:9). That same message is true for us today. We have friends who are suffering due to the attacks of Satan.

In today's verse Satan is identified as a dragon who is raging a war against Jesus and all those who follow Him. From the beginning he has waged this war against us, so how are we to cope? How do we combat his attacks and come out living a victorious life?

Daniel also faced roaring lions. He faced them, but they did not devour him. Why? Because he faced them on his knees. When Darius threw him in the lions' den for refusing to stop praying, Daniel was already "prayed up." Prayer is our primary weapon to defeat the enemy from having his way with our lives. Because of this fact, we must be consistent and faithful to God through prayer. Of all the quotes I've heard about prayer relating to Satan, my favorite is from Samuel Chadwick. He said, "The one concern of the devil is to keep Christians from praying, he fears nothing from prayerless study, prayerless work, or prayerless religion. He laughs at our toils, mocks at our wisdom, but trembles when we pray."

RESPOND

Have you made the devil tremble lately? Take some time right now to praise the Lord for the victory He gives you over the devil. Ask Him to be with those you know who are suffering from Satan's attacks. Finally, pray that God will strengthen you through time with Him so you can have consistent victory over the devil.

REMEMBER

Prayer turns Satan, the roaring lion, into a kitten.

The Good Shepherd

Read

You prepare a table before me in the presence of my enemies. You anoint my head with oil; my cup overflows. — Psalm 23:5.

Reflect

The degree to which the shepherd would go to protect the sheep from any kind of danger was unmatched. During the summer months the shepherd would often direct his flock to the high country where the sheep could graze on "table-like" plateaus. Before he took his flock to the plateaus, he would scout out the area to see how good the vegetation was and to search for any poisonous vegetation. He would also search for any predators.

The shepherd would do his best to prepare the land for the sheep, but he would also prepare the sheep. During the summertime flies were plentiful, so the shepherd would pour oil on the sheep to help prevent parasites and insects from harming them.

Are you drawing the parallel yet? Jesus is our Good Shepherd, and He thinks of everything to protect us. He knows what kind of attacks we need to guard against. He has overcome every attack from the evil one and knows every trick he will try to pull to make us fall. Therefore, He wants to anoint us with the Holy Spirit to protect us. He's looked ahead. He knows what is coming our way. If we are to overcome the attacks of the enemy, we must be bathed in or controlled by His Spirit. Only when we let Him prepare us can we handle the attacks of the enemy.

Respond

Take time right now to thank and praise God for His wonderful protection and thoughtfulness. Ask Him to help you follow His leading in your life today. Ask Him to guide you in preparation to overcome any trial that lies ahead. Trust Him in all things.

Remember

Let Jesus be your Good Shepherd today.

Love Doesn't Honk!

Read

Dear friends, let us love one another, for love comes from God. Everyone who loves has been born of God and knows God. — 1 John 4:7.

Reflect

Imagine you're dating your soon-to-be wife. You drive up to her house to pick her up, and as you pull into the driveway, you honk the horn and yell, "Come on!" Is that love? No. Love would get out of the car, walk up to your sweetheart's door, and knock on it gently. Then when she opens the door, love would escort her very respectfully out to the car and open the door for her, closing the car door behind her. Then, as the two of you drove away, love would compliment your sweetheart for her beauty and grace.

Love respects and reverences intimately. It doesn't honk, and it isn't rude. Yet, that's how many of us treat God, believe it or not. When we come to church, we often say how wonderful God is. We like to hang around people who love Him, and we even sing about how great He is. But we don't talk to Him. And when the pastor is still preaching at a quarter to twelve, we look at our watch and wait impatiently.

Many of us think we're loving God when we take the time to go to church. And, in our own way, we are. But God is wanting relationship with us, and honking and tapping our feet just won't do. Love will seek to build relationship with Him. It will spend more time in His Word, allowing the Holy Spirit to teach and guide. Love will reverence His presence both in and out of church.

Respond

How is your love walk today? Do you think there is room for improvement? Why not spend some time with God right now and thank Him for His grace and love. Become a better lover by simply showing your love to Him. Ask Him to forgive you for the times you haven't been as loving as you should have been. Then, pray that He will demonstrate His love through you everyday.

Remember

God loves to spend time with you. Return the favor.

Give Tom a Break

Read

Now Thomas...said to them, "Unless I see the nail marks in his hands and put my finger where the nails were, and put my hand into his side, I will not believe it." — John 20:24-25.

Reflect

Because Thomas is my name, I'm always tempted to give the apostle Thomas a break. I like to think of him as a seeker of truth. Okay, enough of my pulling for Thomas. He was a doubter. He had to see to believe. He didn't have the greatest faith in the world. But one thing he did have going for him: He was not unwilling to believe but desired to know more in order to believe.

I suppose Thomas was a bit of an intellectual who needed some tangible facts. He weighed the evidence and ended up falling before Jesus and saying, "My Lord and my God" (John 20:28). And Jesus graciously gave Thomas the facts, not because He had to, but because of His love. From then on, Thomas believed by faith because of the facts that were given him, just like thousands have done since then.

We can learn from this lesson today that God has a special interest in doubting Thomases. Those who doubt matter to God. Therefore, they should matter to us. Isn't it good to know that God, who knows the hearts of doubters and how hard they are, still cares enough about them to patiently wait for them to come to Him? That is where we come in. We're the messengers. We are to take His message to the Thomases of this world. We are to patiently wait and pray until they respond to the Holy Spirit.

Respond

Are you a doubting Thomas, or do you know some doubting Thomases? Pray for His Spirit to work in and through you and then thank God for His patience with you. Confess to Him the times you have not taken the time to share your faith when you felt you should. Ask Him to give you the words to say to your doubting friends.

Remember

Be patient with the unbelievers in your life — one of their names might be Thomas.

First to the Lord

Read

And they did not do as we expected, but they gave themselves first to the Lord and then to us in keeping with God's will. — 2 Corinthians 8:5.

Reflect

I'm reminded today of the young county agent who went to visit a wealthy farmer. The farmer took him around his farm and showed the young agent his booming crops, his fat cattle, and his well-kept equipment. After seeing all the farmer had, the young agent said, "God has really blessed you with a lot." But the self-made old farmer replied, "God? Where do you think those crops would be without my hard work? What do you think those buildings and that equipment would be if it wasn't for me?" To this, the young agent replied, "Ask me that in a hundred years."

You've probably noticed that people can get wrapped up in possessions...literally. They think they own possessions, when actually the possessions own them. Their love for possessions steals their joy for giving, so they struggle with it. They haven't come to the point of realizing that everything they have was ultimately given to them and belongs to God.

The truth is, God doesn't need your gifts. Your possessions don't mean that much to Him, but you certainly do. He wants you to first give yourself to Him. After you do that, giving your possessions becomes an expression of gratitude to Him. We all need to give so we can be reminded of how short life is, and that what we do for Christ is all that will last through eternity.

Respond

A hundred years from now it won't really matter that you wore designer jeans or drove a fancy car. All that will matter will be who you loved and how you invested your life for the kingdom of God. So ask God to show you what and where to give. Praise Him for what He will do with your gifts in the next hundred years. Pray that He will guide you in your giving today.

Remember

Give your life to Jesus today, then giving to others will be a joy.

No Dead Ends in Christ

Read

What does the worker gain from his toil? — Ecclesiastes 3:9.

Reflect

Today's devotional writer, Solomon, has a way of making us look at things in plain old black and white. Here is the richest man of his day asking if it is really worth the effort. It reminds me of the street sign that read, "Dead End," on which someone had added two more words — "What isn't?" Actually this is the theme of Ecclesiastes: life is a dead-end street without God. Solomon repeatedly mentioned the vanity of life outside of God's will and protection. And how true that is. No matter how you slice it, when it's all said and done, without Jesus you're walking down a dead-end street.

Just like me, you're interested in a life full of meaning. Your work can and should be one of the most meaningful parts of your life. What should you gain from your work? Integrity, dignity, balance, accomplishment? Unfortunately there is a flip side — frustration, stress, disappointment, and discouragement — but don't look at the minuses as all bad. It is by them that you grow. Through challenges and having to go beyond your personal comfort zone, you lean more heavily on God and draw closer to Him.

Don't look at your work today through the cynic's eyes. If you do, you will stare at a "Dead End" sign. God has a purpose in placing you where you are right now. His work in that place is your responsibility. He has entrusted it to you. It's His gift for you to gain insight.

Respond

Have you ever struggled with your work as a dead-end street? Have you occasionally lost your vision for ministry where you work? If so, renew yourself in the purpose God has for you and the joy He brings when you trust Him. Confess the times you haven't followed His Word. And pray for those you know who think their life is a dead-end. Ask God to give you the words to say to them that will encourage and strengthen.

Remember

There are no dead ends in God's service, and working for Him is a pleasure.

Give Your Testimony

Read

He replied, "Whether he is a sinner or not, I don't know. One thing I do know. I was blind but now I see!" — John 9:25.

Reflect

Many were trying to argue with the former blind man about who Jesus was or wasn't. The blind man just simply told them what had happened to him. He didn't know all there was to know about Jesus, but he did know one thing — yesterday he couldn't see, but today he could. Jesus entered his life and made a difference. What a testimony!

Many believers know they should be sharing their story about what Jesus has done for them, but they don't think people are interested because they don't have a dynamic "blind man miracle" testimony. The truth is, we all have a testimony like that, because we all came out of darkness into the light.

A common fear some Christians have about sharing their testimony is what others may think of them *if* they do. What they forget is that they are presenting Jesus, not themselves. We should be grieved not because we are rejected, but because Jesus is rejected.

Respond

Never forget that the one thing that is unique about you is your own personal testimony. Let me give you a simple outline in case the opportunity arises for you to share your faith with others.

1. Tell them briefly how your life was before you knew Jesus.
2. Tell them how you became aware of your need for a Savior.
3. Tell them how you committed yourself to Jesus Christ.
4. Tell them what your life is like now that you've given your life to Jesus.

Practice this method over and over until it becomes a natural way to share your faith. Then pray for those who will cross your path to have hungry hearts.

Remember

Look for opportunities to share your testimony today.

Memories

Read

But remember the Lord your God, for it is he who gives you the ability to produce wealth, and so confirms his covenant, which he swore to your forefathers, as it is today. — Deuteronomy 8:18.

Reflect

Memories are funny things. I can remember a telephone number from years ago, but I can't remember a name I heard two minutes ago. Some students can remember test facts for an hour, but forget everything they studied and answered correctly on the test within a week.

One of the things God uses to bless and keep us on track as believers is our memory. In the Old Testament He had Joshua place stones by the Jordan River to remind them of the miraculous crossing into the Promised Land. In Deuteronomy 6, God instructed parents to talk about His laws to their children so they would not forget Him. But if there is one thing the children of Israel had, it was a poor memory. Throughout the first four books of the Bible, time and time again, God warned them to never forget Him because He was the source of their strength and power. But Israel forgot, and they paid a high price. They were defeated by other nations and taken captive.

It is interesting that the times Israel was most susceptible to forgetting God were during times of prosperity. When things were going well, they began trusting in themselves instead of God. Have you ever been like that? Sometimes we forget God when things are going well for us. But God isn't like us, because He never forgets.

Respond

When you stop to think about it, God has only been good to you. He is your creator, provider, protector, savior, benefactor, and source. But we can be selfish and forgetful in our imperfect state. It is so easy for us to zip along with our many activities and leave Him out of the loop. So confess to Him those times that you have forgotten Him. Thank Him for His gracious memory and goodness. Then, pray that He will use you today to remind someone else of His love.

Remember

Always remember God — He always remembers you.

UNDER CONSTRUCTION

READ

To keep me from becoming conceited because of these surpassingly great revelations, there was given me a thorn in my flesh, a messenger of Satan, to torment me. — 2 CORINTHIANS 12:7.

REFLECT

Orange barrels and pylons on the road can be a pain when you're trying to get somewhere. Even though you know in your heart construction is necessary for a better future, you don't want it interfering with your plans. It slows you down and messes up your agenda. But for safety's sake you slow down because you're in a construction zone. The orange barrels and pylons are there for a reason, to get your attention, to remind you to be careful, and to keep you from being hurt.

No matter how pain and destruction come, physically or emotionally, they can take the wind out of our sails. Sometimes it is simply a result of being human. We live in a sinful world, and wherever there is sin, eventually there is pain. By its very nature, sin destroys. Think about it. When have you ever habitually sinned that you didn't destroy or take steps to destroy or cause pain for someone? I have seen relationships, reputations, and spiritual renewal destroyed by sin. Sin destroys — period.

Whenever pain and destruction occur, we can choose to let God build character. I know what you're thinking, "I've had enough character building!" The truth is, God is the one who is building the character in you. And His character goal is for you to be like Jesus. Where destruction shows up in your life, God begins the work of construction.

RESPOND

Are you under construction today? God is at work! He has a purpose that He is working out and you are a part of it. He promises to work it out for your good if you will love Him more and more. So be patient when you're in a construction zone.

REMEMBER

Slow down and let God do the construction work in your life that needs to be done.

Keep Your Perspective

Read

But thanks be to God, who always leads us in triumphal procession in Christ and through us spreads everywhere the fragrance of the knowledge of him. — 2 Corinthians 2:14.

Reflect

Even though my birthday falls in the middle of August, it isn't my favorite time of the year. It was during that time of the year that I trained the hardest when I was running competitively. I remember running the cross country course and watching the football players suffer through the excruciating heat as well. I also remember thinking that if I could just get through this month of heat, it would be a lot easier and rewarding when the races began. I knew when the fall came, the cool weather would make it much more comfortable to run. It was that perspective that kept me going.

Perspective is what we need when we feel like quitting. Paul gives his perspective in today's verse. He knew that as long as he was doing what pleased God, God would lead him to victory. God uses us to spread His message, and as long as we do this and keep His perspective, He causes us to be successful. If we lose our perspective and quit, however, we never discover what God has for us.

When you are in a trial and a test of endurance, it is the knowledge of Him that keeps you going and secures your faith. Knowing that God works everything to your good (see Romans 8:28) and that it is His desire to bless you is the perspective and motivation that will give you the strength to continue His work.

Respond

What are you facing today that makes you want to quit? Is it bigger than God? Of course not. Do you need to pray for His perspective? His perspective will encourage you. If you spend some time in His Word and study how He has been faithful to help others who were in difficult situations, you will be encouraged to trust Him. Let God know how grateful you are for His presence in your life.

Remember

When you keep your perspective and refuse to quit in the midst of a trial, God gives you supernatural strength to obtain the victory.

Counsel from the Master

Read

And David inquired of the Lord, saying, "Shall I pursue this band? Shall I overtake them?" And He said to him, "Pursue, for you shall surely overtake them, and you shall surely rescue all." — 1 Samuel 30:8 NASB.

Reflect

When David returned to Ziklag and found the city burned and his family gone, he experienced every emotion that you and I would have. He was angry and distressed and at a loss of what to do. So what did he do? He went to the Lord for counsel. He did not act on his emotions and immediately pursue the enemy. He did not fly off the handle and act out of revenge. He knew that the answer to this storm would come from the Master over the storm. So he prayed. And even when his own men turned against him, he did not plot or try to politic his way into safety. Instead, he prayed. He sought the One who had the answers instead of making up his own answers.

You and I can learn a lot from David's prayer. When he prayed, he asked questions. It's better to ask honest searching questions of God than ignore Him and act like everything is okay — or turn from Him and try to get through it on our own.

God expects us to ask questions. He wants to dialogue with us. Job asked God questions about his situation. The entire book of Habakkuk is a dialogue between the prophet and God about the crisis God's people were going through. The secret to getting through a crisis is gaining the wisdom of the One who sees the end from the beginning. And you do that by asking Him questions, reading His Word, and then listening to His Spirit.

Respond

Today as you pray, take time to praise and thank God for His goodness to you and His willingness to listen and communicate with you. Ask Him to forgive you when you have not acted according to His will. Then pray that He will guide you through the crises that come your way.

Remember

Jesus is the Wonderful Counselor who wants you to seek His wisdom in the storm.

He Really Loves You, Man

Read

Whoever does not love does not know God, because God is love. — 1 John 4:8.

Reflect

Have you seen this commercial? A father and his two sons are on a dock fishing. One son tries to con his dad out of his beer by telling him that he loves him. Funny commercial, but a poor definition of love. In fact, the words "I love you" are thrown around today like yesterday's socks. Everybody says it, but few really know what it means. A young boy says he loves a young girl in hopes she will return the favor and say those words to him. With that motive, he is saying it so he can hear it, not because he loves her. The guy in the commercial doesn't love his dad, he loves beer. So when it comes to love today, for many, talk is cheap.

Today's verse says that whoever does not love does not know God because God is love. His love is much deeper and stronger than the romantic love the world exalts. It is the love that moved Jesus to the cross. God's love is sacrificial and powerful. God's love is holy. It is separated high above all forms of human affection. That is why when we know God, we find love much more fulfilling. His love is not selfish. It is not self-seeking, is not easily angered, keeps no record of wrongs, doesn't delight in evil but rejoices with the truth. And it always protects, trusts, hopes, and perseveres. God's holy love never fails. (See 1 Corinthians 13:5-8.)

Respond

Praise and thank God for His powerful, sacrificial love. Ask Him to forgive the times you have manipulated others instead of loving them. Pray He will guide you in His holy love today. Then put your arm around someone and say, "I really love you, man" — and mean it!

Remember

When we love others out of God's holy love, we are showing them that we know God and that God loves them.

Time Is Ticking Away

Read

There is a time for everything, and a season for every activity under heaven. — Ecclesiastes 3:1.

Reflect

I bought this great little book on time management one summer...hopefully I'll find time to read it someday. Have you ever felt that way? You get in the same-ole, same-ole routine and feel like your time is slipping away? Solomon, the writer of Ecclesiastes, was one who wanted to avoid the same-ole, same-ole lifestyle of his day. He wanted to find out what life was all about. He had the best job in town (king), and he had all the money he needed at his disposal. (He made about four and a half billion dollars a year.) He could afford this effort.

Solomon knew what a heavy schedule was all about. He had 700 wives and 300 girlfriends and ran the kingdom of Israel. It can be assumed his days were very busy. But as he examined life, he determined that time is appointed by God and is a ground-leveling factor that equalizes everyone. All of us have 24 hours in a day. We are all given 168 hours in a week. For some of us time flies, while for others time drags. To the student on summer break, three months goes fast. For the expectant mother who has swollen feet in her last trimester, three months is a long time.

How you manage your time often determines how you manage your life. Waste your time; waste your life. Master your time; master your life. When you spend time alone with God, He gives you direction for your life. Therefore, time alone with God will guide you on how to spend the rest of your time.

Respond

The question you and I must ask ourselves is this: What time is it for us? Time has begun for you and me, but it has not ended. We know that God has established an appointed time for our birth, our life, our death. He has placed eternity in our hearts. But a time will come when God will say, "That's it, time's up." When that time comes, what will you say to Him about how you managed your time?

Remember

Time is ticking away. Use it wisely.

The Cure for Stress

Read

But now in Christ Jesus you who once were far away have been brought near through the blood of Christ. For he himself is our peace. — Ephesians 2:13-14.

Reflect

I'll never forget what happened one day when I was growing up. The telephone rang and it was a neighbor telling us that their daughter was missing. We lived out in the country, and all the neighbors converged on the house of the missing girl. We spread out and walked through the fields, woods, and roads in our area calling her name...fearing the worst. After several hours the girl was found, alive, scared and unharmed. She had run away from home and then got lost. The parents felt relief and anger at the same time. But when they were reunited with the girl, their most intense stress was relieved.

Separation causes stress. If a husband and wife decide to separate, the stress is often devastating to all family members, including grandparents. When a child runs away from home, the loving parents go through a tremendous ordeal until their child is found safe and sound.

But the greatest stress was what befell mankind when we were separated from God. The devastating results have been incalculable, but God, in His mercy, has provided the way back to Him — through the shed blood of Jesus Christ. When we find our way home to the Father, all stress flies out the window in the wake of the peace that passes all understanding. Now Jesus gives us peace amid the storms of life and the ability to stand righteous before God for eternity.

Respond

Meditate for awhile on the reality that Jesus is your peace. He has given you righteous standing before God, authority over the enemy, and has even taken away the sting of death and the grave. Turn your challenges over to Him and allow His peace to replace any stress in your life.

Remember

God is not "stressed out" by the pressures you feel today. Let Him take your load.

Unconditional Love

Read

This is love: not that we loved God, but that he loved us and sent his Son as an atoning sacrifice for our sins. — 1 John 4:10.

Reflect

Have you ever been in a hospital to visit a friend who just had a baby? Remember when they showed you the baby and said, "Isn't she cute?" You looked down on that chunky, wrinkled, red, stinky little newborn and said, "She's a doll." When you did that, you showed the excited new parent and baby unconditional love.

Unconditional love is a decision. It's not a feeling. When you love unconditionally, you decide to love. You make up your mind to love. Notice how the apostle John said that it's not love just to love the One who loved you. True love, John says, is to love the ones who don't love you. God did this by having Jesus pay the debt for our sin before we even knew we were sinners. We all looked like red, wrinkled babies, but He chose to love us anyway. He is still doing it today.

When you consider what Jesus gave up to show His love for you and me, it is nothing short of incredible. He lived in heaven with God. There was no sin there, and He lived on a plane of luxury we can't even comprehend on earth. To top that off, everything centered around Him in heaven, and He came to earth to serve and die. But He gave it all up because you need a Savior. He didn't have to, but He did. He decided to love you when you didn't even have a clue!

Respond

When Jesus walked the earth, He challenged us to show love to others and expect nothing in return. I invite you to praise and thank God for deciding to love you. Ask Him to help you have that same type of love for those He brings your way today. Unconditional love chooses to love because God is love.

Remember

God has decided to love you today, so decide to share that love with someone else.

THE COSTLIEST GIFT

READ

But just as you excel in everything — in faith, in speech, in knowledge, in complete earnestness and in your love for us — see that you also excel in this grace of giving. — 2 CORINTHIANS 8:7.

REFLECT

The story is told of Billy and Ruth Graham going to church one Sunday. At the time of taking the offering, Billy reached into his pocket and pulled out a ten dollar bill. When he saw it was a ten, he flinched and hesitated, but then went ahead and placed it in the offering plate. Ruth asked him why he hesitated when he first saw the bill. "I originally thought I was pulling out a one dollar bill," Rev. Graham said. So Ruth replied, "To God, you were."

Giving is an indicator of love. To love is to give. When a young man wants to impress a girl, he will give her things and do things for her to show his love. The same is true for parents who give to their child. The joy of giving comes from a heart of love. In the same way, when we love God, we will do service and give our money and time to demonstrate our love for Him. When we do this, we not only further His kingdom work, we also become witnesses by demonstrating our love through giving. That makes giving money to God's work in the church more than just raising funds for programs. Giving is a sacred act; it is worship unto God.

RESPOND

God's demonstration of giving wasn't money, it was His only Son. What a gift! He chose the costliest gift to give to you and me. Take a moment today to praise and thank Him for His gracious gifts. Ask Him to forgive you for the times you haven't given to Him. Finally, pray that He will help you grow in love so that you show your appreciation more to Him. And remember, the next time you reach into your pocket or agree to volunteer, He sees your heart!

REMEMBER

When you give, give as an act of worshipping and loving God.

Don't Be a Know-It-All

Read

This is what the Lord says: "Let not the wise man boast of his wisdom or the strong man boast of his strength or the rich man boast of his riches." — Jeremiah 9:23.

Reflect

Have you ever been around people who know it all? You know the type. They ask you a question and when you give them an answer, they're quick to disagree with you. Then you wonder, *Why in the world did they even ask my opinion?*

We may not want to admit it, but we all need God's guidance in our lives. Even the "know-it-all person" needs outside help. The encouragement God's Word has for us is that He wants to guide us through life. He knows life's pitfalls and potholes, so He is able to give us guidance to overcome them and live in victory and fulfillment.

In today's verse, Jeremiah is basically telling us that we are nothing without the Lord. If we have wisdom, if we have strength, if we have riches, we only have them because He allowed us to have them. If we see anyone boasting about themselves, what they have, their abilities or possessions, they are not wise. If we are wise, we will never forget that God is everything to us.

Respond

Do you ever come across as a know-it-all? Get honest with yourself. Do you spend more time talking than listening? Are you letting God guide you or are you guiding yourself and trying to guide others? Do you find yourself bragging about yourself more than giving God credit for what you have and who you are? Ouch. If this is truly you, at least on occasion, take a moment right now to be still and meditate on the awesomeness of God. Praise and thank Him for wanting to have a personal relationship with you. Commit yourself to honor Him with your life. Oh yeah, and make a new commitment not to act like a "know-it-all" today. Instead, act like you know the One who truly knows it all!

Remember

God is the only true Know-It-All.

Service With Style

Read

In Joppa there was a disciples named Tabitha (which, when translated, is Dorcas), who was always doing good and helping the poor. — Acts 9:36.

Reflect

Dorcas probably isn't a household name to you, but she had a style about her that made a significant impact on those around her. Dorcas wasn't known for her singing ability or communication skills. She wasn't recognized for her physical beauty or dynamic personality. She was known for her service. Dorcas gave when her receiver could give nothing in return. She made robes and articles of clothing for widows and needy people in her hometown of Joppa.

Dorcas' approach to evangelism was very practical. I suppose if you hung around her, it would be very hard for you to observe her activity and not get a glimpse of the love of Jesus which inspired her. She used acts of service to speak love to those who were in need. She would meet a person's physical needs and in the process point them to the One who could meet all their needs.

There is no one way to evangelize. Different people respond to different styles of presenting the message of Jesus Christ. The important thing is that the message of God's love which lives in us is shared with others. Each one of us needs to have a style, or an approach, to share the love of God. Our style is the hook that draws others to see their need. It helps us earn the right to share Jesus in such a way that others will listen.

Respond

What's your style? Have you ever considered that you have one? Do you take bread to neighbors on occasion to show God's love? Have you thought about practical evangelism? Pray for God to lead and guide you in building relationships with those who may not know Him today. Make a list of those in your neighborhood and at your place of employment who could use a "Dorcas touch." Then be sensitive to reach out in love.

Remember

God has given you a personality and a style all your own to share the Good News.

Love is Better

Read

If I speak in the tongues of men and of angles, but have not love, I am only a resounding gong or a clanging cymbal. If I have the gift of prophecy and can fathom all mysteries and all knowledge, and if I have a faith that can move mountains, but have not love, I am nothing. — 1 Corinthians 13:1-2.

Reflect

When I was about three years old, I remember my dad coming home from a hard day's work, taking off his tool belt, pulling off his work boots, and sitting in the red vinyl chair that faced the television. I remember putting my feet in those big boots and walking around the house. Sometimes I'd even put on his hard hat and act like I was a lineman like he was. Those were special "dad toys." The best part, though, was climbing up in his arms and letting him rock me to sleep. The security of his love was unmatched in my life.

Now, suppose my dad had come home one day and said, "Tom, I'm going to leave my boots, hard hat, and tools here for you to play with, but I'm not coming home anymore. You can play with them whenever you want, but I'm not going to be around." Do you think that would have been okay with me? Not on your life! It wasn't the gifts and toys that made the relationship, it was the presence of Dad's love.

It's the same way often with our spiritual gifts. Stop and ask yourself: Am I using my gifts out of love for my Lord and His people? Or am I blowing my horn and just making noise? God designed our gifts, both spiritual and natural, as channels for His love.

Respond

All the gifts God gives us are meaningless without His presence. Take some time right now to repent for any godless noise you may have made recently! Then pray for those who need to experience God's superior love today. Ask God to use you to show His love to someone who doesn't know Him.

Remember

Don't clang: love.

A Confrontational Guy

Read

"Woe to you when all men speak well of you, for that is how their fathers treated the false prophets." — Luke 6:26.

Reflect

There once was a man with a big heart, a big mouth, and sometimes he didn't work in sync with others. His name was Peter. No one loved Jesus more and wanted to express it more than Peter. When others questioned Jesus' identity, it was Peter who said, "You are the Christ, the Son of the living God." It was also Peter who stood and spoke boldly at the feast of Pentecost, where over three thousand people came to know Jesus as their Messiah.

Peter was confrontational, and for some people his style would be a major turn-off. But there are many who need a Peter in their lives, to get them straight in their spiritual walk. So why are we afraid to confront people who need a wake up call? Because we want them to like us. And, "Woe to us," Jesus said, when this is always the case.

There are people around us every day who are facing eternal separation from God. If they are trying to live "good lives" to win God's favor and have never been born again, they need someone who will take the risk and confront them with the truth. If they are a believer but are destroying their life with some awful habit, they need someone willing to take a risk. The good news is that we have the great "Risk Taker" living in us! He will open the door and give us the wisdom to confront.

Respond

Do you know people who say they're Christians but don't act like it? Are there people at work or next door who are struggling with life? If you know anyone like this, they may need you to be Peter in their lives. It might anger them, but if done properly, they could get real with Jesus in a new and fresh way. The key to confrontation is to pray and seek God to guide your words and timing. He will show you how, when, and where, to wisely confront.

Remember

Confrontation seasoned with love can rescue someone from the pits of hell.

STICK TO YOUR BOUNDARIES

READ

So I made up my mind that I would not make another painful visit to you. — 2 CORINTHIANS 2:1.

REFLECT

I have a boundary that is very important to me. It involves my time. The boundary is this: I will not write, do office work, or engage in anything work-related during the hours in which my children are home from school and until they go to bed. This provides time with them and opportunities for my wife and me to go out on dates. It also keeps me from being so consumed with my work that it could be interpreted that work is more important to me than they are. This is not always possible due to unforeseen interruptions, but it is a goal. And as I live by it, both my family and I are blessed.

Now, do I still have work to do during that time I'm spending with my family? Yes. Deadlines. Projects. They all stack up and cry out for my time. And guess what, they'll always be there. But there won't always be a little girl who wants me to swing her or a son who wants me to throw a ball with him. Setting boundaries for yourself is easy; sticking to them can be difficult. But if the boundaries are biblical, setting them is the right thing to do and keeping them brings the favor of God on your life. Biblical boundaries are rules you make for yourself in order to protect and provide for a fulfilling and effective Christian walk. Setting boundaries for yourself gives you freedom and protects you from overextending yourself.

RESPOND

Pray and ask God if there are biblical boundaries you need to set in your life. If you have messed up because you violated your boundaries, repent and receive forgiveness and new direction from the Holy Spirit today. Pray that God will guide and strengthen you to stick to your biblical boundaries.

REMEMBER

Boundaries protect you from harm and provide a better life for you.

THE JOY OF THE LORD

READ

Nehemiah said, "Go and enjoy choice food and sweet drinks, and send some to those who have nothing prepared. This day is sacred to our Lord. Do not grieve, for the joy of the Lord is your strength." — NEHEMIAH 8:10.

REFLECT

Do you remember the "God is dead" theme that rang out in the rebellious sixties? Pastor and author Chuck Swindoll tells of seeing a bumper sticker that said, "God is back, and boy is He mad." Sometimes I wonder if this is what the Jews of Nehemiah's day thought when they were finally reunited with God. It was the people who had left God; He didn't leave them. So when they reunited to worship, Nehemiah's message was "Rejoice. God is waiting for you with open arms to forgive and forget. And as you rejoice, you will find strength."

Too often we tend to look at joy only as an emotion. But joy is one of the most powerful resources available to the Christian. With the decision to be joyful, we can snuff out the enemy's attacks. We can extinguish his darts of despair and eliminate the intimidation factor he often uses to cripple us. Joy is a powerful tool for believers. But joy is simply a drummed-up emotion if it isn't flowing from the One who supplies the joy. When we trust God, we rest in His joy and strength.

RESPOND

You know, God didn't die in the sixties. There were just many who rejected His truth and lost their opportunity for joy. How is your joy level today? Are you facing some difficult times? Take a moment or two to stop and praise God for the joy He makes available through trusting Him. Ask Him to forgive you for the times you haven't trusted Him the way you should. Rejoice in the way He has blessed you today and allow His joy to be your strength.

REMEMBER

Joy is a fruit that never goes out of season.

MISUNDERSTANDINGS

READ

Our conscience testifies that we have conducted ourselves in the world, and especially in our relations with you, in the holiness and sincerity that are from God. — 2 CORINTHIANS 1:12.

REFLECT

Have you ever been misunderstood to the point that you wanted to throw in the towel and say, "What's the use?" Paul reveals in his letter to the Christians at Corinth that he faced the same frustration. They were accusing him of deception and not living up to his word. Paul had promised them he would come to see them, but then his plans had changed. Therefore, some of them accused him of having worldly motives and being insincere in his efforts.

A false accusation is enough to make you want to never visit them, isn't it? It would have been easy for Paul to say, "Listen, if you don't understand that sometimes plans have to be changed, then I don't need to come to you anyway." But Paul looked into his heart and concluded that his conscience was clear. He had not neglected them on purpose, and his motives toward them had always been pure. Therefore, he just explained the best he knew how and asked for them to accept it.

When you feel attacked by a misunderstanding, you need to look into your conscience and determine if your motives were pure. If you need to confess — confess. If you need to explain — explain. If you need to seek forgiveness — seek it. Search the motives of your heart and allow God to reveal to you any impure attitude. Have a clear conscience to do what God has directed you to do.

RESPOND

Do you feel like you're alone and nobody is on your side? They may give you "surface" support, but deep down you don't feel they are in your corner. Examine your heart and keep on going. You are not alone. God knows your heart, and He also knows what it feels like to be misunderstood. Pray today for His strength and that He would guide you to continue following Him and to be faithful.

REMEMBER

Identify misunderstanding quickly and set it right — with God first and then others.

O LORD, IT'S HARD TO BE HUMBLE

READ

Be completely humble and gentle; be patient, bearing with one another in love. Make every effort to keep the unity of the Spirit through the bond of peace. — EPHESIANS 4:2-3.

REFLECT

A popular country song in the eighties had lyrics that said, "O Lord it's hard to be humble, when you're perfect in every way." The humorous lyrics of the song probably led to its instant popularity. Another aspect of its popularity might have been that when you heard the song, you thought of people who appeared to feel that way about themselves. The song could make you laugh, but the truth is, some of the toughest people to endure are those who are stuck on themselves.

The people in my life who have impressed me the most never tried to. They were humble. They knew who they were and didn't feel compelled to be anyone but themselves. They understood that without God they would be nothing. They knew He was the One who gave promotions and saw the secrets of the heart, so they lived their lives for no one but Him. They consciously put God in control of their lives. And knowing He was in control, they were calm in crisis and strengthened when discouragement came their way.

One of the promises in the Bible to humble people is that God will lift them up and exalt them (see Luke 14:11). He notices humility. He also notices if it is real or not. Humility means knowing the awesomeness of God, knowing who you are in Christ, and then being yourself to the glory of God.

RESPOND

Does position and notoriety matter to you? Is it important that people know who you are and your position? The Bible says to humble ourselves (see James 4:10). So let God know from your heart how great He is and how worthless you are without Him. Pray for Him to use you to — humbly — touch others today.

REMEMBER

It's not hard to be humble when you walk in the presence of Almighty God.

What's Your Opinion of Sin?

Read

So I tell you this, and insist on it in the Lord, that you must no longer live as the Gentiles do, in the futility of their thinking. — Ephesians 4:17.

Reflect

Before I became a Christian I didn't think I was that bad of a person. I knew what sin was, but it didn't bother me that much because, compared to everyone I hung around, I was pretty good. I learned that the comparison game is a deception. Whenever we compare ourselves to others, we are using a measuring stick that is never accurate. Satan loves for us to evaluate ourselves by comparing ourselves to others, because when we do, we are using the wrong standard. Thus, we never get a true picture of our condition or an understanding of what God desires our lives to be.

I gave my life to Jesus when I became aware of how my sin would eventually destroy me. The main difference I have noticed since that day is in my thoughts about sin. Before being saved, it didn't bother me — in fact I loved it. Deep in my heart it left me empty, but the temporary enjoyment was all I was after. Since I've given my heart to Jesus, I hate sin, because my sin is what caused Him to be crucified. Sin doesn't fit in my life, not only because of what it does to me, but even more because of what it did to Jesus.

I now see clearly that sin is a trap to distract me from real living. Have I messed up and sinned since then? Unfortunately yes. But my attitude toward sin is altogether different. That's one way I know Jesus is living in my heart, because I'm thinking the same way He does about sin.

Respond

Are you still vulnerable to the sin that tries to destroy you? Are you thinking correctly about sin? Do you hate it? Thank Jesus for the price He paid for your sin. Ask Him to help you resist it today and help others who are playing games with sin to resist also.

Remember

Love God and Hate Sin.

God's Delivery Service

Read

The righteous cry out, and the Lord hears them; he delivers them from all their troubles. — Psalm 34:17.

Reflect

Do you remember the story of the guy who lost control of his semi truck going down a mountain? The truck ended up going over the side of the mountain and the driver was thrown out. As he was flying through the air to his ultimate death, he miraculously caught a branch. Holding on for dear life, he saw his truck explode at the bottom of the mountain. In despair he cried out, "Is there anybody there?" To his surprise the voice of God answered and said, "I'm here and I'll help you." The truck driver replied, "Great, come and help me." God said, "Okay, here's what I want you to do. First, let go of the branch." The truck driver cried, "Is there anybody else there?"

God has been in the delivery business for a long time. He delivered the children of Israel from Egyptian slavery. He delivered Daniel in the lions' den, and He delivered Shadrach, Meshach and Abednego from the fiery furnace. He can deliver anytime, anywhere, under any circumstances.

God desires to deliver you from any sin that is hindering you and from any attack of the devil that is causing you pain or harm. Our Scripture verse today says that if you cry out to Him, He will hear and deliver you from all your troubles.

Respond

Will you allow God to deliver you from the things that are holding you back today? Some things that bind us and keep us from serving God are pride, fear, unhealthy relationships, money, drugs, alcohol, and there are many others. Are you willing to release those things that are binding you and allow the Holy Spirit to set you free? Confess the times you have been unwilling to let God take control of your life and allow Him to come in and change your heart now.

Remember

Deliverance from all evil is God's plan for you!

Passing the Legacy

Read

Tell them that the flow of the Jordan was cut off before the ark of the covenant of the Lord. When it crossed the Jordan, the waters of the Jordan were cut off. These stones are to be a memorial to the people of Israel forever. — Joshua 4:7.

Reflect

I love the story about the little girl who asked her mom why she always cut off the end of the ham before she put it in the oven to cook. The mother replied, "That's what my mom used to do and the ham always came out tasting delicious." So the little girl asked her grandmother why she cut off the end of the ham before she put it in the oven to cook. The grandmother said, "That's what my mother always did, and it tasted so good." Finally, the little girl went to her great-grandmother and asked the same question. "Why did you always cut the end of the ham off before you put it in the oven to cook?" Her great-grandmother looked at her and said, "Well sweetheart, my pan was too short to hold the whole ham, so I had to cut the end off to make it fit."

Traditions are good when they are meaningful. As believers we need traditions that will help us remember what God has done in our lives. For example, the members of our family celebrate our spiritual birthdays. We have birthday parties for the days we were born again just like we do for our physical births. We sit around the table and let the one who was born again on that day tell what God did in their life.

Respond

If you can't remember the date of your spiritual birthday, pick one from around the time of year you decided to give your life to Jesus. If you are single or your family doesn't have any spiritual traditions, spend a little time thinking about what you would like to do. God is pleased when we pass on to our children the great things He has done for us.

Remember

Traditions are good when they point back to what God has done in your life.

THE PRACTICE OF SERVANTHOOD

READ

Your attitude should be the same as that of Christ Jesus: Who, being in very nature God, did not consider equality with God something to be grasped, but made himself nothing, taking the very nature of a servant, being made in human likeness. — PHILIPPIANS 2:5-7.

REFLECT

I love servants. They make me smile. Recently I visited with the president of an organization who manifested servanthood. He had been out in the field of work, at power meetings, trying to make things happen for his company. When he came back into the office he saw one of his assistants working their tail off to make the company succeed. He stopped, went into his office, dropped off his laptop, and changed his clothes. Then he came out to the assistant's office and asked if he could borrow the assistant's car for about half an hour.

The executive then walked out of the office building, drove his assistant's car to the nearest car wash, and cleaned that car inside and out. He came back into the office and said to his assistant, "Thanks for the car. Why don't you take the rest of the day off and let me cover for you?" Not the normal conduct for a CEO, but what a message it sends to all of us: I may be your boss, but I'm also your servant.

Most people like servants. Some take advantage of them. Some are suspicious of them. Some ignore them. But most appreciate them. So the question is not, "Do you like them?" The question is: "Are you one?" Jesus was equal with God. He had the position. But He valued you and me more than the position. That is ultimate servanthood. It is the attitude we are to embrace everyday.

RESPOND

How are you doing with this servanthood attitude thing? What is your position? Are you using it as a platform to serve others? Do you spend time thinking how you can make someone's day, or how you can make yourself look good? The answer to that question will reveal how much you think like a servant. In your time alone today, ask God to help you be a better servant to those around you.

REMEMBER

You're probably never more like Jesus than when you are serving.

Contented in His Strength

Read

I can do everything through him who gives me strength. — PHILIPPIANS 4:13.

Reflect

I remember well when my wife Rhonda first quoted this verse in public from memory. We were on a ski trip and I wanted her to ski with me. Rhonda likes to take her time down the slopes and enjoy the swishing sound of the skis. She likes to go down the easiest slopes so she can stop and look at the scenery. On the other hand, I'm a daredevil. I want to go as fast as I can, as steep as I can, for as long as I can.

On this occasion, we were skiing together. I told Rhonda to go ahead and I would follow behind. Unfamiliar with the ski area, she asked me if a particular trail was "a green." I remember saying, "Oh yea, it's green all the way to the bottom." In a couple of minutes I realized I was wrong and my wife was headed down a "blue/black." (Let's just say, that's not good.) When I caught up with her, I heard her quoting today's verse, "I can do everything through him who gives me strength." She's really good at scripture memorization when she's under pressure!

But isn't today's scripture a great encouragement? To know that when you depend on Him and trust Him, there is nothing out of your reach. When you allow Him to strengthen you, your potential increases. Paul knew this. He wrote these words from a jail cell. The prison bars he saw did not intimidate or threaten him. His physical limitations could not weaken His inner strength. He saw the prison not as a confinement, but as an opportunity. With that attitude working for him, no wonder one of the jail keepers became a Christian when he was chained to Paul (see Acts 16:22-34).

Respond

Do the slopes of your life look steep and treacherous? Read today's verse again and be encouraged. Thank God that He has provided you strength to get through today.

Remember

You can do *all* things through Jesus who gives you strength.

God's Work Involves You

Read

So God created man in his own image, in the image of God he created him; male and female he created them. — Genesis 1:27.

Reflect

One of my fondest memories of growing up was working with my dad on the farm. I can't honestly say that I always liked it, because I was a kid, and kids like to play when there is work to be done. But he balanced the play and the work for me in order to prepare me to be a man. And when we worked together, I was never worried about the work, because he was with me.

This was not only true with work, but also with what he loved. He taught me what to love. For example, he loved my mom (They've been married over 57 years at this writing), so I loved my mom. He also taught me how to treat people, to show everyone respect and honor.

God established work long ago in the Garden of Eden, and He started with man. We don't always like the way He works with us, because we're just like kids. We want to have our way, our playtime, and get our desires met when it's time to work. But God is patient and He works with us, giving us the responsibility to carry on His work. He also works with us on what we should love. He loves all of us, and He wants us to love each other. According to 2 Corinthians 5:20, we are His representatives on this earth to spread His message of love.

Respond

God's work is centered around relationships. Think about it, if you had given your Son to die for someone, so you could have a relationship with them, wouldn't that be your quest in life? So, it is with God. He wants a relationship with you. Why don't you spend some time with Him right now developing that relationship? Thank Him for His love. Confess to Him the times you have done things to hurt the relationship. Pray for those you know who need a relationship with Him.

Remember

God wants to work with you and show you how to love like He does today.

The Highest Purpose

Read

If I give all I possess to the poor and surrender my body to the flames, but have not love, I gain nothing. — 1 Corinthians 13:3.

Reflect

He was one of the nicest guys I ever knew. He had it all. He was successful, talented, had a good, solid family background, and had all the money one could ever need. If you were to meet him, you would be attracted by his hospitable personality. He was undoubtedly the best musician I have ever been associated with, past or present. There were no limits to what he could accomplish or where he could go. But then it ended. His life turned inward. He got caught up in himself. All the love he had seemed to change its focus.

He developed a hatred and intolerance for those who didn't see things his way. His world became small and narrowed down to just himself. His cause in life was himself. And he eventually died at the age of twenty-nine. When I heard the news of his death, I remember thinking, "What a waste." Loving yourself because God loves you is good. But loving yourself alone is a waste.

One of the most disheartening things in life would be to give your life to something, only to find out in the end that your purpose in life was wrong. During New Testament times there were many who were burned at the stake, but the martyr who had no love, Paul says, died in vain.

Respond

God has called us to His highest purpose: love. Make a list of people you love and people who love you. Praise God for providing His presence through them in your life. Ask Him to forgive the times you have been caught up in yourself and ignored the opportunity to love others. Then pray that your life will be a manifestation of His love to those with whom you come in contact today.

Remember

It is difficult to see clearly when your eyes are solely on yourself.

Introducing the VIP

Read

He was not the light, but came that he might bear witness of the light. — John 1:8 NASB.

Reflect

If a VIP (very important person) were to come to your house, chances are you would make some preparation for the visit. You would clean your house from top to bottom. You would prepare the best meal possible. You would go the extra mile. Why? Because if you didn't, you might suffer great embarrassment. That is what John the Baptist tried to do for the people of Israel. He wanted to pave the way for the VIP and save them embarrassment by preparing them with the message of repentance.

John the Baptist's role was to make the nation of Israel aware of the coming of Jesus on the scene. He was to reach out to the people and be the primary witness of the Messiah's arrival. John the Baptist showed the attitude we must have if we are to be an effective witness when he said, "He (Jesus) must increase and I must decrease" (John 3:30).

If we are to reach out to those who need Jesus, we must earn the right to be heard, and we earn that right through a humble attitude. Our egos must be taken off the throne of our lives or we will misrepresent Him altogether. Jesus never drove Himself into the lives of people. He drew them through a humble spirit. We must have the same attitude that He had when we tell people about Jesus.

Respond

Do you know of someone who needs to be introduced to Jesus? Have you taken time to consider that you might be the one God wants to prepare the way? If you do prepare the way for Jesus to work in their life and your friend becomes a Christian, you can be sure they will be eternally grateful. So try introducing the VIP of your life to them today.

Remember

You may be the one who prepares the way for Jesus to touch someone today.

JULY 10

House Cleaning

Read

You were taught, with regard to your former way of life, to put off your old self, which is being corrupted by its deceitful desires. — Ephesians 4:22.

Reflect

I once read about a strange custom followed by an Italian town. At midnight on New Year's Eve, the streets are cleared. There is no traffic, no pedestrians, and even the police take cover. Precisely at midnight, the windows of the houses fly open. With laughter, music, and fireworks, each family member tosses out old dishes, disfigured furniture, and any thing else that reminds them of something in the past year. They are determined to wipe out their memories. Once they have thrown out the old, they are ready to begin with the new.

Wouldn't you love to be able to throw out some of the old? That is exactly what we are to do every day as believers. We are to confess and agree with God about our sin. We are to get rid of it through the avenue of confession, and He promises to throw that trash as far as the East is from the West. (See Psalm 103:12.)

The challenge for many of us is that we often can grow callused to our sin, to the point that we begin to accept it as part of our lives. We toy with it, justify it, rationalize it, and convince ourselves that our sin isn't a sin. It is then that we become desensitized to evil and caught in Satan's steel trap of sin.

Respond

Spend some time with God right now and thank Him for His unconditional love. Ask Him to help you take an honest look into your heart. As painful as it may be, ask Him to help you repent of all the sin that you have given in to. Confess your sin to Him as soon as He reveals it to you, and with all that is within you turn away from it. Let Him take the trash of your life and give it a big heave!

Remember

When is trash day at your house? Everyday!

"Love in Action"

Read

This is love for God: to obey his commands. And His commands are not burdensome. — 1 John 5:3.

Reflect

I'll never forget the night my wife Rhonda and I left the church we had served for years to go to Kansas City to further my education. The night we left, the church threw a big party in our honor. We found all the gifts given and nice words said very humbling and undeserved. At the close of the evening we were given a going away present, a check for $1,000. We were blown away. I will never forget the memo line on that check — it read, "Love in Action." From that moment on I have measured my own love not by what I say, but by what I do to demonstrate it.

How do you know when people love you? Do you know it because they tell you? Some of you would say yes, but some of you would say, "Just telling me isn't enough, you need to show me." God says if we love Him, we will show it. We will show it by our obedience. But it's much more than just our obedience. Notice the last part of today's verse. "His commands are not burdensome." You see, those who really love God do not obey Him out of fear but out of love. They obey Him because they want to. It's a joy to go His way because they trust Him and enjoy His company.

Respond

Does your love for God motivate you to obey Him? Why do you serve at church? Because of your deep love and devotion to the One who gave His life for you, or because of the image you want people to see? I know these are searching questions, but they are valid. Spend some time with God now and ask Him to search your heart and motives. Let His Spirit guide you and lead you to a point of assurance that your love is pure and true, and that your works are genuine and faithful to Him.

Remember

Your love will be demonstrated today, not by your words, but by your actions.

Comfort Those in Pain

Read

...who comforts us in all our troubles, so that we can comfort those in any trouble with the comfort we ourselves have received from God. — 2 Corinthians 1:4.

Reflect

At a funeral I watched a widow of three years speak to a widow of three days. "I know how you feel." She said that with such strong emotion, they both wept together. Why did she say that? Because she knew how the new widow felt. Many people at funerals say they know how you feel, but they don't if they've never been there. This woman had been there. So her words carried a lot of weight. "You'll make it," she said, "I know right now, you don't even want to, but you will, it will just be different. A different normal. But you'll make it."

Pain and suffering can give us the capacity to enter into another's sorrow and struggles. If you have suffered the pain of a broken leg and been confined for weeks, you can sympathize with one who is going through the same thing even years after your incident. You can empathize much better than someone who has not felt the pain. And who better to comfort someone who is going through the loss of a husband or child than a person who has been there?

Pain can be a tool by which God grows us into better servants. It humbles the proud and quiets the boasters. Many times when someone calls me to help them and I have no experience, I call someone who has had that experience to go with me. They can minister to the afflicted one in a more complete and meaningful way.

Respond

Do you see people around you being worked on by the tool of pain? Can you identify? If you can, do. Let them know it won't last forever and you want to be there for them. Pray God uses you to minister to someone in pain today.

Remember

If you will let Him, God will take your scars and use them to heal others in pain.

Watch Your Tongue

Read

Do not let any unwholesome talk come out of your mouths, but only what is helpful for building others up according to their needs, that it may benefit those who listen. — EPHESIANS 4:29.

Reflect

"Sticks and stones may break my bones, but words will never hurt me." You probably heard that saying as a child. But as an adult you know it's not true. Words do hurt. They can be deadly. I heard a person say one time, "I'll just explode and then it will all be over." Wrong! The scars that person leaves could take years to heal, and some of them never do.

The tongue is often a reliable barometer of a person's walk with God. It reveals what is on the inside. We can sense their motives by the way they use words, place inflections, and gesture. Is it any surprise then that Paul gives us the admonition in this verse? Paul's desire was to reach out to others for Jesus Christ and to encourage other believers to do the same. He knew that if believers were not careful with their words they could repel seekers after God and would cause other believers to stumble as well. The same thing is true for us today. If we allow things to come out of our mouths that are not becoming to a Christian, we could hinder someone from coming to Jesus or cause another believer to stumble and fall.

Respond

How carefully do you select your words? Do your words go through the "ready, aim, fire" sequence, or is it more like "fire, aim, ready"? All of us need God's strength to control our tongue. Ask Him to help you to be careful with your words. Pray that your words would make Him look good to others. Pray God will give you an open door to reflect His love to them.

Remember

One of the evidences that God is controlling your life is whether or not you have control over your own tongue.

Invitation to Love

Read

Whoever has my commands and obeys them, he is the one who loves me. He who loves me will be loved by my Father, and I too will love him and show myself to him. — John 14:21.

Reflect

Why does a mom love her newborn baby? Think about it: For months this baby brought her back pain, front pain, side pain, top pain, bottom pain — did I miss one ladies? This child has made her body go through all kinds of changes, not only physical changes, but mental ones and emotional ones too. She ate differently, had cravings for strange foods, threw up in the mornings, waddled like a duck when she walked, got punched in the stomach from the inside every day, and couldn't sit down without making plans to stay there for a while. Who brought all that discomfort? The one she kept safe, warm, and fed for nine months. Does she get any thank yous? No. And to top all this off, when the baby arrives, he cries. The room is too cold, the people are too loud, and who does he want??? Mom. Her head is pounding, her back is aching, and she is totally exhausted. So why would a she love someone like this?

I hope you're catching my point. It's really not hard to understand. The mom loves the baby because he's hers. He was made in her image. He's her own flesh and blood. The bond between them is incredible. Together they have been through pain and discomfort that no man should ever try to explain.

So why does God love you? For the same reasons a mother loves her child.

Respond

When He showers His love on you, God gives you an invitation to love Him back. And the best way you can demonstrate your love for Him is by obeying Him. Do you love Him? If you do love Him, show Him today.

Remember

Throughout the day, show your love for your heavenly Father by obeying Him.

Be Real to God

Read

But when the young man heard this statement, he went away grieved; for he was one who owned much property. — Matthew 19:22 NASB.

Reflect

The young man did not have to go away grieved. He could have gone away full of joy and fulfillment. But he left in grief because he knew he could not serve both God and money. Tragically, he chose to serve the wrong master. This story assures us that even the greatest of possessions apart from Jesus cannot give us lasting joy and pleasure.

Jesus knew that the man in this story loved material wealth. When He instructed him to go and sell what he had, Jesus forced him to determine his priorities in life. Even with all his good qualities, this rich young ruler still lacked love for God. No doubt many considered him a godly person, but when he was asked to demonstrate his godliness by giving away his possessions, he failed the test.

It is assumed the man in this story was one of the most respected men in the area. He was as good as any Christian today. But to be respectable in the eyes of men is not the same as being real in the eyes of God. Today the pews of our churches are filled with respectable people. And tragically, they often think being respectable on the outside compensates for not being real on the inside. If asked to demonstrate their commitment in the same way as the rich young ruler, they would find an excuse not to follow God's instructions. They too would go away grieving over something that was never intended to make them grieve.

Respond

Take some time right now to praise God for His priceless love. Then, ask Him to guide you in all your involvements. Ask Him to lead you in all your priorities and thank Him for the fact that He considers you His treasure.

Remember

Being a real Christian in the eyes of God is more important than being a respectable in the eyes of the world.

Modeling Godly Values

Read

Impress them on your children. Talk about them when you sit at home and when you walk along the road, when you lie down and when you get up. — DEUTERONOMY 6:7.

Reflect

Whether you have children of your own or not, you will have daily opportunities to affect a child's life. When a child is standing next to you in the grocery store and you receive too much change from the cashier, it's time to teach values. If children are present in your home and something ungodly comes on the TV, it's time to teach values. When a child is sitting next to you at church and the offering plate is passed, it is time to teach values. God is not as interested in where we teach values, as that we teach them all the time through our lifestyle.

If you are a parent, you will have daily, moment-by-moment chances to impart godly wisdom to your own children. But parent or not, whether you live in an apartment or house, whether you work at home or at an office, you will have opportunities to demonstrate what it is to be like Jesus to the children around you.

In this verse God commands us to always be in the process of teaching His ways to children. Whenever a wrong is committed, we teach children how God hates sin. Whenever someone is blessed, we can teach a child how God's love has helped them. We are to constantly look for teachable moments to make God look good to the children in our sphere of influence.

Respond

Do you make God look good to your children, the children in your neighborhood, church, or school? If you are excited about God, your enthusiasm and love for God is contagious. And no one catches excitement like a child! If you are a parent, begin to look for any opportunity to impart a love for God to them. If you are not a parent, ask God to show you how you can give something of eternal value to children.

Remember

The values our children embrace will shape the future.

Taking Time to Communicate

Read

Making the most of every opportunity, because the days are evil. — Ephesians 5:16.

Reflect

I once heard it explained this way. Communication is like a family going down the river in individual rafts with their arms linked together. If their arms unlink, they drift apart. What is so sad today is that there are many families going down the rapids of life so focused on the rapids that they don't realize they have lost some family members along the way.

One of the biggest challenges to communication is making time to do it. But of all the things vital to a relationship, communication is at the top of the list. We talk a lot about having a time alone with God every day, and that is of the utmost importance. But it is also important to have a time alone with those you love every day. Take the phone off the hook, or better yet, just don't answer it. Turn the TV off and sit down and talk. Have a sharing time — not just about the activities of the day, but of individual feelings about those activities. Ask questions like, "When did you feel happy today? Excited? Sad? Hurt? Angry?" You can be creative about the format, but the main thing is to spend time communicating in an atmosphere of love.

Respond

When you manage your time well, you manage your life well. And the most important thing in life is relationships. And the most dear relationships you have outside of your relationship with Christ are those within your family and friends. How much time are you giving them? Relationships are a priority in life. So spend some time with God right now praising Him and thanking Him for your family and friends. Ask Him to show you the things in your schedule that are not important enough to be robbing you of time with them. Ask Him to give you wisdom and courage to get rid of those things so that you can become a better communicator of His love.

Remember

Time to communicate with those you love needs to be one of your highest priorities.

RESCUED

READ

And when he finds it, he joyfully puts it on his shoulders and goes home. Then he calls his friends and neighbors together and says, "Rejoice with me; I have found my lost sheep." — LUKE 15:5-6.

REFLECT

Sheep that wander can get themselves into the most difficult circumstances. Sometimes they get trapped and need a shepherd to rescue them. Jesus told this story in Luke 15 to help us see that His Father is the Shepherd who wants to rescue us from our wandering helplessness.

I'll never forget the first rescue I ever saw. I was five years old and playing in the back yard on our farm. I heard my brother scream from a wooded area behind our house. I remember seeing my dad carrying my brother and running as fast as he could to the car. My dad was hurdling fences and dodging obstacles on the farm like the best NFL running back you've ever seen. He was yelling at all of us to get in the car because my brother had been bitten by a poisonous snake. We raced to the doctor's office in a 1956 Ford at record speed. My brother was treated and recovered completely. Afterwards, I remember how thrilled we all were. I can still see my father running to rescue my brother, his son.

That's the way it is with all of us, isn't it? We all need to be rescued from the "sin" snake that has bitten us. We all need a father who cares — one who will do anything to rescue his helpless child. We have that kind of Father available to us. God the Father has gone to unmatchable lengths to rescue us from the snakebite of sin by allowing His own Son to die on the cross in our place.

RESPOND

Do you need to be rescued today from some habits that have led you away from the Father and entrapped you? Surrender completely to the loving arms of your Father and let Him rescue you.

REMEMBER

If you need to be rescued today, just call and watch the Father run to you.

New Life

Read

We were therefore buried with him through baptism into death in order that, just as Christ was raised from the dead through the glory of the Father, we too may live a new life. —Romans 6:4.

Reflect

Before I baptize people, we talk about several things to prepare for the ordinance: We talk about who was most influential in leading them to know Jesus. We briefly go over the reason for being baptized and the reality of how we are truly baptized into Christ. We discuss identifying ourselves with Jesus' death, burial, and resurrection. And, of course, we go over the "mechanics" of how to be baptized — hold my wrist in a certain way, take a deep breath, and above all, don't swallow the water! Then I always try to give them assurance concerning the safety issues surrounding the ceremony itself. I often reassure them with, "Don't worry, we've never lost one yet."

When we arise from the waters of baptism, we are symbolically resurrected into Christ's free gift of eternal life. The ceremony is a type of the reality of our spiritual conversion. We were dead, but now we live. To be "buried with him through baptism into death in order that, just as Christ was raised from the dead through the glory of the Father, we too may live a new life." New life in Christ is truly life.

What a picture baptism provides of God's care for His own. Not one who trusts Him will ever be lost. Jesus tells us in John 10:28 that when we trust Him as Savior and Lord, we are placed in His hand and no one will ever be able to take us from His hand. We have a new life that will never end: "I am the resurrection and the life. He who believes in me will live, even though he dies..." (John 11:25). New life.

Respond

Take some time today to thank Jesus for making His life available through His sacrifice on the cross. Praise God for the new life you experience, symbolized in water baptism.

Remember

When we are baptized into Christ, we are blessed with a new life in Him.

ACCOUNTABILITY

READ

Brothers, if someone is caught in a sin, you who are spiritual should restore him gently. But watch yourself, or you also may be tempted. — GALATIANS 6:1.

REFLECT

I have a love/hate relationship with accountability. I love it because when I'm accountable to someone, it makes me better in the area for which I am accountable. I hate it because I have to answer to someone, and if I don't come through, I feel like I've failed. Well, those words are a little strong, because those to whom I have made myself accountable have never allowed my failures to be fatal. In fact, they know that accountability makes the one who is accountable better. As Paul described it, accountability is designed to support and restore. It should neither be too severe, nor too loose. The person being held accountable should be treated gently, with genuine love and concern, so they can be fully restored.

Accountability is rare these days. Why? Because we don't want to make ourselves vulnerable, even if it will help us live above mediocrity. We would rather wear the mask and let everyone think that we have it all together. Being accountable to someone does not mean being judged. It means someone loves you enough to say, "I want you to become better at living this Christian life." Being accountable means being vulnerable, honest, teachable, and available. It means developing a fellowship that digs to a deep level of trust. There is someone in your life who cares for you and wants to have a part in helping you become all God wants you to be.

RESPOND

If you don't have someone to whom you are accountable and you have been slipping in your walk with God, pray that God will lead you to someone you can trust who will help you grow. Pray for those you know who need help in their walk with Jesus. Pray that God will restore them to fellowship with Himself.

REMEMBER

Being accountable is uncomfortable because you are being challenged to rise to a new level of excellence.

Relating to People

Read

Paul then stood up in the meeting of the Areopagus and said: "Men of Athens! I see that in every way you are very religious." — Acts 17:22.

Reflect

Here's Paul, a narrow-minded Jew, a Pharisee for years, an "i dotter and t crosser" of the law for most of his life, in the middle of a bunch of broad-minded philosophers. Have you ever been in that situation? Completely out of place. It probably would have been scary to Paul, but Paul knew he was not alone. God had put him right where He wanted him. So it was time to seize the moment. Paul began by warming up to their sensitivity to religion. Then he steered their attention to the "unknown god" altar and told them who God was.

This is the heart of Paul's message. It is sound theology and easily understood. They listened intently as he quoted some of their own poets (see v. 27-28). Then he challenged them to change their thinking and repent because of God's judgment and Jesus' resurrection. End of speech. Five minutes, tops. Some listened. Some believed. Some dismissed him. But the message went on.

Sounds a lot like church, doesn't it? The speech stops, but God continues to speak. The message is much bigger than the messenger. So the message must get out to every corner of the world — every corner of your world.

Respond

How are you doing in utilizing opportunities you have to relate the good news of Jesus to others? For Paul, it took about five minutes. Maybe now would be a good time for you to think through how you can best relate to those you know who need Him. Start by praying to God and asking Him to give you the right time and best approach to make Him look good in their eyes. Let Him guide you. And take courage — because you're not alone.

Remember

When you go for God, you never go alone.

Can You Change?

Read

Can the Ethiopian change his skin or the leopard its spots? Neither can you do good who are accustomed to doing evil. — Jeremiah 13:23.

Reflect

"We've never done it that way before." Those are the seven last words of a dying church. An unwillingness to change, coupled with an attitude with anyone who tries to initiate change, results in a mediocre church that does the same old thing every week. You can set your clock by it. They will do it the same way until Jesus comes. And if He comes in the middle of their ritual, they'll ask Him to wait.

Changing is always tough when it involves habits we love and have had for a long time. Most often, we make all kinds of excuses for not breaking them. Do any of these sound familiar?

"Well, nobody's perfect."
"That's just the way I am."
"I was born this way; it's in my genes."
"You can't teach an old dog new tricks."

Those excuses come so easily when we are "accustomed to doing evil." But these excuses are nothing more than our self-satisfied sin nature refusing to change. We simply don't want to change because we know it will be uncomfortable and difficult. Unfortunately, we seldom look past the cost to see the tremendous rewards.

Respond

So, can you change? God didn't give you His Word just to provide good reading. He gave it to you to change your life. You can change if you want to badly enough. But realize change doesn't take place overnight — it takes time. Start off with one attitude, then move on. No more excuses! Break the custom of "doing evil" and get to work on a change. Remember, all heaven is pulling for you.

Remember

God does not change, but He is in the changing business.

Spirit of Unity

Read

May the God who gives endurance and encouragement give you a spirit of unity among yourselves as you follow Christ Jesus, so that with one heart and mouth you may glorify the God and Father of our Lord Jesus Christ. — Romans 15:5-6.

Reflect

At times I wish I could have been present on the day of Pentecost when the Church was first established. Picture it with me: Peter gets up to preach a sermon for which he has no notes. He speaks for five to ten minutes about who Jesus was and what He did, and that He was resurrected. Then three thousand people respond and are baptized — publicly taking their stand for Jesus Christ.

Hey, don't stop reading — that's not the end of the picture! A brand new church was born, with three thousand people who had no church building, no pastor, no church bylaws and constitution (which is probably why they got along so well), no committees, and no promise of a future. So what did they have? Jesus. They had the presence of the Messiah in their lives. They had His love, His joy, His faith — and when they exercised those attributes, they had unity. Since then, obviously there have been disagreements along the way. But when the Church functions properly, it is because a spirit of unity prevails.

Are you operating with a spirit of unity, or when things don't go your way, do you pout and pull away from the body? I've got news for you — things will not always go the way you want them to in the church. That's because the church is made up of flawed human beings. I guess that's why Paul mentioned in today's verse that God gives endurance and encouragement with the spirit of unity. In order to have the spirit of unity, we must endure others and encourage them to follow Jesus. But when we have the spirit of unity, we can fulfill the purpose of the Church, which is to glorify God.

Respond

Praise and thank God for the church. It was His idea and it was a great one.

Remember

The spirit of unity will never come by theology, but by God's love, shed abroad in our hearts by the Holy Spirit.

Love Has No Boundaries

Read

Love is patient, love is kind. It does not envy, it does not boast, it is not proud. It is not rude, it is not self-seeking, it is not easily angered, it keeps no record of wrongs. Love does not delight in evil but rejoices with the truth. It always protects, always trust, always hopes, always perseveres. — 1 Corinthians 13:4-7.

Reflect

A few years back I heard Paul Harvey tell a story of a sheriff's election. Two candidates were running for the office and were speaking at a county gathering a few days before the election. The first candidate got up to speak, and during his speech fell on the platform, experiencing what appeared to be a heart attack. Naturally there was confusion on the platform. Then someone rushed from backstage and revived the man. They rushed him to the hospital where he recovered. Who was the guy who rushed out to revive him? His opponent! Have you ever seen love like that? Love without boundaries? Love as a verb?

Many people say "I love you" these days. But love is to be demonstrated. The acid test is: do you really show it to those to whom you say it? Jesus tells the story of the Good Samaritan in Luke 10. It is the story of a man who was robbed and beaten by thieves. A priest passed him by, then a lawyer, but then a Samaritan stopped to help him. So Jesus told us to be like the Samaritan. Ouch! There are too many unloving passersby today, and Jesus wants to show Satan's victim God's unconditional love.

Respond

Can't we just send our money to those who are in need? Do we have to get personally involved? Have you ever said or heard this in or out of your church? If you have, you need to learn from the Samaritan. Perhaps you know some people who have been robbed of joy in their lives. Maybe they have been stripped of self-respect and are beaten down emotionally. Will you walk around them like the lawyer and priest, or will you show them love today?

Remember

The love people know is the love you show. Put feet to your love today.

Invite Some Friends Over

Read

Then Levi held a great banquet for Jesus at his house, and a large crowd of the tax collectors and others were eating with them. — Luke 5:29.

Reflect

Generally speaking, people like to eat. The tax collector Levi knew this. So after he became a Christian, he invited his tax collector friends over for a banquet. Levi created an atmosphere for those he had developed relationships with to come in contact with the love of God. And, he was fortunate to have the best communicator in history scheduled as banquet speaker.

What Levi did wasn't that difficult. He just used food as a platform to get his friends in touch with God. He developed an environment that God could use, and he developed friendships to draw them into that environment. Levi's approach wasn't to force Jesus down anybody's throat, but to let his friends experience Him.

You too can set an environment for your unchurched friends. You don't need to put on a big banquet. Ask a friend to your church. Invite them to a social activity hosted by your Bible study. Invite them to play on a church sports team. Whatever activity you choose, your efforts should focus on getting your unchurched friends in an environment where God can speak to them.

Respond

Think for a moment: What can I do to get my friends in touch with God? What kind of setting would create a comfortable atmosphere in which God could speak to them? Take some time to praise and thank God for the way He spoke to you when you responded to Him. Ask Him to forgive you for the times you have blown opportunities that He has given you to introduce Him to others. Finally, pray for those you have in mind who need Him. Ask God to guide you to help make a significant difference in their lives. By the way, what's for dinner?

Remember

Look for platforms for sharing your faith today.

No Excuses

Read

And now, brothers, we want you to know about the grace that God has given the Macedonian churches. Out of the most severe trial, their overflowing joy and their extreme poverty welled up in rich generosity. — 2 Corinthians 8:1-2.

Reflect

> "When you have experienced the grace of God in your life, you will not use difficult circumstances as an excuse for not giving."
>
> — Warren Wiersbe

Do you like hanging around people who are always full of excuses? You know, the ones who always have an explanation for why they didn't do or aren't doing what they should have done? If you're like me, a little bit goes a long way with people like that. So how do you think God looks at us when we give excuses?

Excuses for not giving are numerous. Sometimes it is a result of poor management, but other times people are just selfish. Giving is a matter of the heart. Paul describes the church in Macedonia as giving even when they were going through a severe trial. They didn't let their circumstances serve as an excuse for not giving. They found a way to give even though they were going through difficult times.

Giving is a "want to" thing. It comes from the realization of how much God has given to you, and it is a natural response to show your appreciation to Him. People who really believe it is more fulfilling to give than to receive understand this natural response. They also understand that you're probably never more like Jesus than when you are giving.

Respond

How is your attitude toward giving? Is your giving attitude one that honors God? Do you give to the right things? Do you look for new areas in which to give? These are good questions to bring before God. Praise Him for His gracious gifts to you. Ask Him to forgive you for the times you've made excuses not to give. Ask for His guidance in how and where He wants you to give.

Remember

Giving is a "want to" thing. Either you want to or you don't. No excuses.

The Peace of Jesus

Read

"Peace I leave with you; my peace I give you. I do not give to you as the world gives." — John 14:27.

Reflect

Imagine how you would feel if the dearest person in the world to you announced they were leaving. Would that disrupt your peace? This is what the disciples were going through when Jesus told them He was going to die. But at the same time, Jesus told them He would be leaving them His peace. How could He be leaving them and at the same time provide them with peace? Simple, His peace isn't like the peace of the world. The peace of the world is based on temporal security and happiness. Jesus' peace is based on the comfort, provision, and protection of the Holy Spirit. The Holy Spirit brings comfort the world doesn't understand.

When things go well, it's easy to feel a sense of peace. But it is an altogether different thing to have peace when everything around us is falling apart. We live in a stressful world that races around at ninety miles an hour, and most of us are equipped to do fifty-five!

The word peace in this verse means to bring together. When we have peace with God, we are together with Him. That's what Jesus does in a life that is surrendered to Him. He brings it together and makes sense out of life. So when we are surrendered to Him, life makes sense. We have peace in Him.

Respond

What causes the most stress in your life right now? Home? Job? Relationships? Finances? Whatever it is, God can handle it. In fact, what you face is no surprise, because Jesus experienced the same feelings. If you depend on Him, He will produce peace in your life. He will bring it all together. Will you let Him do that? Cast your anxiety on Him today. Then, whenever you feel stressed as the day progresses, stop and turn your problem over to Him so He can give you more peace.

Remember

Whenever you begin to feel anxious or tense today, turn to Jesus and receive His peace.

FORGIVE

READ

The punishment inflicted on him by the majority is sufficient for him. Now instead, you ought to forgive and comfort him, so that he will not be overwhelmed by excessive sorrow. — 2 CORINTHIANS 2:6-7.

REFLECT

Forgiveness never comes easy. When you are called upon to forgive someone and to cancel the punishment they deserve, you are tempted to put stipulations on the forgiveness. "I will forgive you if you will change and be more sorrowful." Or, "I will forgive you when I am able to deal with this deep hurt." Or, "I will forgive you, but I will never deal with you again." Such words do not indicate true forgiveness. They are only words. True forgiveness says, "I have the right to punish you in some way, but I waive my rights and you are free from the offense. It's over."

In this scripture, Paul instructed the Corinthians to forgive. One of the reasons the squabble was so painful at the church in Corinth was because it was over one of the members — possibly a leader who had messed up morally. In Paul's first letter to the church, he told them this guy needed to be disciplined because he was giving the church a bad reputation. Evidently, the church did discipline the person involved (notice Paul never mentioned who it was) and the guy was repentant. So Paul then told them "Enough is enough. Let the person involved come back to church."

RESPOND

Some of us would rather quit a relationship than provide forgiveness. Aren't you glad Jesus didn't quit? He valued a relationship with you and me so much that He forgave. If you are going to fully identify with Him, you must be a forgiver too. Praise Him for His forgiveness now. Ask Him to forgive you for the times you have been unforgiving. Ask Him to help you forgive others. Pray that He will help you to always forgive.

REMEMBER

Of all people, believers should be forgiving, for we are the forgiven.

Not Even A Hint

Read

But among you there must not be even a hint of sexual immorality, or of any kind of impurity, or of greed, because these are improper for God's holy people. — Ephesians 5:3.

Reflect

To be authentic as a Christian, we must allow the presence of God's love and the power of the Holy Spirit to refine and purify us. In order to do this we must abstain from any form of impurity. This takes discipline, because immorality is everywhere. We must discipline our thoughts, control our eyes, and force our will to avoid immoral enticements.

Paul uses the words, "not even a hint of sexual immorality." Does that sound like you? Would the people you work with say there is not even a hint of immorality associated with you? When the dirty jokes fly around the office, do you join in? When certain magazines make their way within your vision, are you looking right along with those who don't know Jesus? When the TV screen is full of lust and carnality, do you continue viewing?

God has called you to a higher standard of living. He desires to give you the best. So ask yourself this question: Do I really want to live for Him and deny my selfish desires? There is no middle ground. The answer to that question will tell you where you are spiritually. If you do, all of heaven is behind you cheering you on. But if you just want to please yourself, you are on your own — and in this world that is a scary place to be.

Respond

Take some time right now to spend time with God. Especially if you don't feel like it — you need to! Praise Him for who He is and thank Him for what He has done for you. Ask Him to forgive you for the times you have failed Him. Pray for those you know who are struggling with the pressures to compromise. Ask God to help you be one who reaches out and makes Him look good to others today.

Remember

Someone is watching. Show them Jesus living through you.

Growing Up

Read

But he said to me, "My grace is sufficient for you, for my power is made perfect in weakness. — 2 Corinthians 12:9.

Reflect

I once heard a story about the great Charles Finney. His father was near death and Finney was by his side...silent. He recorded in his journal, "I found myself in the presence of my father, wanting nothing." How much more will the presence of our heavenly Father leave us wanting nothing? Even when we are in pain, His presence makes a difference. No pill will bring us His presence. No psychiatrist can cause us to feel His presence. It is His grace. That is the only way to explain the knowledge and sensing of His presence during suffering.

Paul was probably disappointed that his prayer was not answered in the way he would have liked for it to be answered. But judging by his response to God's answer, he experienced God's presence, which was worth more than what he had requested. He discovered that at his weakest God would provide strength and victory over circumstances.

I'm afraid too many times we pray for a change of circumstances when God wants to give us a change of character in the midst of the circumstances. We pray, "God, I could serve You so much better if I didn't have to work with all these jerks." When God might be saying, "The jerks are not the problem. You need to be a light for Me where I have planted you. Don't make Me look bad by complaining all the time."

Respond

God's grace is amazing. Spend some time praising Him for His unmerited favor toward you. Thank Him for the blessings of today. Ask Him to forgive you for the times you have not represented Him well. Finally, pray for those you know who are going through pain and ask God to graciously grant them the ministry of His presence in their lives.

Remember

God wants you to experience His presence so you can grow up.

God Demands Change

Read

That is why, for Christ's sake, I delight in weaknesses, in insults, in hardships, in persecutions, in difficulties. For when I am weak, then I am strong. — 2 Corinthians 12:10.

Reflect

> "Pain and suffering produce a fork in the road. It is not possible to remain unchanged."
>
> — Tim Hansel

When I ran the 400 meter race in high school, there was a point in that race called the pain barrier. Bill Cosby has called that the point in the race where the invisible bear jumps on your back and weighs you down. I can't say I ever saw the bear, but I felt his weight and he was big! It was at that point when my inner man discussed with my outer man the current and future condition of the ultimate man.

When we are hit with a pain barrier in life, we have several alternatives: (1) We can ask God to remove the pain. (2) We can allow the pain to make us bitter. (3) We can allow the pain to cause us to give up, or (4) We can choose to look past the pain and allow God to strengthen us and teach us.

God demands change — the way we think about life, about Him, about people, and the way we conduct ourselves and make decisions. He can use pain to speak to us in a very significant way. Our pain causes us to say, "I don't ever want this to happen again, and I will take measures to keep it from happening." Then God says, "Okay, let Me tell you the root of all this."

Respond

Praise God for His love and the comfort of the Holy Spirit. Ask Him to forgive you for the times you have not responded the way you should have to pain in your life. Pray for those you know who need to feel His presence and find His truth in their pain. And finally, pray that God will help you change what you need to change in your thinking patterns and in your behavior.

Remember

When you go through pain, you are not alone. God has His hand on the thermostat and His eye on the thermometer.

The Joy of Knowing God

Read

What is more, I consider everything a loss compared to the surpassing greatness of knowing Christ Jesus my Lord, for whose sake I have lost all things. I consider them rubbish, that I may gain Christ. — PHILIPPIANS 3:8.

Reflect

The people who bring me joy in life are those whom I know personally. Now, I know about Abraham Lincoln. I know he was a great man and did a lot of great things, but I don't get a whole lot of joy in knowing about him. On the other hand I know some people who bring me great joy, not because they have done anything great, but because I know them personally and enjoy them. Our privilege as Christians is to know God personally, and no one has done any greater things than He has.

Paul knew firsthand what it was like to have a joyless life. He had been a Pharisee. He had lived a life enforcing strict rules, a rigid lifestyle that snuffed out joy. He knew *about* God during this time, but he did not *know* Him personally. When God interrupted Paul's joyless life by striking him blind on the Damascus road, he had no idea what God had in store for him. In the long run, Paul lost a lot to receive this life of joy. He lost his reputation and he lost his religion, but he gained so much more. He gained a personal relationship with God through His Son, Jesus Christ. He gained a life filled with joy because of the quality of love he received from God.

Respond

Do you know the joy of knowing God personally? If not, all you have to do is to go to Him in prayer and ask Him to come into your heart and take control. When you do this, and mean it with all your heart, you are born again into a new family — God's family — a family that experiences joy. If you already know God, take some time today to share the joy of knowing Him with someone who doesn't. Pray that God will give you an opportunity to share His love today.

Remember

There is no greater personal relationship in all the world than the one you have with Jesus.

Growing in the Word

Read

"Like newborn babes, long for the pure milk of the word, that by it you may grow in respect to salvation." — 1 PETER 2:2 NASB.

Reflect

My father-in-law has a sweet tooth, and my kids love it. Whenever he knows we are coming to his house, he will stock up on ice cream and cookies. It's funny to watch how one of the first things the kids will do when they rush into the house is to check out the refrigerator and cookie jar to see if Papa stocked up for the visit. The problem comes when they're stuffed with Papa's goodies and they lose their appetite for more nourishing snacks like fruits and vegetables.

It's the same way when we are born into the family of God. When we're converted, we develop an appetite for His Word. His Word not only gives life and hope, it nourishes us as Christians. But a tragedy exists today within Christian circles, and it weakens our testimony. The tragedy? I've said it before, and I'll say it again. We often substitute ritual and entertainment in place of feeding on God's Word. And that can corrupt our taste for the truth.

A steady diet of God's Word is a must if we are to mature as Christians. His Word contains milk for spiritual babies and meat for those who are more mature. Without it, we will lose our ability to discern God's voice and truth from the world's. We will become weak spiritually and susceptible to sin.

Respond

How much spiritual nourishment from God's Word do you get every day? Determine today to make a habit of coming to His table every day and feeding on His Word. Pray that God will give you understanding of His Word like never before. Ask Him to direct you to the helps you need to enhance your Bible study. Then, eat the Word and watch how you can be nourished spiritually. Meditate and keep His Word in your heart and it will help you to avoid sin. (See Psalm 119:11.)

Remember

Sweets taste better after a nourishing meal.

POWER TO SPARE

READ

And God is able to make all grace abound to you, so that in all things at all times, having all the you need, you will abound in every good work. — 2 CORINTHIANS 9:8.

REFLECT

On March 5, 1979, an amazing demonstration of power and energy was displayed. Scientists recorded one of the most incredible bursts of energy in the universe. One description of the event read, "The burst of gamma radiation picked up by satellites lasted only one-tenth of a second. However, in that brief instant, it emitted as much energy as the sun does in three thousand years. If the sun had burst out the same amount of energy, the earth and everything in it would have been vaporized instantly."

Isn't it interesting that about the time we think we have learned so much about the universe, something like this happens and we see how much we don't know? To this day scientists and scholars are still trying to figure out what God did on the first day of creation. This is no discredit to them, but it says a lot about the Creator.

It's easy to notice God's creative power in the *universe,* but Paul said that God wants to release His power in our *lives.* Can you intellectually grasp that truth? If you can, how will that change the way you pray? How will that change the way you see yourself? Should knowing that God can do "exceedingly abundantly more than all you think or ask" change your life? (See Ephesians 3:20.) The answer is yes! The challenge for us is to grab hold of the truth of God's power in our lives and start depending on it.

RESPOND

God can do anything in the world around us and whatever He wills in us. Therefore, it is our duty as believers to yield to Him and allow His power to work in us. In your devotional time today, allow God to work in your life. Praise Him for His power. In Jesus' name, invite Him to take control of your thoughts, motives, and actions today.

REMEMBER

There is nothing God can't do, because He has power to spare.

The Sudden Return

Read

Behold, I come like a thief! Blessed is he who stays awake and keeps his clothes with him, so that he may not go naked and be shamefully exposed. — Revelation 16:15.

Reflect

Surprises can be fun, but they can also be traumatic. When I was in college, I went out to my car one morning to find my CB radio had been stolen. I remember feeling like I wanted to cry, hit someone, and scream all at the same time. So many emotions ran through me. But in the end, there was nothing I could do. The radio was gone.

Have you ever had anything stolen from you? Do you remember the feeling you first had when you realized you had been violated? You were probably shocked, angry, and sad all at the same time. That's the way a thief leaves you. The return of Jesus Christ is referred to as a thief coming in the night. It will be unexpected by many. It will undoubtedly leave behind many with sadness, fear, and anger, but it will rescue many who have trusted Him.

For those who are ready, Jesus will be coming "like a thief" to establish His will on the earth. So His warning in Scripture is intended to make those of us anticipating His return ready. In order to be ready, we should live everyday anticipating His return. "Therefore keep watch, because you do not know on what day your Lord will come," Jesus tells us in Matthew 24:42. And, "It will be good for that servant whose master finds him doing His will when he returns," He added in Matthew 24:46.

We should be thinking about His return and what we want Him to find us doing when He returns!

Respond

What is God's will for you today? What would He find you doing if He came tonight? Take time to thank God for His faithfulness to carry out all He has planned for your life. Ask Him to forgive the times you haven't followed His plan. Make a new commitment to discover His plan and do it everyday.

Remember

Jesus is coming — it could be today.

Unending Love

Read

Love never fails. But where there are prophecies, they will cease; where there are tongues, they will be stilled; where there is knowledge, it will pass away. — 1 Corinthians 13:8.

Reflect

When it comes to presents, I can't remember the ones I have received over the years. The birthday and Christmas presents I received during my childhood have faded. In fact, I would he hard pressed to remember just a few of them. But the thing I do remember most is my parents gift of love. I was never short on feeling loved and can't remember a day growing up in their house that I didn't hear the words, "I love you." I remember how they expressed their love countless times by giving me presents or doing things for me. Well, all those presents are all gone now. But the thing that still remains is the memory of their love.

God has given us all gifts — more than we deserve — to build the kingdom of God and minister to others. His gifts are powerful and life-changing, and we should never take them lightly. When the Holy Spirit operates a gift through you to touch a person's life, it is an awesome moment. But when all things are complete and we enter eternity, these gifts will cease. The one thing that will remain will be the love in which the gift was given. It will always be remembered, throughout eternity.

Respond

If love dominated your thoughts every minute of every day, how do you think it would change your behavior? Mediate on that thought today. Let God's eternal love dominate your whole being. Then praise and thank God by showing love to those around you, even the most difficult person. You know, the one you just can't stand. Give them a gift they will always remember: the gift of God's eternal love.

Remember

The power of love can melt the hardest heart and restore the most destroyed relationship.

The Power of Giving Sacrificially

Read

For I testify that they gave as much as they were able, and even beyond their ability. Entirely on their own, they urgently pleaded with us for the privilege of sharing in this service to the saints. — 2 Corinthians 8:3-4.

Reflect

Can you imagine receiving a gift from a beggar or someone who is in poverty? This is what Paul experienced from the church in Macedonia. To receive a gift from such a source is truly humbling. When you are on the receiving end of one who sacrificially gives to you, there is no way to express the feeling adequately.

The church in Macedonia knew what the joy of giving was all about because they had experienced the grace of God. God's grace is a great motivator. In fact, they would have felt left out if they didn't give. They had seen what God had done through Paul's ministry in their own lives, and they wanted to be a part of bringing that same joy into the lives of others.

What keeps people from having the same attitude toward giving as the Macedonians? You would think that if people had lots of money, they would be more apt to give, and that those who have little would be prone to give less. But here was a group of people who were at the poverty level, enthusiastically giving to Paul's ministry. Why? Because they weren't pressured to give — they wanted to give. Their desires and God's desires were one in the same. They had learned from their mentor Paul of their unpayable eternal debt.

Respond

Outside of your children or a family member, how long has it been since you gave sacrificially? Pray that God will guide you to be a giver who will honor Him like the Macedonians did and thank Him for all His blessings in your life.

Remember

Giving sacrificially is precious to the Lord and brings great blessing on your life.

Rejoice in the Lord

Read

Rejoice in the Lord always. I will say it again: Rejoice! — PHILIPPIANS 4:4.

Reflect

One day I talked with three men who had just lost their jobs. None of the jobs were related; all lost their jobs through no fault of their own. None knew the other talked with me; they just simply crossed my path and let me know of their loss. I sensed their hurt, their shock, their depression...but interestingly enough, their hope. One even said, "I was really depressed for a while, but now, it's funny, I'm excited about what the Lord will do in my life through all this." Crazy? I don't think so. You see, this is the kind of stuff joy is made of.

When you are up against the wall and have to depend on God, you discover He is enough, and that is a joyful thing. Take a good look at this verse again. Remember that a prisoner wrote this. If Paul could make rejoicing a habit of his life while in prison, so can you! He teaches us through this verse that rejoicing is a choice, not a result of everything going smoothly.

Whenever I think about rejoicing, I think about singing. A song expresses joy so well. Now I know you might be thinking, "But, Tom, I can't sing." Oh, but you can. Animals can't sing, pews can't sing, even Bibles can't sing — but you can. If you know the Lord, you have a song in your heart just waiting to come out. Singing it (even in the shower) is a way to rejoice. And another thing, your rejoicing is piped into the speakers of heaven. God rejoices when He hears your rejoicing.

Respond

Today's assignment: Rejoice! Are you in prison? Rejoice! Do you have a job? Rejoice! Have you lost your job? Rejoice! Rejoice in the Lord always, whether you feel like it or not. Choose to rejoice and see if He won't lift your hopes and give you a fresh perspective. Try a song or two today while you are driving or alone. Let your voice sing God's praise and picture His smile of approval.

Remember

You have something to sing about. Start tuning up!

A Most Important Evening

Read
"Are you not much more valuable than they." — Matthew 6:26.

Reflect
Let me tell you about one of the most important nights in the life of the Hufty's. My wife, son, and I were sitting in our family room watching TV when in walked our daughter. Her face was serious as she said, "Mom, Dad, I need to talk to you, just the three of us." For months and weeks preceding this night she had told us she wanted to talk about becoming a Christian.

We walked into the living room and Mackenzie sat us down. "I've been thinking about this for a long time," she said, "and I really want to become a Christian." We talked for quite a while that night. We read Scripture and talked some more. Finally, she asked, "Could I pray and ask Jesus to come into my heart?" We knelt down next to the couch and made the angels sing. Without a doubt, Mackenzie's prayer was the sweetest words Rhonda and I had heard spoken all year. It was an evening we'll never forget. Why? Because the most important decision our daughter will ever make was made that night. The best part was watching how the Holy Spirit drew our daughter to Jesus, until finally she couldn't live another day without having Him in her heart and knowing God for herself.

Jesus said that even though God made everything, He made us special. In comparison to the birds of the air and all the rest of His creation, we are much more precious to Him. Why? Because He wants to have a relationship with us. And the most important thing in life is having that relationship and developing it. Are you?

Respond
Take some time to spend with God today praising and thanking Him that you are His valuable and precious child. Confess the times you have allowed the clutter of your life to distract you from spending time with Him. Finally, ask Him to help you focus on what's important today, because today could be an important day for someone's eternity.

Remember
As you face the day, walk in the knowledge that you are special to Someone special.

UNDERSTANDING OTHERS

REFLECT

If you have any encouragement from being united with Christ, if any comfort from his love, if any fellowship with the Spirit, if any tenderness and compassion, then make my joy complete by being like-minded, having the same love, being one in spirit and purpose. — PHILIPPIANS 2:1-2.

REFLECT

Several years ago I facilitated a marriage retreat for a former church I had served. It had been at least six or seven years since I had seen any of these people. We had a blast. I gave them several personality questionnaires and tried to make it fun. At one point I was explaining my own personality type, that one of my weaknesses was not being sensitive to others. I knew that sometimes I could become too focused on a task and completely ignore people and offend them. While I was speaking, a lady off to my right innocently burst out, "Oh, so that was it." I turned to her and said, "What was it?" She said, "Tom, for the longest time I thought you just didn't like me." It had been seven years that she thought I didn't like her.

Misunderstandings are one of Satan's best tools. And once a misunderstanding has taken place it is many times impossible to correct it. In fact, in most efforts to make things straight we often make them worse. Misunderstandings can hurt deeply and paralyze a relationship for years. That's why it is important to understand others. This takes time and patience, but you will avoid offenses and enhance your relationships.

RESPOND

When you are in a conversation, do you listen carefully before you respond, or are you forming your response before the other persons is finished speaking? Isn't it great that God has gone to the greatest limit to understand us? He became flesh. He was misunderstood Himself. He was the victim of bad press and it wasn't His fault. He loves you and has a tremendous plan for your life. Thank Him for His understanding of you. Confess to Him the times you have failed to seek understanding from Him. Ask Him to help you show understanding to others today.

REMEMBER

Misunderstandings are one of the devil's greatest tools – so avoid them today.

Consecration

Read

Then Joshua built on Mount Ebal an altar to the Lord, the God of Israel.
— Joshua 8:30.

Reflect

Consecration not only means to get rid of all the sin in our lives, but to replace doing the wrong things with doing the right things, which is what the altar on Mount Ebal symbolized to Joshua. When Israel was defeated at Ai, he did not hesitate to go directly to the Lord with his problem. The Lord told him that one of the Israelites had sinned and disobeyed Him by taking some of the spoil of Jericho. This was the cause of Israel's defeat at Ai. Joshua immediately took action to set things right by locating the transgressor, Achan, and allowing God's judgment to fall on him and his family.

The story of Achan teaches us how one man's failure can defeat a whole nation. But as we continue reading the eighth chapter of Joshua, we also see how repentance and dependence on God can turn defeat into victory. God will always honor repentance. He is the God of a second chance. What is so troubling today is when believers know better. They get involved in sin, justify it, and rationalize it. This angers God. His judgment is sure, no matter how long it seems to tarry. It will come, and it will be painful.

Respond

Are you so sensitive to the right things that you have developed a hatred for sin? If you are still toying with sinful habits, take time right now to confess them to God and get rid of them. Be rude to that sin. Get rid of it and replace it with what you know is right. Peace will come when you act in faith and obedience to God. Build your own altar of submission to Him today.

Remember

Consecrate yourself today so you can serve God without reservation.

Serve Somebody

Read

No one can serve two masters. Either he will hate the one and love the other, or he will be devoted to the one and despise the other. You cannot serve both God and money. — Matthew 6:24.

Reflect

I once heard a preacher say, "The only freedom we have is to choose whose slave we will be." Powerful statement. Who are you serving?

Bob Dylan wrote a song several years back entitled "Serve Somebody." Dylan has been a controversial figure over the years, but the lyrics of this song could not be more accurate. The narrative of the song refers to different types of people — some wealthy, some famous, some brilliant. However, they all have one thing in common. They have to choose whom or what they will serve. One line of the song says, "It may be the devil or it may be the Lord, but you're still going to have to serve somebody."

Jesus follows the thought of serving some*thing* in this verse. He gave the example of serving either God or money. The two are opposites in what they produce in your life. If you serve money, you will become greedy and lust for more. If you serve God, you will be a giver and give more. And Jesus said you can't be totally devoted to both. You will either hate God and love money, or you will hate the love of money and love God. (Remember, it is the love of money that is evil, not money itself. Money is a neutral commodity. It becomes filthy lucre when used for immoral purposes, but it is blessed when used for the kingdom of God.)

Respond

Check your heart regarding your attitude toward money and your attitude toward God. Thank Him for His patience with you and your selfish desires and ask Him to cleanse you from the times when you have been too selfish with what He has given you. Ask Him to help you serve Him in sincerity and truth today. Pray to be a witness to others in your giving. After all, to be most like Him you must give.

Remember

There is no one better and easier to serve than Jesus.

GET ORGANIZED

READ

But everything should be done in a fitting and orderly way. — 1 CORINTHIANS 14:40.

REFLECT

The Odd Couple was a successful TV series in the early seventies. It focused on two guys: one a neat freak and the other a slob. Everyone laughed at the combination because it was so true to life. We all have a tendency to be one way or the other. Some of us are very organized and structured, while others are very sloppy. Felix Unger was tremendously organized, but he wasn't any fun and had no social life. His roommate, Oscar Madison, didn't have an organized bone in his body, but had lots of friends and was fun to be around.

God loves both types of people, but He loves us too much to allow us to go unbalanced. Part of cleaning up the clutter in our lives is to develop a plan to get organized. Different people organize themselves in different ways, and no one way is the right way to do it. If you are a disorganized person, don't turn me off and start praying yet. Maybe you just need to surround yourself with some people who have the organizational skills that you lack to help you get organized. What you need is a system that works for you. If you take the time to plan and then work your plan, you will find that organization relieves a lot of stress in life, and God will bless your efforts.

RESPOND

You and God are not an "odd couple." He is in the process of grooming you into an obedient child who follows His plan. Take a moment or two to praise and thank Him for the plan He has for your life. Let Him know how you want to follow it. Ask Him to forgive you for the times you have allowed the enemy to confuse and distract you. Then ask Him to help you get focused and organized today.

REMEMBER

God wired you in a unique way so you could honor Him in a unique way.

On to a New Level

Read

Walk in the way that the Lord your God has commanded you; so that you may live and prosper and prolong your days in the land that you will possess. — DEUTERONOMY 5:33.

Reflect

If you have ever seen a preschooler take his first steps, you probably saw a parent or another adult holding out their arms around the child, ready to catch him if he fell. The parent encouraged the child to stretch his horizon to a new level of living but was always there in case he stumbled. And the parent's hands were not only outstretched to soften the fall but to pick up the child after he fell.

It is the same way when we start walking with God and living according to what He commands. He periodically challenges us to a new level of living, but He doesn't abandon us. Quite to the contrary, He surrounds us with His presence. Nothing on earth pleases Him more than a heart that desires to follow His will.

God never drives us to His will; He draws us to it. He will never push us; He just gently pulls us in His direction. The problem comes when we consistently resist His tender tug. For some reason, once we resist His will it becomes easier to resist His will again, even to the point that it becomes a habit. If we don't watch out, we will become callused to His will. That's when we lose ground spiritually and forfeit the new level of living the Holy Spirit was calling us to.

Respond

God has given us His Word and His Spirit to find a fulfilled life within His will, and He challenges us to follow His plan. Are you? If not, why? What part of your life causes you trouble spiritually? If you are being hindered because of an area of weakness or sin, ask God to gently rescue you from those ungodly desires that tend to control you. Only He can deliver you. He wants you to overcome and go to the next level as much as you do.

Remember

New levels of obedience are sometimes difficult, but bring you to a new level of living.

Intimidating Giants

Read

Do not fear their intimidation, and do not be troubled, but sanctify Christ as Lord in your hearts. — 1 Peter 3:14-15 NASB.

Reflect

Intimidation does more to weaken the Christian than almost anything. Goliath intimidated the entire army of Israel. Jezebel intimidated the mighty prophet, Elijah, so much that he ran and hid in a cave. And how ironic it is that Peter would write these words since it was "bold" Peter who warmed himself at the fire on the night Jesus was taken captive, intimidated to the point of cursing to show he was not a follower of Jesus.

By our verse today, we can tell Peter had learned his lesson. He not only said that intimidation is nothing to fear, but he gave us the ingredients to overcome all intimidation. He said, "Sanctify Christ in your hearts." That means to hold Jesus in reverence, get closer to Him than ever. Isn't it interesting that the one who conquered Goliath spent years "sanctifying" the Lord in his heart as a shepherd before he was ready to face that giant?

Respond

Who or what giant is intimidating you now? Here are four suggestions for your prayer time today:

1. Isn't it great to know we don't have to fear anything? The psalmist said, "The Lord is my light and salvation, whom then shall I fear?" (Psalm 27:1). The answer is NOTHING. Thank God for that.
2. Sanctify also means to separate. It's important that we separate our hearts from the mindset of the world and join the mindset of Christ. Confess to God when you've chosen the way the world thinks over the way God thinks.
3. Pray for some of your closest friends who may be experiencing intimidation. Pray that God's presence in their lives might drive out their fears.
4. Pray for strength to overcome the things you fear.

Sanctify Christ in your life. Then SLAY THAT GIANT!

Remember

Don't be intimidated today, because greater is He that is in you, than he that is in the world. (See 1 John 4:4.)

He Kept on Knocking

Read

But Peter kept on knocking, and when they opened the door and saw him, they were astonished. — Acts 12:16.

Reflect

Everyone wants their prayers to be answered, but not every answer is what they expected! Luke writes about Peter's deliverance from prison that "Peter kept on knocking" at the door. When I read that I thought, "Thank God he kept on knocking." I believe answers to our prayers often knock on our heart's door and after going to the door and hearing the answer we say, "That can't be the answer." When we do this, we are doing one of several things with God's answer. Either we don't believe the answer, we don't expect the answer, or we won't accept the answer. Peter kept knocking. After those inside had discussed and theorized about what or who was outside knocking, they finally decided that it must be the answer they had been praying for, and they were astonished!

What have you been earnestly praying for lately? Have you heard the answer knocking on your heart's door? Were you satisfied with the answer? Did you believe it? Was it what you expected? Can you accept it? Those are tough questions, but they are questions that, if answered honestly, reveal your heart. God wants to approve the sincerity of your prayerful heart. He wants to grant your request with the answer that is best, not necessarily with the answer you suggest.

Respond

When God answers, open the door. You'll be astonished! He is interested in your prayers. Thank Him for always wanting the best for you. Take some time to confess to Him the times you've shut the door on His answers. Now pray for some of those you know who need Him. Ask God to use you to make Him look good and attract them to Him. Finally, pray for yourself and your pressing needs today.

Remember

When God answers your prayers, be thankful.

THE SANCTITY OF LIFE

READ

For you created my inmost being; you knit me together in my mother's womb. — PSALM 139:13.

REFLECT

One of the most awesome experiences in the world is having a baby. (Not a statement widely used by mothers while in labor, however.) The adjustment and change that takes place for new parents dims in the creation of a new life. A baby can cause a mature, macho (whatever that is) man to act like a goofy idiot. And the responsibility of taking care of another life brings a new kind of joy and significance into the life of a parent. There's just nothing else like it!

But wait. One of the most erroneous things a couple can think is, "We did this all by ourselves." The psalmist wants to correct that kind of thinking in our society. Who knitted you in your mother's womb? God did. You can do nothing on your own. He knew you before you were known. You never have to send God a birth announcement or a note that says, "We're expecting." He is not surprised by the new arrival. He knows. He knows everything. Not only does He know that child before it is born, He knows how that child will turn out. He knows it all.

The word "created" in the verse above has an interesting meaning — "to create and still hold the title to." In other words, the psalmist is saying, "Lord, you not only know me and have formed me, but you own me." God sanctified life from the beginning. He holds life in a highly honored position. He is the giver of life and the owner of life.

RESPOND

Are you letting God deal with you as the creator and owner of your life? If He hasn't already showed you, ask Him to reveal His plan for your life, the plan He formed before time began. Enjoy life today knowing that you are the beloved child of the Creator and Owner of the Universe!

REMEMBER

In your physical birth, God gave you life; in your spiritual rebirth, He gave you eternal life.

The Adventure of Being Contagious

Read

"Or suppose a woman has ten silver coins and loses one. Does she not light a lamp, sweep the house and search carefully until she finds it?" — LUKE 15:8.

Reflect

Not long ago Rhonda and I led a marriage retreat. Friday night went very well. We laughed a lot, shared with all the couples, and gradually built a rapport with them. On Saturday morning a man showed up by himself. He had not been there the previous night, but he had heard about the retreat from a friend at work. Since his marriage was falling apart he thought he'd give the retreat a shot. After about thirty minutes he became so uncomfortable that he go up and said in a loud voice, "This is not for me," and started to walk out.

I caught the man at the door and told him I didn't want him to feel uncomfortable and that I wanted to help him. We talked for awhile and he eventually left. However, two days later he came to another meeting and gave his life to Jesus. As the scripture was shared with him about what Jesus had done for him, he said these words, "I'm 51 years old. Am I the stupidest man in the world that I didn't know this about Christ?" You see, he was a seeking soul looking for a willing witness. He was that lost coin wanting desperately for someone to share the truth with him.

To be a contagious Christian you must first become a willing witness. That means you start looking for God to work around you in everyday situations. Whenever God sees you are a willing witness, He will bring a seeking soul to you. You may not know you are going to meet a new brother or sister in Christ that day, but afterward you will know your meeting was designed in heaven.

Respond

Just as the woman entered into the adventure of searching for the coin, so we need to enter into the adventure of becoming a willing witness for God. Pray He will lead you to someone who needs Him today. Then get ready for the adventure.

Remember

When a willing witness finds a seeking soul, a divine encounter takes place.

Committed to the Dream

Read

"Come, let us rebuild the wall of Jerusalem, and we will no longer be in disgrace." — Nehemiah 2:17.

Reflect

Martin Luther King Jr. coined the phrase, "I have a dream," yet he never saw his dream fulfilled. And so it is with many dreamers. But the truth about fulfillment is that it does not come in seeing something completed, but in fulfilling our part of the dream. God's purpose for us is that we are committed to the completion of His dream.

When God selects people to carry out His plan, He chooses those who have no interest in making themselves look good. Rather, He chooses those who simply want to honor and please Him. It gave Nehemiah deep satisfaction to please God, to see that God's city of Jerusalem was no longer in ruin and disgrace with no wall around it.

God is looking for people who are committed to His dream. He is not interested in our ideas. He is interested in His ideas being worked out through our lives. Those leaders who followed Nehemiah caught his enthusiasm because his focus was simply to "no longer be in disgrace." The same thing occurred with Martin Luther King Jr. Those who followed him caught his vision and carried on his dream after he was killed. This generally happens when the visionary is wholly dedicated to God's dream and not their own reputation.

Respond

Consider the commitment necessary to carry out the dreams God has put in your heart. What walls does He want you to rebuild? Are you giving it your best? Ask Him to help you to build walls that will protect you from being influenced by those who ignore or oppose God. Also, ask God to give you the strength and courage to be an influence on those who do not know Him. Finally, ask Him to enhance your commitment to His dream for your life.

Remember

God's dream for you is the burning desire He has placed in your heart.

Hanging Around Godly People

Read

Do not be misled: "Bad company corrupts good character." Come back to your senses as you ought, and stop sinning; for there are some who are ignorant of God. — 1 Corinthians 15:33-34.

Reflect

The most important decision you will make in your life is what you do with Jesus Christ. The second most important decision you make is whom you marry. The third most important decision you will make is whom you choose to hang around. The reason, of course, is that the group of people you hang around often influences your thinking. And if they influence your thinking, they can influence your behavior.

For example, say you get married and you start hanging around people at work who don't believe in marriage. They may tell you that marriage is old-fashioned and doesn't make any sense anymore. Feeding your mind with those types of thoughts day in and day out is not healthy and can lead to an unhappy marriage.

However, the opposite is true also. If you have people around you who are authentic, who have integrity and do what they say, that will rub off on you. Now I'm not leaving out the element of choice. Of course, you can be in a crowd of negative people and refuse to let it rub off on you, but if you are around them habitually, watch out!

Respond

So, with whom do you spend most of your time? Negative or positive people? People who have godly values or people who have their own values? Age has nothing to do with this. Peer pressure has no age limits. Whom you choose to be around often determines whom you become. If you spend a lot of time hanging around believers, it can serve to strengthen you to be a witness to the unbelievers God brings into your life. Ask God to help you to be influenced by the right people, but not only that, ask Him to help you be a good influence for Him today.

Remember

Ten years from now, you will be the essence of the material you have read and the people with whom you have spent your time.

We All Need Support

Read

If one falls down, his friend can help him up. But pity the man who falls and has no one to help him up! — Ecclesiastes 4:10.

Reflect

"He ain't Heavy, He's My Brother" was a popular song in the seventies. It started with the words: "The road is long with many a winding turn." That is the way of life — a long road with turns that can cause you to lose your way or stumble and fall. It's important that when you experience those turns you have someone close by to help you. It is important that you have a friend who is not someone with all the answers, but someone who will help carry the load.

Solomon did not say, "If one falls down, give him an outline of things to do to get back up," or "share your experience with him" or "explain to him what is happening." All of those responses may be noble, and sometimes needed, but when your friend is down on the ground, he just wants an understanding helping hand.

We all need to be carried sometimes. That is why fellowship is so vitally important to sustain us as believers. And when we fellowship beyond talking about the weather and eating, we can develop relationships that will give us strength, encouragement, and support when the road gives us a sharp turn.

Respond

Everyone needs someone to love and encourage them in the faith. Even Jesus asked Peter, James, and John to stay with Him and pray for Him the night before He was crucified. Do you have a brother or sister who picks you up when you fall? Pray for God to send you one if you don't. When you were lost in sin, Jesus picked you up and held you, never to allow you to fall into that lost state again. Now He wants you to do the same for others in need, just like the Good Samaritan in Luke 10. Ask God to cross your path with someone in need today so you can support them and pray for them.

Remember

When you see a person who has fallen into a ditch on the road of life, don't throw stones, throw ropes.

Out of the Comfort Zone

Read

"Then you will know which way to go, since you have never been this way before." — Joshua 3:4.

Reflect

When the children of Israel crossed the Jordan River, most of them were entering new territory. Only two had been there before — Joshua and Caleb. But crossing the river was only the physical part of the move. There would be some emotional strain to the move as well. Canaan was not a paradise, and God would use the struggle to possess the land as a vehicle to refine the nature of His people. There would be pain and failure as well as joy and success. There would be an improvement in life from the past 400 years, and in the end the struggle would be well worth it.

What do you do when you come to a place or situation in life where you have never been before? How do you respond when you're asked to step out of your comfort zone? How did the children of Israel know what to do? They followed the ark of the covenant, which symbolized the presence of God. The same is true for us. We must follow the leadership of God when we face something we've never faced before.

Are you facing a new challenge in your life today? Do you wonder what God is thinking about your situation? Rest assured, He is considering your plight. Do you think He wants you to cross over into new faith experiences? Without faith in God it is impossible to please Him (Hebrews 11:6). That's what leaving your comfort zone and rising to a new level of living is all about — faith in God. If what He has called you to do agrees with the Word and the Spirit, just take a deep breath, put your life totally in God's hands, and do it. You will never possess the promised land if you don't!

Respond

Spend some time with God right now thanking and praising Him for the challenges He has laid before you. Ask Him to give you the strength and courage to follow through with what He wants you to do.

Remember

When you leave your comfort zone with God, you can't go wrong.

God Reveals Himself

Read

Surely the Sovereign Lord does nothing without revealing his plan to his servants the prophets. — Amos 3:7.

Reflect

Let me tell you a little bit about Amos. He was a farmer and a prophet. He said a lot of things that you and I only think about saying. I guess one reason I like him is because I'm a farm boy and Amos uses a lot of rural illustrations. He was not formally trained as a prophet, but God revealed Himself to Amos and told him that He wanted him to preach to the people. During the time of Amos' preaching, there was a lot of interest in religion, but the interest was shallow.

God's message to Israel through Amos was simple: You are God's chosen people — start acting like it. Where there is privilege, there is also responsibility. Amos put it something like this: If you see two people walking together, they must have had an appointment. If you hear a lion roar, there must be prey not far away. If a bird gets in a trap, someone set the trap. In other words, look around you, for God is revealing Himself to you. But you must look for Him. When you do, you will see Him in everything.

The problem was, nobody listened to Amos' message. God was trying to warn the nation of Israel to return to Him and listen, but they didn't. Ultimately, the Assyrians destroyed them. God desires to reveal Himself to you and keep you from harm also. You just need to look for Him. He reveals Himself first to give you His plan for your life, and then to give you the wisdom and strength to do what He's called you to do.

Respond

Are you looking for Him? Thank Him for revealing Himself to you. Ask Him to forgive the times when you have ignored Him. Pray that He will give you courage to obey Him today.

Remember

God desires to reveal Himself to you, not just in prayer, but throughout your day.

Caution: God at Work

Read

Continue to work out your salvation with fear and trembling, for it is God who works in you to will and to act according to his good purpose. — Philippians 2:12-13.

Reflect

The first time I ever saw one of those "Have patience, God isn't finished with me yet" bumper stickers was on a beat up old Plymouth, double parked on a one-way street. I remember thinking, *I wonder if God is going to work on your parking habits next.* The truth is, God is always at work in our lives. We may not notice, we may choose to ignore it, but He is at work in us. In fact, He is trying to help us fulfill the purpose for which He created us. He had a purpose for our life before we were even thought of. Tragically, many believers search for that purpose all their lives without consulting or seeking God.

What is His purpose for you? You are to be a reflection of Him. That means your job is to be, first and foremost, a follower and reflector of Jesus Christ. You accomplish that through the various opportunities He gives you daily to "work out your salvation." God is working in you to produce love, righteousness, and the fruit of the Spirit. He has gifted you to do His work, but if you neglect your gift or refuse to do the work, your life will be unproductive and joyless.

Respond

What are you working out today? When you know and understand your purpose, you experience joy when you do it. If you refuse to fulfill your purpose in life, you will be frustrated. Take a moment right now to thank God for working and continuing to work in your life. As you go through your day, look at ways you can fulfill that purpose and experience the joy He intended for you to have. And remember: "Be patient, God isn't finished with you yet."

Remember

God wants to work in your life today. Work out what He works in.

Joined and Held Together

Read

From him the whole body, joined and held together by every supporting ligament, grows and builds itself up in love, as each part does its work. — Ephesians 4:16.

Reflect

I have had the opportunity to work with many talented artists in the music field while serving in ministry. God uses many of these musicians in a great way. Those who impressed me most were not the ones who pushed themselves or were concerned about how many records they sold. Rather, the ones who impressed me were the ones who said, "Tell me what to do, I've just come to help." God uses our talent to grow the Church much better when it is accompanied by a genuine spirit of love and humility.

God is love. So if the body is to grow effectively, it must be under the direction of the Head, who is Jesus. He has modeled to us the ultimate example of love, laying His life down for us and becoming the greatest servant of all. Therefore, if the Church is going to grow, we must live our lives daily as demonstrators of His love, laying our lives down for our brothers and sisters — or the unbeliever next door who desperately needs to see Jesus' love in action.

You can be the most gifted person in the world and not be a loving person. Your gift makes no impression on God and no impact on the world if it is not packaged in God's love. The Church will not grow and flourish through its polished talent. It will grow because of its genuine love. This is the power that joins us and holds us steady forever — God's love.

Respond

How is your church doing in the area of "the greatest of these?" Is it building itself up in love? Spend some time during today's devotional thanking God for the way He loves you and the leadership of your church. Pray for your pastor. Ask Him to forgive you for the times you haven't demonstrated His love to those around you. Finally, look for opportunities today to put your love into action.

Remember

People may see and admire your talent, but they will remember and cherish your love.

Let Peace Rule

Read

Let the peace of Christ rule in your hearts, since as members of one body you were called to peace. And be thankful. — Colossians 3:15.

Reflect

Are you a worrywart? Did you worry last week? Today? The past hour? If worry takes up a lot of your "think time," you probably are a worrywart. Worry is the result of not allowing the peace of God to rule your heart.

The word rule in our verse today means to preside over. It carries with its meaning the picture of an umpire presiding over a game. During Paul's day, the umpires or judges of the Greek games occasionally rejected contestants who weren't competitively qualified. On other occasions they rejected those contestants who broke the rules. The peace of God is to be the umpire of our hearts. When we allow His peace to rule in our hearts and minds, His peace disqualifies thoughts of worry and rejects them. His peace will also throw out any thoughts which are stealing our joy or disrupting our peace.

Can you identify times when your mind is consumed with thoughts that disrupt your peace? Do you have the strength to reject those thoughts and allow His peace to rule in your heart? I'm not talking about a blind denial of reality. I'm referring to a trust in God that sees how much greater the Answer is than your problem — which relieves your anxiety. The circumstances of life are temporary. The peace of God is permanent. And He promises you will live in His peace if you will just trust Him with all your heart.

Respond

Take some time right now and evaluate your thought patterns. Ask God to show you the thoughts that disrupt your faith and joy so you can throw them out of the game! Praise God for the fact that He knows your thoughts. Thank Him for the relief from stress that He makes available to you by living in His peace. Let His peace preside over your life so that you will be free to help others who are seeking peace also.

Remember

Trust God with every detail of your life — with all your heart — and let peace rule today.

Bring Glory to His Name

Read

Who will not fear you, O Lord, and bring glory to your name? — Revelation 15:4.

Reflect

I believe a young executive can live a life of integrity in the workplace without being dishonest — and still be successful. If I didn't, I would have nothing to write about. I believe a teenager can stand strong in the face of peer pressure and refuse to have sex or do drugs. If I didn't, I wouldn't have a testimony to share. I believe a single adult can stay pure in the pressure of temptation. If I didn't, I wouldn't have a song to sing. I believe these things because I've seen the power of God work in the lives of people who victoriously overcame these pressures and difficulties — giving glory to God.

The book of Revelation was written to encourage believers who were being persecuted by the enemy through the world system. For example, we face these decisions every day...whether to cut a compromising deal, to flirt with temptation, to lie to protect ourselves, or to try to satisfy our fleshly lust through inappropriate behavior. But the Holy Spirit gives us discernment to the lies of the enemy. The truth is: We can win if we will let the Spirit of God who lives in us control our lives. Thus, we can bring glory to the name of the Lord.

Respond

Are you bringing glory to the name of the Lord, or are you struggling with the pressure of the world system? Does it look like the easy road is the best road? Have you entertained thoughts and actions that, as a believer, you never thought you would? Stop! Slow down! Be alone with God for awhile. Begin to praise and thank Him for His unconditional love. Then let Him reach down and calm you, so you can choose to go His way regardless of the circumstances. As you experience His love and peace, you will make the right choices and bring glory to God.

Remember

When you listen to the tempter, you listen to a loser who wants to make you a loser. When you listen to God and obey His voice, you bring glory to His name.

Responding to Pain

Read

Three times I pleaded with the Lord to take it away from me. — 2 CORINTHIANS 12:8.

Reflect

Paul wrote thirteen books in the New Testament, but Second Corinthians is where he revealed the most about himself. Paul's life was not going according to plan. In fact, things were so miserable that he begged God to take the pressure away from him. But God replied that His grace was sufficient to see Paul through to victory. In other words, "Paul, you have everything you need to see this through successfully."

Paul's incredible commitment to Jesus resulted in pain — pain of rejection, ridicule, and imprisonment. How did he respond? He responded to pain in the appropriate way. He prayed. He continued to study the Word. He continued to preach and teach. He continued to go where the Holy Spirit led him to go and do what the Holy Spirit told him to do. I know that is easier said than done, but what is the alternative? More pain.

Pain is not something we like to handle. It interrupts our plans and can wear us out mentally. But if we do not handle pain God's way, it will multiply. When God said that His grace was sufficient, He didn't mean a sufficiency to suffer and suffer and suffer. He meant a sufficiency to get stronger and wiser and more powerful in God until the battle was won.

Respond

How do you respond when the pinch of pain comes on the scene? Do you seek God? Do you pray for His wisdom and strength to overcome whatever is assailing you? Do you continue doing all the things you should be doing: praying, studying the Word, and being a witness? Ask God to help you respond to pain in the right way today.

Remember

Don't let pain take advantage of you — take advantage of it and grow stronger in God.

How Much Is Enough?

Read

A greedy man brings trouble to his family. — Proverbs 15:27.

Reflect

He went to my church. If you would look at him your first impression would be, "He's a success." But somewhere along the line, he lost his touch. His debt grew. He made some bad decisions. And before he knew it, he had lost it all. Embarrassed by failure, he abandoned his family. Sad. But greed is a silent killer. As long as you have a lot of money, you don't notice it, but when you start losing it and panic for more, the greed monster strikes.

In Joshua 7 we read about a man named Achan, a man whose greed brought the deaths of himself and his family. Achan's trouble began when he pilfered forbidden silver from the ruins of the fallen city of Jericho, in direct violation of God's command. This greedy act not only resulted in the death of his family, but it also resulted in the defeat of Joshua's army in their next battle. Thirty-six innocent soldiers died because of Achan's sin.

What a tragedy. Can you imagine the shock of learning your son or husband died in battle because of another man's direct violation of God's command? Greed is the desire for more, an excessive, unsatisfied drive to possess. When greed takes over your life, it distorts your priorities and strains your relationships. It can overshadow common sense and put an entire household at risk. Achan probably thought he was taking Jericho's forbidden silver to help his family. But in his greedy blindness, he purchased his family's death.

Respond

How much is enough for you? The writer of today's devotional verse, Solomon, had possessions galore — and family stress. Hmmm. Ask God to show you any areas where greed has taken hold of your heart and repent of any hurt or harm you have brought to others because of greed. Then, take God's anecdote to greed — give something of value to someone who doesn't expect it.

Remember

Greed is the silent killer that is defeated by a lifestyle of giving.

Refreshing Our Hearts

Read

Your love has given me great joy and encouragement, because you, brother, have refreshed the hearts of the saints. — PHILEMON 7.

Reflect

There is no joy outside of love. Have you ever had a friend like the one mentioned in this verse — who refreshed your heart? That's what Paul said about his friend Philemon. It was Philemon's love that refreshed Paul and gave him such "great joy and encouragement."

Being loved and loving brings tremendous joy to our lives. However, the problem for many is that they will not let God love them. They refuse to accept His love because they think that if they start loving Him, He will ask them to be a fanatic or something strange. Thinking God will ask you to be a fanatic is misunderstanding who He is and what He is about. His first priority is to have an intimate relationship with you. Then He wants you to know the joy of loving as He loves you by bringing others to know Him.

What would you think if I told you that God has a priority list? At the top of His list is to love you and bring joy to your life. But the catch is that you have to slow down long enough to let God love you. Remember, there is no joy outside of love, and if you love Him, you will experience joy.

Respond

Take some time to praise and thank God for the joy you experience through His love and presence in your life. Thank Him for those you love and those who refresh your heart. Now ask Him to forgive you for the times you have refused to love Him the way you should or allow Him to love you. Pray for those you know who need His love in their lives today.

Remember

Someone today needs to know they are loved. Would you give them that message?

Well Done!

Read

Do you see a man skilled in his work? He will serve before kings; he will not serve before obscure men. — PROVERBS 22:29.

Reflect

What do you think employers look for when they hire new people? They search for people who can use what they know to benefit the business. Employers are highly practical. They couldn't care less if you know the seventh letter in the Greek alphabet. They want to know if you have the skills and are able to apply them to enhance their work. Does this sound unspiritual?

Using your skills in practical, productive ways will be rewarded. Jesus said that those who are faithful with the talents and abilities He gives them will hear the words, "Well done, good and faithful servant." Remember, you were given the skills you have to develop and use to their maximum potential. If your skills become dormant, you will gradually lose them. Therefore, it is a must that you sharpen the rough edges of your God-given skills and get plugged into a place where those skills can bring God glory. When that happens, you will experience a fulfillment inside that brings a tremendous amount of satisfaction.

Respond

What skills do you have that people around you aren't aware of — because you hide them? It's time to bring those gifts out of the closet and use them. Are you unhappy in your job? If you are, it may be because your skills aren't being developed and used to maximum capacity. Search and find a way to develop and use those skills. You'll start enjoying life much more when you start practicing them regularly. Your boss will even take notice at the difference in your work — not to mention all those who will benefit from your faithfulness to use what God has given you. God has gifted you in a special way so you can do His work and make Him look good to others.

Remember

A man skilled in his work will serve before kings, but God's the one from whom you want to hear, "Well done."

COURAGE

READ

"Be strong and very courageous. Be careful to obey all the law my servant Moses gave you; do not turn from it to the right or to the left, that you may be successful wherever you go." — JOSHUA 1:7.

REFLECT

It has several names: Bravery, Valor, Audacity, Heroism, Confidence, Guts, Grit, Backbone, Spunk, etc. No matter what you call it, it's the missing ingredient in many lives today — sadly, many of those are Christians. It's the presence of mind against all odds and another word for inner strength. What am I talking about? Courage. It makes the physically challenged reject the odds set against them and keep on going. It's what helps every married couple having trouble reject the option of divorce. It's what encourages the widow and orphan to face tomorrow. It's courage, and it's missing.

David had courage as a small boy. Elijah had it when he was outnumbered by the prophets of Baal. Moses had it when he stood against Pharaoh. And Joshua had it when he led the children of Israel into the Promised Land. The fact is, it is impossible to live victoriously for Jesus without courage.

In our effort to change our world for Jesus Christ, we are educated enough. We have the message, but we often lack the courage to take a stand. What can we do to increase our courage level? God told Joshua to "be careful to obey." First, we must be obedient in our daily disciplines of prayer and Bible study. These disciplines strengthen our ability to be courageous. Then we must act in faith to do what God directs us to do. Finally, we can stand confidently in knowing that "Faithful is He who calls us, and He will bring it to pass." (See 1 Thessalonians 5:24.)

RESPOND

The most courageous act in history was when Jesus left heaven to come and die for the sins of the world. Take some time right now to thank Him for His example. Read Joshua chapters 1 and 2. Ask God to help you be courageous to do His will today. Then, be strong and do it.

REMEMBER

Be strong and courageous — God is with you as He was with Moses and Joshua.

Don't Miss This Wedding!

Read

"Let us rejoice and be glad and give him glory! For the wedding of the Lamb has come, and his bride has made herself ready." — Revelation 19:7.

Reflect

Have you been to many weddings? I've been to some very memorable ones. I've seen the best man pull a ring out of a Cracker Jack box and give it to the groom for his bride. I've heard the song, "Come on Baby Light My Fire," played during the lighting of the candles. I've even seen a bride arrive in a horse-drawn buggy, and the bride and groom leave the church in the same carriage. And of course, my wedding day was one of my best days ever.

As Christians, our best days are still ahead of us. In fact, today's scripture tells of that day when we, the Church, the Bride of Christ, will finally be united with Jesus for all eternity. It will be the time of rejoicing that we all have longed for. All sin and evil in our lives will be gone, and we will forever be with God the Father. At that moment, in the most spiritual and truest sense of the phrase, we will be without spot or blemish.

The Church, with all its trials through the years, is still the heartthrob of the Bridegroom. Whether the Church is located in Liberty, Missouri, or in a poverty-stricken area of the former Soviet Union, Jesus still looks on her and says, "She's worth my love, I will be faithful to her." What a thought! The One whom we have forsaken so many times, whom we have ignored because of the distractions of life, remains faithful for eternity. What a beautiful picture of God's love for you and me!

Respond

What a hope you have in eternity! As you spend time with God today, get a little heavenly-minded and think about your coming glorious wedding day! Thank Him for waiting patiently for you, His bride, throughout the ages. Give Jesus praise and thanksgiving for His faithful love. Finally, in all you do today, make an effort to make His Bride look good for the upcoming wedding.

Remember

Wedding bells are ringing — eternally — so let them ring through your life today.

But Where Is...Wherever?

Read

As they were walking along the road, a man said to him, "I will follow you wherever you go." Jesus replied, "Foxes have holes and birds of the air have nests, but the Son of Man has no place to lay his head." — Luke 9:57-58.

Reflect

While Jesus was on His way to Jerusalem, He encountered a man who volunteered to follow Him wherever He was going. But Jesus must have detected something in the motivation of this man's heart to make the reply: "The Son of Man has no where to lay his head." You see, to really commit yourself to Jesus means you have to be willing to give up security as you know it and rely totally on Him. This man might have been caught up in the popularity of Jesus and the great works He had done, really only wanting to keep company with a popular leader. Regardless of his reasons, Jesus challenged the man's commitment to "wherever" by telling him he would have to give up some comforts in order to follow Him.

Have you ever said, as this half-hearted disciple said: "I will follow you wherever you go," but then when you discovered where "wherever" was, you lost interest and wandered back into the status quo? True commitment means that you will do whatever it takes to be what God wants you to be. It means you are open to change. It means you are willing to have your will broken so His will can dominate your life. It means total trust.

Respond

Have you set a limit on "wherever" God wants to send you? First, thank Him that He always has your best interest at heart and will never ask you to do something He won't equip you to do. Praise Him for His willingness to trust you with His will. Ask Him to forgive you for the times you have fallen short of doing what He asked of you. Now pray that God will show you where "wherever" is for you today. It may be a friend at work. It may be a private place to pray. It may be a generous gift or an encouraging word.

Remember

Today be open, and let God lead you to...wherever.

Now I Lay Me Down to Sleep...

Read

Jesus said to her, "I am the resurrection and the life. He who believes in me will live, even though he dies; and whoever lives and believes in me will never die. Do you believer this?" — John 11:25-26.

Reflect

"Now I lay me down to sleep, I pray the Lord, my soul to keep. If I should die before I wake..." If I should die? I remember praying that prayer as a child every night before I went to bed. Did I really believe I was going to die in my sleep? No, not really. Did I think about it often? No. Was that going to change the way I lived? Not hardly. I was a kid, and no one feels more immortal than a protected child. But because I learned the prayer by routine as a child, it reminded me that death was going to happen. And aging has a way of making you think about it more often.

Our verse today is part of an experience Jesus had with the death of someone He loved dearly. When He arrived on the scene, Mary and Martha were going through a tremendous grieving process. Their brother, Lazarus, had died just a few days before. They were angry and were blaming Jesus for not being there to heal him. (see v. 21, 32.) So Jesus comforted them with the words of today's scripture verse. When He asked Martha if she believed His words, she replied, "Yes, Lord" (v. 27). On her faith, Jesus raised Lazarus from the dead.

Whenever we are faced with disease, discouragement, or even death, our hope comes from the words of Jesus, "I am the resurrection and the life." Martha put her faith in Jesus' words, and He honored her trust.

Respond

Begin praising and worshipping God that no matter what comes your way, Jesus is the resurrection and the life for you today. Thank Him that you will live with Him for eternity, and in the meantime, He withholds no good thing from you as you love and obey Him.

Remember

Tonight you can lay down to sleep...in perfect peace.

It's Great to Be Clean

Read

You are already clean because of the word I have spoken to you. — John 15:3.

Reflect

"Cleanliness is next to godliness" is a phrase that mothers used to say to get their children to wash. Even though it is not a quote from Scripture, spiritually it is biblical. To be pure in your thoughts and behavior is to be Christlike. To be clean from sin is to know His forgiveness and His fellowship.

Here are some reasons why it is important to be clean from sin. First, sin destroys any chance to live a fulfilled life. After David's tragic sin with Bathsheba, his life took a tailspin filled with pain and regret. Second, unconfessed and uncontrolled sin wipes out any possibility to have a close and growing relationship with God. Therefore, you must always confess and forsake the sins that try to conquer you. David also knew that when he wrote, "Create in me a clean heart, O God, and renew a right spirit within me. Do not cast me away from Your presence." (Psalm 51:10-11).

Time and time again the Scripture reminds you that it doesn't make any difference if your vessel is chipped or cracked, all that is required to be used of God is that it be clean. You may have done some terrible things, and you may think that God cannot use you, but the truth is, you have done nothing that He cannot forgive and cleanse. If you have admitted your sin to God and committed yourself to forsake that sin, He will use you.

Respond

Are you clean before God? Have you confessed all of your sins to Him? If you are sincere and want to be used by God, He will honor your confession. There are probably people around you today whose lives are filled with sin. They need the influence of someone who knows the joy of what it means to be clean before God. Take some time to pray for them now. Ask God to use you to honor Him today.

Remember

Keep your heart pure and clean from all sin today so you can walk with God.

Heaven on Earth

Read

Then I saw a new heaven and a new earth,...He who was seated on the throne said, "I am making everything new!" — Revelation 21:1,5.

Reflect

What happens after this judgment stuff is over? Three words: HEAVEN ON EARTH! Have you ever wondered what heaven will be like? According to today's verses, everything will be new as we experience heaven on a recreated earth. In Revelation 21:3 John tells us that one day we will dwell in the presence of God, as Adam did, in a glorious city. There will be no more sadness because God will wipe every tear from our eyes. There will be no more death, mourning, crying, or pain. Why? Because in that day, the old order of things will have passed away (v. 4). Other verses in this chapter tell us the city John saw descending from heaven will have walls of jasper, gates of pearl, streets of gold, and that there will be no more night! Then he concludes the chapter by saying that nothing impure will ever enter it (v. 27). What a place! But that's not all.

John continues in Revelation 22 with another list. In verse 2 he tells us we will have full access to the tree of life on our new heavenly earth. In other words, what was lost in the Garden of Eden because of sin will be restored. Secondly, the curse put on the first man and woman in Genesis 3 will be lifted (v. 3). Finally, we will be able to stand before God face-to-face without fear or shame. Sound like a place where you'd like to be? Me too! How do you get there? One word. JESUS!

Respond

If you've never made a commitment of your life to Jesus Christ, you can do it right now, because He's listening. When you come to Him in prayer, all of heaven pays attention. If you have a personal relationship with Him and this devotion has made you homesick for heaven and excited for our new heavenly earth, stay faithful. Heaven is closer than you think.

Remember

Throughout the day, be conscious that your real home is heaven.

ANDREW'S LIGHT

READ

The first thing Andrew did was to find his brother Simon and tell him, "We have found the Messiah" (that is, the Christ). — JOHN 1:41.

REFLECT

I often say that the people in my life who have impressed me the most never tried to. Why? Because they were humble. Andrew was that way too. He had to be one of the most humble guys in the New Testament, for all through the gospels he was referred to as "Simon Peter's brother." Everyone knew Peter — exuberant and boisterous. Peter naturally drew people to himself, while Andrew faded into the background — sort of an "easy-to-miss" type guy.

Do you think Andrew ever got tired of hearing, "Oh, you're Simon Peter's brother?" Having lived with Peter all his life, Andrew knew there would be only one seat for him once he brought Peter to Jesus...the back seat. But Andrew was not concerned with himself, He introduced Peter to the Messiah, and as he might have expected, Peter became the major player.

Some people do not go into the army unless they can be an officer, some refuse to join the team unless they can be the star, and some only get involved in evangelism if they can be the evangelist. But the one who truly reaches out is the humble-hearted who doesn't care so much about position but about people who need to know Jesus. Position meant little to Andrew; all he wanted to do was to be a contagious Christian. In fact, almost everywhere you saw Andrew's name in Scripture he was bringing someone to Jesus. Oh, that we could be remembered that way!

RESPOND

Take some time right now to pray and thank God for using an "Andrew" in your life. Ask Him to help you be more like Andrew by bringing people to Jesus today.

REMEMBER

Be humble-hearted today, like Andrew, and watch the light of Jesus begin to shine.

THINK BIG LIKE GOD

READ

Now to Him who is able to do exceeding abundantly beyond all that we ask or think, according to the power that works within us. — EPHESIANS 3:20 NASB.

REFLECT

I challenged about twenty young people with this verse several years ago. I asked, "If money was no problem, what do you think God would want to do in your youth group?" After several weeks of praying about it and having Bible studies on this verse, they felt God was leading them to host a youth conference. A year later more than five hundred teenagers were at their church. This event went on for a couple of years and hundreds of teenagers were touched through their efforts. Why? Because they started thinking big.

Let me give you a thought you may not have entertained in awhile. Your God is BIG! So how does that affect you? How big do you think? How big a part does imagination play in your life? Paul said that God is able to do more than we ask or think — abundantly more, exceeding abundantly more. In other words, we cannot exhaust God's ability to "do" in our lives. His well can never run dry. There is nothing we can ask or even think to ask that God will say, "Oh, I don't have the ability to do that." So, in light of this verse, are you thinking too small? Is it possible that God wants you to ask for something big?

RESPOND

There's one catch to all this: He is able to do "according to the power that works within us." How much of God's power is at work in you? Are you walking in purity, using His power to overcome sinful habits in your life? Do you make it a habit to pray daily? Do you allow Him to control you? If so, ask Him to give you some thoughts that will enhance your service to Him. Start praying that God would give you His BIG ideas!

REMEMBER

You cannot think or ask for anything too big for God to accomplish.

It's Party Time!

Read

"I tell you that in the same way there will be more rejoicing in heaven over one sinner who repents than over ninety-nine righteous persons who do not need to repent." — Luke 15:7.

Reflect

Are you into partying? God is! Not just partying to party, but partying for a reason. For God, changed lives is reason to celebrate. You see, God is into change, especially when the change involves someone turning from sin to Him.

Over the years God has allowed me to see many people repent. One of them was at one of our outreach events. Rhonda counseled a young girl who gave her life to Jesus. The girl came up to me after she had talked with Rhonda and said, "I wanted to tell you that I've just given my life to Jesus." I said, "Oh, that's great!" I continued, "You may not know this, but there are angels in heaven having a big party right now over your news." She smiled and said, "That's exactly what your wife just told me." (Great minds think alike!)

Just imagine for a minute all of heaven breaking out into one gigantic party with your name in lights! You're the one making news in heaven, and the place is going wild with joy! I don't know all that goes on at those parties, but I know they're parties like we've never seen before.

Respond

In all three of Jesus' stories in Luke 15, He says a party was given. Why? Because a life was changed. God is into changing lives. And I'm sure you have people in mind who need a life-changing experience — friends at work or family members, perhaps your husband, wife, or child. Whoever they are, start praying for them now. Ask God to work in their lives. Don't give up! Keep searching, keep looking, keep praying, and continue to be a contagious Christian. And when it happens, have a party!

Remember

A life changed by Jesus Christ is the greatest reason to celebrate.

The Power of Vision

Read

I can do all things through Him who strengthens me. — PHILIPPIANS 4:13 NASB.

Reflect

"I think I'm going to explode!" Have you ever made that statement? Just think about it for a minute. It implies that there is a strong force within you that you can't control. You could probably explain your feelings better by saying, "I think I'm going to implode," because of all the pressure you feel from the outside. But in truth, we as Christians have a force within us that is more powerful than the pressures around us. We just need to stay in touch with that power — the power of the Holy Spirit who lives within us.

The Living Bible paraphrases this verse in this way, "I can do everything God asks me to with the help of Christ who gives me the strength and power." Regardless of the translation you use, this verse means that believers have all the power within them that they need to meet the demands of life. And knowing this, you can have an attitude of victory for the future.

The future will make demands on you. However, God's power is always available to you. Maybe you have tried to handle the pressures of life without His strength and guidance and have become stressed out. Getting in touch with God's power starts by taking a look at situations from His perspective. Receiving God's vision for that set of circumstances not only enables you to cope, but is the first step in finding His plan for your future.

Respond

Another secret to getting in touch with God's power is to break the old habit of self-reliance and depend on Him. Pray that He will give you His vision for your life today. Then ask Him to help you live your life with confidence in Him and His Word. Choose today to let Him be the authority in making your future plans.

Remember

There is no limit to what you can do when you are in touch with God's power.

YOUR NAME IS CHRISTIAN

READ

I urge you to live a life worthy of the calling you have received. Be completely humble and gentle; be patient, bearing with one another in love. — EPHESIANS 4:1-2.

REFLECT

Before dropping my kids off at school for some activity I often say to them, "Remember your last name." They usually reply, "Don't worry, I will dad." Why do I say that? Because they are carrying the "Hufty" name, and I don't want them to do anything to embarrass it. To the contrary, I hope they will do something to enhance it. In the same way, we are to honor the name we carry that identifies us with Jesus.

Paul urges us to: "live a life worthy of the calling." What is our calling? We are called to be Christians. That means Christlike. To live a life that is like Christ we must be completely humble, gentle, patient, and willing to bear with one another in love. This kind of love doesn't happen over night. It is developed over a lifetime by the Spirit of God who indwells us and the circumstances which bring His love to the surface of our lives.

Paul also says we are to: "bear with one another in love." That can be a wearisome task if it means bearing with someone who is difficult to love. I can put up with a lot if I really love someone, but if I don't.... The only way to act on God's Word is to remind myself that He loved me and cared for me when I did not deserve it — and was probably being a jerk as well. This truth causes me to get rid of my selfish attitude. And I can take joy in bringing honor to the name Christian by bearing with someone else in their struggle.

RESPOND

Are you bringing honor to the name Christian? How are you doing with those you rub shoulders with every day? Are you loving them by being humble, gentle, and patient with them? Determine in your heart today that you will bring honor and joy to God by offering service to those He brings to you.

REMEMBER

Live your life worthy of God's call, bearing the struggles of others and bringing honor to His name.

Reaping What You Sow

Read

Remember this: Whoever sows sparingly will also reap sparingly, and whoever sows generously will also reap generously. — 2 Corinthians 9:6.

Reflect

Being raised on a farm I can fully understand the principle of reaping what you sow. If my dad went out to plant corn and only put a few seeds of corn in the ground, we could expect only a small amount of corn to be harvested. But if he put a lot in the ground, we could expect a lot in return. The same is true in the Lord's work — the more generous you are in planting yourself in His work, the more you can expect in return.

When you understand the grace of God, giving becomes a part of who you are — not just something you do. Givers release their resources as a natural part of their Christian lifestyle. The fact that they receive blessings from God when they give is simply a fringe benefit. And the blessings they receive back may not be material. The thing to remember is, you can't out-give God.

The opposite of generosity is selfishness. Selfishness comes naturally to all of us, whereas generosity has to be practiced in order to become a habit. Generosity is a big deal to God. Why? He is always looking for seed scatterers. Many people want God to give them more money so they can buy more "stuff" for themselves, but God is looking for those who want more money to sow into His kingdom. And when they do that, He supplies their needs superabundantly anyway!

Respond

Would you describe yourself as generous or selfish? Do you sow sparingly or lavishly? Ask God to forgive you for being blinded by what you don't have. Then praise and thank Him for all the things He has given you that money can't buy — strong relationships, spiritual gifts, good health, friends, and a good church. Now take a moment to pray for those you know who are in need. Ask God to give you a generous spirit to minister to them.

Remember

Sow whatever you need today and tomorrow your needs will be met.

Bitter Sweet

Read

I took the little scroll from the angel's hand and ate it. It tasted as sweet as honey in my mouth, but when I had eaten it, my stomach turned sour. — Revelation 10:10.

Reflect

God's Word is compared to milk, meat, and honey in Scripture. We are commanded to "eat" the Word and to share it with others. To eat it means to receive it. God does not force feed us with His Word, but rather hands it to us and gives us the choice to receive it. The Word, if we receive it, can have different effects, depending on the condition of our lives. To some, the Word will bring sorrow. To others, the same Word will bring joy. God's Word contains sweet promises, but it also contains bitter judgments.

Consider this phrase: "God is near." If this were said to a widow who had just lost her husband in a car accident, it would be very comforting. But if the same words were said to someone who had been intentionally and habitually sinning, the words would ring with frightful judgment.

The themes of mercy and judgment run throughout the Bible. And the mixture of the two can be baffling at times. We see the same thing in the book of Revelation. It can only be understood by recognizing that God, while He executes judgment on those who refuse to repent of their sin, will be merciful to those who do repent.

Respond

The question you must consider today is: How does God's Word affect you? As you spend time in His Word, do you sense His comfort or His warning? You wouldn't know much about Him if not for His Word, so let Him know how you appreciate its role in your life. Pray that God would use you to share His Word today with someone who needs some encouragement or a warning to get on track.

Remember

Allow God to use you to be Jesus, the Living Word, in your world today.

Earnest Prayer

Read

So Peter was kept in prison, but the church was earnestly praying to God for him. — Acts 12:5.

Reflect

Peter was in prison across town. Although chained to guards, he slept. He could well be called the sleeping disciple, because he also slept in the Garden of Gethsemane on that cool spring night when the Roman soldiers arrested Jesus. But this night when he slept he probably remembered what Jesus had told him: "When you were young, you went where you wanted to go, but when you are old they will take you where you don't want to go" (John 21:18). Peter probably thought, *I'm still young. It can't end here,* and he slept in peace.

The church never raised a hand to help him, but across town they earnestly prayed for him. They didn't pray, "Lord, bless him while he's chained to those two guards." No. They prayed, "Lord, deliver him." An earnest prayer is one that demonstrates total dependence on God to work. It is powerful because those praying know their only hope is in God.

They knew Peter was in a situation that no man could help. His trial was the next day and the sentence was pretty much decided. So God chose to wait until everyone could see that He was the only one who could make a difference. That's the way of God. He lets us exhaust all our own efforts so that our total dependence is cast on Him. He hears not only our prayers, but the earnestness of our prayers. And when He has our complete attention and all our hearts, He acts (Psalm 37:5).

Respond

Grocery-list praying doesn't have the impact earnest praying does. Earnest praying is not only totally dependent on God, but focused on specifics and persistent. Do you have some specifics to pray for others today? Ask God to forgive you for the times you have been selfish in your praying. Now pray earnestly for someone you know. Finally, take a moment to pray specifically for your own needs.

Remember

When you pray earnestly, you are totally dependent on God.

THE SCARLET CORD

READ

The men said to her, "This oath you made us swear will not be binding on us unless, when we enter the land, you have tied this scarlet cord in the window through which you let us down." — JOSHUA 2:17-18.

REFLECT

"Okay, guys, remember when you see the scarlet cord hanging out the window, protect that place because the one who lives there protected us." The marching orders were clear. Jericho would fall, but one spot would be marked — Rahab's place. How would it be marked? With a scarlet cord.

At the time, Rahab probably didn't understand the full significance of that scarlet rope hanging out of her window. But it was more than a signal of her location; it was an act of faith. The scarlet rope was a sign that she believed God to be God. Rahab knew Jericho would fall. And she knew that she and her family would never be the same.

Rahab understood she would never have the same neighbors, never live in the same place, and never worship any other gods. But how surprised she must have been when she realized that God would enable her to get her life back together in such a way that she and her loved ones would become a major part of the Jewish family. Her name would go down in history as a prostitute saved by the grace of God. She would also be remembered as one of the world's most unusual mothers. She would become the mother of Boaz, which made her the great-great-grandmother of King David, one of the direct ancestors of Joseph, who was the husband of Mary, the mother of Jesus.

RESPOND

The scarlet rope was risky for Rahab, but she knew the only way life would get any better was to exercise some faith. What a wonderful example. Spend some time alone with God and thank Him for the faith He has in you today. Admit to Him the times you haven't demonstrated faith. Now, make your scarlet cord this time of study and prayer. Then go forward and be full of faith.

REMEMBER

Exercise your faith today — it builds spiritual muscle — and God will be pleased.

Conflict Resolution

Read

Let us therefore stop turning critical eyes on one another. If we must be critical, let us be critical of our own conduct and see that we do nothing to make a brother stumble or fall. — ROMANS 14:13 (PHILLIPS).

Reflect

If you want to turn someone off quickly, never admit when you are wrong. That is one of the quickest ways to put distance and mistrust in a relationship. Eventually, communication will come to a standstill and discussion will come to a halt because the other party will say, "What's the use?"

Usually a person who never admits they're wrong is a poor listener. While another person is expressing their view, the "infallible" one is thinking how they can defend themselves. They are preparing their response instead of listening to the other person speak. Their goal is to win. Thus, the argument continues and communication ceases.

Paul was no stranger to conflict. In this verse he gave some thoughts on how to handle conflict more effectively. First, he said you should take a look at yourself before you start criticizing someone else. You are fallible — which may come as a blow to you — but it's the truth. Second, you need to be in control of your emotions. If they are out of control, it becomes easy to say things you will regret. So if you feel you're losing it, stop and assess the gravity of the situation. Ask yourself, "Is this really that big of a deal, or am I just trying to get my way?" Finally, try to look at the situation from the other person's perspective. You may discover an entirely different motive behind their behavior than you originally thought.

Respond

Pray today that God will give you an understanding mind and a willing heart to please Him in all your relationships. Choose to listen and refuse to be critical. Pray for God's grace to help you grow in grace. Always be aware that every time you point your index finger at another, three other of your own fingers are pointing back at you.

Remember

When conflict arises, don't fight a battle to win — seek restoration.

Cheerful Giving

Read

Each man should give what he has decided in his heart to give, not reluctantly or under compulsion, for God loves a cheerful giver. — 2 CORINTHIANS 9:7.

Reflect

I find it very easy to give to my children when they demonstrate the proper attitude toward me and others. But when their attitude becomes sour, I find it difficult to reward them. Now, don't get me wrong. I still love them like always. I still provide for them without question. But I will not reward a bad attitude.

Just as I find it difficult to reward my children when they have a rotten attitude, I find it enjoyable to reward them when they are demonstrating the right attitude. When they build each other up, share, and cheerfully contribute to the health of the family, it's a joy for me to reward them. In fact, you can't stop me from rewarding them. And guess what! It's the same way with God when we are cheerful givers.

Giving is a lot like love — it never diminishes us and only helps our spiritual situation. Therefore when we give, it should be with a cheerful attitude because we know that we will benefit just as those who receive the gift, if not more. Giving money, time, and your gifts to the work of the Lord is a "heart" thing. God is much more concerned about the attitude of your heart than he is about the amount of money in your offering envelope. Which are you more concerned about?

Respond

If you give because you feel you have to, that should be an indication that you need to check out your motive in giving. "Have-to-giving" isn't "cheerful giving," and cheerful giving is what God loves. Take some time right now to praise and thank God for all He has given you. Be specific. Then pray and ask Him to forgive the times you haven't given cheerfully. From now on, consider giving to be a privilege.

Remember

God loves a cheerful giver. Cheers!

WHO'S THE BOSS?

READ

Serve wholeheartedly, as if you were serving the Lord, not men. — EPHESIANS 6:7.

REFLECT

There are few things more frustrating than having to work with a jerk. But when that jerk is your boss, you have a real challenge. This is especially true when you have to do jobs you detest and it seems that seeing you suffer gives your boss pleasure.

But wait a minute. As a Christian, who is really your boss? Christianity teaches that it is always God's will that we do our best, regardless of who our earthly employer is. So when we encounter jerks at our work, we should always be able to draw satisfaction from the fact that, when all is said and done, we are really working for God. Mediocrity is the nature of the world system, not of those who belong to Jesus Christ. Your loyalty to Him should know no bounds. And when you are submitted totally to Him, work takes on a whole new purpose.

One of the most exciting things about working for Jesus is the retirement plan benefits. Not only that, He gives you purpose in your work. When others see your good work, it glorifies our Father (see Matthew 5:16) and your job can become His harvest field.

RESPOND

Jesus not only expects the best you have to offer, He enables you to perform your best as you depend on Him. No one could ask for any more in a superior. So when you go to work today, remember for whom you work. When you obey your immediate superior, you are pleasing your ultimate Boss. If you have a tough time working for your earthly boss, remember they are not the one for whom you really work. And your job is to please Jesus first. When you do that, He will take care of the rest (see Matthew 6:33).

REMEMBER

Work for your audience of One today. Give Him your best and see the difference it makes in your job.

While You Were Sleeping

Read

"To the angel of the church in Sardis write...Wake up! Strengthen what remains and is about to die, for I have not found your deeds complete in the sight of my God." — Revelation 3:1-2.

Reflect

The city of Sardis was surrounded by steep cliffs, which made it impregnable. Yet in 549 B.C., Cyrus and his army of Persians climbed the steep cliffs to surprise the sleeping inhabitants of the city and capture them. Even more amazing is that the people of Sardis failed to tell their children to watch and not be overly confident of their position. In 214 B.C., just over two centuries later, Antiochus the Great surprised the city again by leading his army to scale the cliffs at night while Sardis was sleeping.

In this passage, Jesus tells the church in Sardis to "Wake up!" The Church is to be like an army that is always prepared for the spiritual attacks of Satan — which are very sneaky. He waits until Christians have fallen asleep spiritually to deceive them, and then when they wake up, they're bound.

How do you know if you've ever fallen asleep spiritually? You go through the same old routine of going to church, singing the songs, and hearing the sermon, but no change takes place. If that describes you, wake up! The enemy could be climbing the walls of your life, getting ready to attack. Be on the alert, because the enemy doesn't make a lot of noise. The Lord promises a reward to those who do not fall asleep spiritually. He promises that you will be clothed in white robes and your name will be in the book of life. (See Revelation 3:5.)

Respond

Spend some time alone with God right now praising and thanking Him for His protection. Ask Him to help you to stay alert to the spiritual things going on around you. Pray that you can be a help to others to stay awake spiritually.

Remember

STAY AWAKE!

THE "BUILD UP" RULE

READ

Therefore encourage one another and build each other up, just as in fact you are doing. — 1 THESSALONIANS 5:11.

REFLECT

We have a rule in our house that goes like this: Inside these walls we build up. We made this a rule because of what goes on outside the walls of our home — the world's system is aggressively trying to tear us down. In the workplace no tears are shed when someone climbs the ladder over us, unless they are our tears. Everyone is out for number one. So, we decided in the training of our children we would be aggressive as well by instituting a mandatory rule of encouragement. Home is the place you'll find it. Everyone from Dad to baby knows, "When I get home, I'll be safe from attack."

One important thing to remember about the "build up" rule: Just because you have the rule doesn't automatically mean it will always be followed. There will always be challenges, but when you have the rule, it helps you remember what you're up against outside the walls of your home.

Here is another important aspect about the "build up" rule. It must be modeled by the adults in the home if it is ever going to happen in the lives of the children in the home. If you don't show your spouse and children respect, you cannot expect them to be respectful.

RESPOND

Today's verse closes with the assumption that the believers are already building each other up. Are you? Let me ask you some questions to help you evaluate yourself. Are you more encouraging at work or at home? Do your children hear you say complimentary things about your mate, to your mate? Do you brag on your mate to your kids? Do you habitually (everyday) let your kids know how proud you are of them, and how unconditional your love is for them? How did you do? If not so good, you can start today. Praise and thank God for what He has given you, and pray He will guide you on how to build up the ones you love.

REMEMBER

Whether you are at work or at home, live by the "build up" rule today.

SEPTEMBER 20

God's Will Is His Word

Read

All Scripture is God-breathed and is useful for teaching, rebuking, correcting and training in righteousness. — 2 Timothy 3:16.

Reflect

I love the story of the little boy who said God answers prayer five different ways: "Yes"; "No"; "Wait"; "I have something better for you"; and "You've got to be kidding!" You know, for a little guy, he wasn't too far off. We sometimes wonder what God is saying to us when we pray and nothing happens. It may be that each of these answers could represent what God says privately as He convicts us to study His Word and wait for His confirmed will.

The Bible is God's guidebook. If you want to know His will, read it. God made sure of that when He inspired its writers through the supernatural influence of His Holy Spirit. This guaranteed the accuracy and trustworthiness of its every word. So we should want to become so familiar with the Scriptures that we know them inside and out, because God's Word is His will, and His will is His Word. Want to know why things in your life either are or are not working? Look in God's Word. Want to know where man came from, what to do now, and where we're going? Look in God's Word. Want to know how to beat the devil? Look in God's Word.

Respond

God doesn't want us to be in the dark. So if it seems He isn't revealing His will to you right now, there may be several reasons why. Here are a few:

1. He might be preparing something else for you that you haven't even thought of yet.
2. You might need to make an adjustment in your attitude.
3. You might already know something God wants you to do, but you've refused to do it.

There may be other reasons you can think of, but one thing is for sure — God's will is consistent with His Word. In fact, God's will is His Word.

Remember

When you want to know God's will, get into His Word.

THE GOOD SHEPHERD

READ

"When he puts forth all his own, he goes before them, and the sheep follow him because they know his voice." — JOHN 10:4 NASB.

REFLECT

I'm so glad Jesus described Himself as a shepherd. The shepherd leads his sheep in the best way possible. The sheep don't have to break down gates or fret over any obstacles because they have the constant company of the shepherd. And that is exactly the way it is in our relationship with our Savior. When we have a decision to make that is in keeping with His will, the circumstances will fall in line.

God doesn't want you to be confused when it comes to pleasing Him. He wants to guide you down the path that leads to life. Therefore, when He guides you in a certain direction, He says He will go before you. That means you won't have to unlock any doors or jimmy any windows, because He is the God of the open door (see John 10:9 and Revelation 3:8).

If you find yourself having to push down barriers and run over people to accomplish a goal, it could be that the Good Shepherd isn't leading you in that direction. Or, it could be that you're not going about it His way. Regardless of which of these reasons it possibly could be, you need to make an adjustment through seeking Him.

RESPOND

One of the toughest things about making decisions is trying to discern what is and what isn't of God. This is where intensive prayer comes in. If we are to distinguish the origin of outside circumstances, we must seek Him diligently until we hear His voice and know His peace. Seek God's face today. Confess anything in your life that may prohibit you from hearing Him. Seek Him with your whole heart. Ask for His wisdom in decision making. Ask Jesus to be the Shepherd of your life and guide you through the open door of His will.

REMEMBER

Trust Jesus for everything today. Follow Him as a sheep would follow the shepherd.

SEPTEMBER 22

Heaven's Symphony

Read

So in Christ we who are many form one body, and each member belongs to all the others. — Romans 12:5.

Reflect

Have you ever gone to hear the symphony and the only one who played was the drummer? Would you block out a night on your entertainment calendar to hear seventy-six trombones play by themselves? Probably not. Why? Trombones are designed to fit into a symphony, providing a full and beautiful sound, and I don't think their sound alone would be enjoyable for long.

In the same way, the individual church members who make up the body of Christ all have unique, individual sounds. But when we tune up and play our music together, we blend in a powerful God sound. God didn't design the Church to be a "one-man band," but a symphony. There is no room in the body of Christ for solo acts. We are to harmonize with the other members. And no gift should be viewed as more important simply because it is more public or more recognizable.

When God "gifts" someone, He expects them to use that gift with love in order to honor Him. Whenever they exercise their gift in the church, it shouldn't be to make themselves look good. It should be to accompany Jesus, our only soloist, and make Him sound good to the listening world. Then, when we all use our gifts in love, we have a powerful symphony.

Respond

Evaluate how you view your gift. Do you want to be praised, or would you rather hear people praise God when your gift is used? Do you get put out when your gifts go unnoticed, or are you satisfied and happy that you will receive your reward from the Father in heaven? These are hard-hitting questions, but it is vitally important that we have the proper attitude about the use of our gifts. Let God be Lord of your music today. Play in tune. Play your part.

Remember

Your gifts were given to accompany Jesus and harmonize with the body of Christ.

The Discipline of Contentment

Read

"When I saw in the plunder a beautiful robe from Babylonia, two hundred shekels of silver and a wedge of gold weighing fifty shekels, I coveted them and took them. They are hidden in the ground inside my tent, with the silver underneath." — JOSHUA 7:21.

Reflect

When a friend of mine would see someone with a nice car, he used to say, "I wish I had that car and he had a better one...now that's not coveting...is it?" Basically, coveting is an uncontrollable compulsion to possess something. It is not simply admiring something or just appreciating it. Coveting goes much deeper. The one who covets has the attitude of, *I have to own it.* That's what Achan had in our verse today — and it cost him and his family their lives.

We live in a society that endorses the mind-set that things bring happiness — "If I just had more things, I would find contentment." But if you base your happiness on things, you will never have enough to satisfy, because there are unlimited things to possess. Thus the more things people have, the more discontented they become, because they want even more. Covetousness and greed are closely related. If greed is one of your weaknesses, then you probably covet things too.

The opposite of covetousness is contentment. Have you ever wondered how people made it in "the olden days" when they had to get by with so little? They had to learn the discipline of contentment and how to do without. It forced them to be creative and also taught them the value of the things they had.

Respond

Have you learned the discipline of contentment? When you see something you want, do you put off getting it or do you pursue possessing it with a passion? Our passion as Christians is to follow God, not our selfish desires. When we do, we realize how He "supplies all our needs according to His riches in Christ Jesus" (Philippians 4:19). Pray that God will give you an attitude of contentment. Throw off any desires that will not honor Him, and be thankful for and content with what He has given you.

Remember

It's okay to have possessions, but it's not okay for the possessions to have you.

The Great Escape

Read

He who dwells in the shelter of the Most High will rest in the shadow of the Almighty. I will say of the Lord, "He is my refuge and my fortress, my God, in whom I trust." — Psalm 91:1-2.

Reflect

One year during the hurricane season, my family took a vacation to Florida (not too bright, I know.) On the night Hurricane Erin abruptly changed course and turned inland, we found ourselves on a mission to find a safe place before it hit. We drove to the Georgia state line, stopping at every motel before we found an available room. Everyone was driving north to avoid the storm's destructive path. I raced into a motel lobby at 3:30 a.m., just ahead of another escapee, to snatch the last room. I remember telling the guy that I was sorry I got the last room, and then feeling badly later because I really wasn't sorry. The next morning on TV I saw the devastating path of Erin's destruction and thought, *Who could have survived that blast if they were in its path?* I remembered thanking God that we were notified and we were spared.

The psalmist shares a very comforting promise from God — if you live your life close to God you will find rest, because He will be your refuge, fortress, and security. That's what dwelling in the shelter of the Most High is all about. Isn't that great? God wants to protect you. He wants you to experience safety and rest, and He will provide it for you as you trust in Him.

Respond

Aren't you glad God has notified you about the coming calamity on the earth and that He has provided a way for you to escape? Take some time to praise and thank Him for His grace and mercy. Ask Him to forgive the times you have disregarded His warning to you. Pray He will use you to bring honor to His name and bring others to Him to be saved also.

Remember

Dwell in the shelter of the Most High today so any storm that comes will not touch you.

Fellowship with Meaning

Read

They devoted themselves to the apostles' teaching and to the fellowship, to the breaking of bread and to prayer. — Acts 2:42.

Reflect

One of my favorite sayings goes like this:

> To live above with those we love, O, that will be glory.
> To live below with those we know, well, that's another story.

Isn't that great! We all know people who get on our nerves — those people we enjoy being around for maybe...two minutes. Now getting along with God may not be a problem for us, but getting along with some other believers may be tough. Why? Here's my theory: The closer we get to God, the more divine we see He is; and the closer we get to others, the more human we see they are. But the honest truth is: We need each other, and we need to have fellowship with other people.

Fellowship is defined as "having in common." It also means "to share." And true fellowship fills one's inner need for love and acceptance. The Church today is filled with people who look contented, but on the inside they are crying out for someone to show them that they care. Fellowship demonstrates caring.

Besides filling the need for love and acceptance, fellowship also fills the need to be heard, to be encouraged, to feel support, to be reproved, and to be held accountable. Are these needs being met in your life? Have you found the fellowship you need to help you grow as an authentic Christian? Your growth as a believer depends largely on the people with whom you choose to fellowship.

Respond

Praise God for His willingness to have fellowship with you through His Son. Then confess the times you have not lived in fellowship with Him and the times you did not fellowship with other believers. Determine in your heart that you will walk with God and have regular, quality fellowship with other believers to remain strong in the faith.

Remember

Fellowship doesn't mean having food at church, but sharing, caring, and supporting each other.

LOVE WHAT GOD LOVES

READ

They said to me, "Those who survived the exile and are back in the province are in great trouble and disgrace. The wall of Jerusalem is broken down, and its gates have been burned with fire." — NEHEMIAH 1:3.

REFLECT

It was a day when the enemies of God were laughing at His people. The great city of Jerusalem was no longer beautiful. It lay in ruins and the people of God were powerless in the eyes of all those who looked on. They needed a leader, someone who was willing to face the opposition and take a stand for God.

Nehemiah was the one God chose. He had every natural reason to stay aloof from the needs of his people. He lived in comfort and was trusted by the king. Why would he want to leave that comfort to face the incredible challenge of rebuilding the walls of Jerusalem? I'll tell you why: Nehemiah loved Jerusalem. And, he couldn't stand to see God embarrassed. If he had his way, no one was going to make a mockery of God and what God loved.

Nehemiah got involved because he loved what God loved. No comfort he experienced in the king's palace could compare to the discomfort he experienced when seeing his greatest love, God himself, mocked by those who didn't know Him.

RESPOND

What does it take to make you leave your comfort zone? If you're like Nehemiah, it probably takes something you love very much to push you to face a challenge. It could be that God presents these challenges in our lives to reveal how much we do love Him. Has God set a challenge before you that will reveal your love for Him? Spend some time praying that God will give you a passion for Him and His cause. Ask Him to help you understand when new challenges before you are a test to prove your love. Finally, take a stand today and make Him look good to others.

REMEMBER

Love what God loves and you will do what pleases Him.

What Do You Know?

Read

And when the seven thunders spoke, I was about to write; but I heard a voice from heaven say, "Seal up what the seven thunders have said and do not write it down." — Revelation 10:4.

Reflect

My parents taught me a lot, but I remember times as a child when I wanted to know more and they would not tell me. I would try to wear them out with the whiny, one-word question, "Why?" But they would reply, "You'll understand that when you're older." What they were trying to help me understand was: Some things were not "age appropriate" for me.

The same is true for spiritual things. There are some truths we need to know and understand now, but according to God, there are other things we don't need to know now. Instead, we need to have faith in the place of understanding. Daniel experienced this frustration when he asked to understand all the future prophesy he was seeing. God replied, "Go your way, Daniel, because the words are closed up and sealed until the end of time" (Daniel 12:9).

At the beginning of Revelation, John was told to write what he saw. But when the seven thunders spoke, he was instructed to stop writing. It is senseless for us to speculate why he was instructed to stop writing. One thing we do understand from this instruction is that God is both a revealing God and a concealing God. He gives us enough knowledge to have faith if we choose, but conceals enough for us to understand that He is God and He is sovereign.

An old, wise preacher once told me that he didn't worry about the things in the Bible he didn't understand. He said, "The parts that give me the most trouble are those that I do understand, like how I need to win over the flesh and trust God with relationships."

Respond

Do you have more trouble obeying the things God has revealed than understanding the things He's concealed? Ask God to help you walk in what you do know today.

Remember

Obey what He reveals to you, trust Him when He conceals from you.

The Heart

Read

The heart is deceitful above all things and beyond cure. Who can understand it? — Jeremiah 17:9.

Reflect

I used to never take personality tests for one simple reason...I just didn't want to. I was scared of them! But now I take every test I can get my hands on. Why? I don't know everything there is to know about me, and I'm interested in learning more. Today when I can find a test that will help *me* understand *me* and the kinds of things God has built into me, I take it. When I get the results, the test shows me how I can give what I've discovered about myself back to God.

Have you ever felt like kicking yourself in the seat of the pants because you did something that you didn't believe you would do? Join the club. This is just one aspect, I believe, of Jeremiah's "mystery of the heart". So I suppose what I'm saying is, the more we can know about ourselves, the better. And, I have found the ultimate personality test: it's called the Word of God. God's Word reveals what's really going on. It cuts through all the veneer and reveals to us our thoughts, motives and attitudes.(See Hebrews 4:12.)

Jeremiah said the heart of man is prone to evil and without outside help it is hopeless. He asked, "Who can understand it?" Only the One who made it can fully understand it. You can't trust yourself. You must trust God to handle your heart.

Respond

Does your heart play tricks on you? Do you entertain thoughts that have no business in your mind? If so, ask the One who made you for help. Read Psalm 139 during your devotional time today and let Him search your heart to cleanse you from any evil thing. Then make a commitment to meditate on holy and pure things as your day progresses, inviting God's life-changing power to purify your heart and mind.

Remember

God made you and He knows you better than you know you.

GOOD SOIL

READ

"Others, like seed sown on good soil, hear the word, accept it, and produce a crop — thirty, sixty or even a hundred times what was sown." — MARK 4:20.

REFLECT

I was raised on a farm where we grew row crops like corn and soybeans. A lot of variables determined whether or not we had a good crop — things like the amount of rainfall, the amount of damage by insects, and oh yes...the creek. The creek ran right through our bottom ground, and it seemed to overflow its banks every year. When it did, part of the crop washed away and we were given a literal witness of Jesus' words in today's verse. As a result of the creek's flooding, some seeds tried to grow through the rocky soil the overflow left behind. So we always knew where we would get the worst yield — from the rocky soil produced by the creek's damage. Those rocky soil stalks were always the sickest in the whole field.

Jesus compared our spiritual growth to that of seeds growing in the ground. The seed is God's Word and the soil represents our hearts. Some "hard soil" hearts never produce because Satan snatches the Word before it can take root. Still others are "rocky soil" hearers who are open to God's Word, but they don't last long because when hard times come, they fall away. Then there are those "thorny soil" hearers who hear the Word, but allow the worries of life to choke out the effectiveness of the Word in their lives. Finally, there are those "good soil" hearers who receive God's Word and allow it to change their lives completely. They produce fruit. And no storm or creek can harm them because their lives are planted on the good bottom land foundation of His Word.

RESPOND

Are there some creeks running through your life that wash away what God has taught you? Have you abandoned any of His teaching because of hard times? Take some time to be alone with the Sower and let Him speak to you through His planted Word. Read through Mark 4:1-20.

REMEMBER

Make certain your heart is good soil in which God plants His Word today.

A Good Reason to Be Baptized

Read

Then Jesus came from Galilee to the Jordan to be baptized by John. — Matthew 3:13.

Reflect

Do you remember trying to please your parents and make them proud of you in public? I remember times in school when I was either playing sports or singing in concerts that I couldn't wait until the events were over to learn what my parents thought of my performance. A parent's approval is one of the most important needs of a child's life. The same thing is true spiritually. As a child of God we desire the approval of our heavenly Father, and one of the most significant ways to get it is to be baptized. Baptism symbolizes three major strongholds of the Christian faith. First of all, it symbolizes cleansing from sin. Second, it symbolizes our identification with the death, burial, and resurrection of Jesus Christ. And third, it identifies us publicly with Him.

Jesus gave us the example of baptism. For those who are believers and have not been baptized, this should be reason enough. However, another phenomenal thing happened when Jesus was baptized in the Jordan River by John. For the first time in Scripture God the Father is recorded as saying, "This is my Son in whom I am well pleased" (Matthew 3:17). Now, if God was so pleased with His Son — including baptism — shouldn't all believers want to follow the Lord's example?

Respond

If you are a believer and have postponed baptism, is it because of pride or fear? Pray and ask God to show you the reason so you can work with Him to get it out of the way. Then arrange to be baptized. It is a very meaningful and important experience for a believer. If you have obeyed God in this area, maybe there is someone you know who hasn't who you can pray for. Then evaluate your overall obedience to God and pray that He will use you to point others to Him.

Remember

Baptism doesn't make you a Christian, but it lets everyone know of your commitment to Christ.

Make God Look Good

Read

We are therefore Christ's ambassadors, as though God were making his appeal through us. We implore you on Christ's behalf: Be reconciled to God. — 2 CORINTHIANS 5:20.

Reflect

As a father I'm always pleased when I hear someone say, "Your son is so well mannered." I usually smile and wonder if they saw the right child. But there is a sense of pride when you hear something like that about your son or daughter, because all the effort you've put into them is somehow paying off in the real world. It makes you feel like a good parent and it also makes you look good. The same thing is true spiritually.

As God's children, we are Jesus' ambassadors or representatives in this world, so our job is to make Him look good to people we meet. It is our responsibility to spread the message of God's desire to reconcile the world to Himself, because if we don't do it, no one will.

The word reconcile means "to bring back a former state of harmony." Because of sin in the world, man is separated from God. But God has made it possible, through the work of Jesus on the cross and in His resurrection, to change thoroughly the relationship between God and mankind. Are you, as one of His ambassadors, spreading that message?

Respond

When people watch you day in and day out, do they see a loving God living through you? Do they see a person who cares? Chances are, if they know you're a Christian and you don't act like you care about them, they probably won't think your God cares either. This truth really helps define our Christian mission! Spend a moment or two alone with God right now and thank Him for reconciling you to Him through His Son, Jesus. Ask Him to help you show His love to others. Pray for those who are watching you. Then, make the Father look good to the world today. Because if you don't do it, nobody will.

Remember

It's your mission everyday to make your heavenly Father look good to others.

God's Blanket of Love

Read

...to grasp how wide and long and high and deep is the love of Christ. — Ephesians 3:18.

Reflect

When the snow comes down in large fluffy flakes, it makes me want to go out and play in it. Isn't it interesting how those flakes fall from heaven one piece at a time and make such a beautiful blanket of white for us to enjoy? Sometimes God's love is the same way. It comes a piece at a time to blanket us so we can enjoy a warm and pure relationship with Him.

When I became a Christian years ago, I never dreamed He loved me as much as He does. But over the years, as I've tried His patience and experienced His forgiveness, I've learned that His love goes far beyond what I could ever imagine. I don't know if I will ever grasp how wide and long and high and deep is the love of Christ for me. In fact, the longer I live and the more of His love I experience, I know that I'm just catching a glimpse of Him. What I do understand is, the more I experience His love for me, the deeper and higher I can see.

Another thing I've learned over the past twenty years of my new life is that when I don't spend time with Him, I don't grow in His love. Spending time with God is the most important thing we will ever do, because that is the foundation for the rest of our day — for the rest of our life. It's futile to go about handling our daily lives without first hearing from the One who knows the end from the beginning and everything we need to know in between.

Respond

Spend some time today thanking God for His unfathomable blanket of love. Then read 1 Corinthians 13 and choose to show His love to everyone who crosses your path today.

Remember

His beautiful quilt of love comes to you a piece at a time.

Be Real

Read

But one thing I do...I press on toward the goal to win the prize for which God has called me heavenward in Christ Jesus. — PHILIPPIANS 3:13-14.

Reflect

Former Atlanta mayor and United Nations ambassador Andrew Young told those of us gathered at a pastors' conference about his daughter's missionary call to the African nation of Uganda. When she revealed this to him, Mr. Young acknowledged her noble ambitions, then asked her to reconsider. He went on to explain how foreigners, black foreigners included, would most likely be mistreated. But to this his daughter replied, "Daddy, I'm going to Uganda. God has called me." Not wanting to hurt his daughter's feelings, he gave her a second reason not to go. "Not only foreign blacks, but women in general are mistreated there," he continued. "So now you have two strikes against you. You might even be killed." But to this his daughter replied again, "Daddy, I'm going to Uganda. God has called me."

Over the course of time, Mr. Young's daughter did indeed go to Uganda. He very candidly shared the thoughts he had the day he saw his daughter off. "I had always wanted her to be a respectable Christian," he told us, "but not necessarily a real one."

The apostle Paul said that real Christians always do one thing — they press on to what God wants them to do. That's what makes them real. And that is what made Andrew Young's daughter real.

Respond

Are you real? Are you pressing on to what God wants to accomplish through you? He may not be sending you to Uganda, but He is sending you somewhere. It will always be to your family. It may also be to your neighbors, to the nursery at your church, or to your business community downtown. Take some time today to ask God what your heavenly call involves. Press on and surrender completely to God's will — the greatest blessings of your life await you!

Remember

Be real.

Be Strong

Read

"Be strong and courageous, because you will lead people to inherit the land I swore to their forefathers to give them." — Joshua 1:6.

Reflect

Getting used to a new leader can be quite an adjustment, especially when that leader has to follow in the sandals of someone like Moses. Not too many guys could follow the parting of the Red Sea. Nevertheless, God chose Joshua to do just that. He didn't possess Moses' personality, but he had a passion to do what God wanted. He had an uncompromising spirit that God could use during that time of history. But like any leader, Joshua needed encouragement, because he would inevitably face discouragement like all leaders do.

Discouragement is part of the package that comes with leadership. Even the best leaders have periods of discouragement. Joshua probably had private times of questioning and wondering how he got into his position in the first place. From time to time he may have lacked confidence in himself. But he had seen God work in miraculous ways in the past. And, he had gone to the funerals of thousands of friends who had voted against him some forty years earlier. These experiences, coupled with the promise of today's verse, gave Joshua the confidence to lead. He knew God was in total support of him. Therefore, Joshua believed he could move ahead without reservation.

Respond

What gives you confidence when God is nudging you to make a move for Him? Do you find confidence in His Word just like Joshua did? You should, because God's commandments are His enablements. In other words, when you obey His commands, He enables you to carry out His will. And before He gives you an assignment to carry out His will, He prepares you for the mission. Praise and thank God for His confidence in you. Trust Him to give you the strength and courage today to carry out His plan for your life.

Remember

When God gives you a mission, He prepares you for it in advance.

WAIT...GOD IS WORKING

READ

Yet those who wait for the Lord will gain new strength; they will mount up with wings like eagles, they will run and not get tired, they will walk and not become weary. — ISAIAH 40:31 NASB.

REFLECT

Have you ever been in a conversation with someone and you knew their mind was a million miles away from what you were saying? That can be frustrating, but it's even more frustrating when the person you're talking to is God. When He is silent, or it seems He is a million miles away, a feeling of despair can overwhelm you. However, you must realize that God is silent for a reason. Perhaps He is waiting for you to make an adjustment in your walk. Or maybe He just wants you to wait — wait and trust in Him.

In today's verse, Isaiah encourages us to wait upon the Lord, to draw strength and confidence from Him as the fruit of waiting. When God is speaking, wait. When God is silent, wait. Intertwine yourself with the Lord and wait, because He is always listening, and He will answer on time.

RESPOND

Have you gone through a time when it seemed like the heavens were silent? Did you wonder if your prayers were going any higher than the ceiling? Perhaps you feel that way now. Don't fret! Remember, God is working. Your responsibility is to make any adjustments necessary to conform to His will, and wait. Spend some time right now to praise and thank Him for His willingness to speak to us through His Word. Confess to Him the times you have failed to wait on His best for you. Read His Word. Then ask Him to show you today any adjustments you need to make in your life to get in the center of His will. Finally, pray He will give you the strength and courage to obey His direction.

REMEMBER

God is listening and He's working, so just wait.

Consider It All...What?

Read

Consider it pure joy, my brothers, whenever you face trials of many kinds, because you know that the testing of your faith develops perseverance. — James 1:2-3.

Reflect

I remember my first ride in a small-engine plane. I went up with a couple of pastor friends on a windy day. You're probably aware that small planes and windy days don't go together too well. But when you add to that undigested fried chicken.... Well, we weren't into our wind-tossed adventure ten minutes before something got tossed...namely my lunch. I survived, my friends laughed, and my lesson was learned. Never eat a big meal just before you go small plane flying on a windy day!

Life is a lot like our small plane was on that windy day. Sometimes you get tossed from one emotion to another and it seems like solid ground is nowhere around. You feel sick and no one around seems to care. How can you have a good attitude when your day goes like that? With JOY. James says, "Consider it all joy." Why? Because rough weather doesn't last forever, and if you stick it out with a good attitude, the rough weather experience will teach you a lesson that will help you in the future. James calls this learned lesson, perseverance.

Respond

Do you feel like your life is being tossed around right now? Are you sick of life the way it is? Look up, it won't last forever. When you consider it all joy, you can know you're being shaped for a better day. So take some time right now to praise and thank God for His wonderful love for you. Thank Him for the patience He builds into your life through tough times. Also take some time to confess the times you've fallen short of what He wanted. Finally, pray for those you know whose lives are being tossed around. Ask God to become a stabilizing force of joy in their storms today.

Remember

When the winds of opposition toss you around, you can trust your pilot Jesus to land you safely on the ground.

HAPPINESS IS ...

READ

"Watch out! Be on your guard against all kinds of greed; a man's life does not consist in the abundance of his possessions." — LUKE 12:15.

REFLECT

If someone asked you, "What are you waiting for to enjoy life?" what would you say? Some would say, "When I reach a certain financial plane, I'll be happy." Or, "When I climb the corporate ladder and reach a certain position, I'll be happy." Or, "When I get the things I've always wanted, I'll be happy." Others might say, "When I find that person who will fulfill my life, I'll be happy and satisfied." And others will say, "When I reach my goals, I'll achieve happiness and enjoy life." These may be noble quests, but none of them can bring total happiness.

Notice how Jesus points out in our verse today that happiness in living isn't found in gaining possessions of any kind. You won't find true fulfillment in making a name for yourself, you'll find it in making Him look good to others. You won't find fulfillment when you reach some plateau. You find it in the growth and service opportunities that lie along the climb. You find it in the struggle. Think of what James said, "Is your life full of difficulties and temptations? Then be happy, for when the way is rough, your patience has a chance to grow. So let it grow, and don't try to squirm out of your problems. For when your patience is finally in full bloom, then you will be ready for anything, strong in character, full and complete." (James 1:2-4 TLB)

RESPOND

Happiness is for today. It isn't something you arrive at; it's something you decide. In your work, in your home, in your social life, in your whole life, happiness is not to be put on hold. It isn't just for the TGIF weekends. It's for now. And it's for you. So give up living for possessions and a better day. Take hold of the prize possession — Jesus — and be happy today!

REMEMBER

Happiness exists now, knowing you are Jesus' most precious possession.

Motivation Factor

Read

Do not work for food that spoils, but for food that endures for eternal life, which the Son of Man will give you. On him God the Father has placed his seal of approval. — John 6:27.

Reflect

I have a good friend who is a mascot for a professional sports team. He is a Christian. He gets paid to act goofy. He uses his platform as a mascot to speak to thousands of kids every year. Why? He is motivated. What motivates him? God has put in him a burden to use whatever position God gives him to reach his corner of the world. What a great idea!

Whether you are a college professor or a ditch digger, your work is important to God. It makes no difference if your pay is a four or six-digit figure, God watches the way you work. This leads to the obvious question: What is your motivation in your work? Do you dread going to work each day or are you a workaholic? Somewhere in between is where God wants you to be.

In our verse today, Jesus refers to two different kinds of people. One is motivated by putting physical food on the table, while the other is stimulated by eternal treasures that we can't see right now. Also, you see here that there are two kinds of food mentioned — physical food that is necessary, but not the most important, and food for the inner man that is essential for life. Natural food sustains temporary life, but Jesus' food gives eternal life.

Respond

Which kind of food are you working for today? Surely your job provides food for the table, but are you using it as a ministry? If you dread work today, stop and take a look at your motivation. It just may be that your vision of that workplace is stained by the wrong motivation. You can color that job with gold if you realize how important it is to Jesus that you make His ministry a part of it. Now go out there and enjoy working!

Remember

Whatever you do, do it with all your heart, as if you were working for the Lord and not men.

TRUE PROSPERITY

READ

"Do not let this Book of the Law depart from your mouth; meditate on it day and night, so that you may be careful to do everything written in it. Then you will be prosperous and successful." — JOSHUA 1:8.

REFLECT

For too many, the idea of prosperity is what keeps them going. But whose idea is it? We live in a world of competitive success values. Many believe if they're gifted in making money, they are successful. But that's not success in God's eyes. God isn't interested in our position or personal wealth. He is interested in transforming us into His image and in helping us learn to serve Him in the most effective way. This is the biblical understanding of prosperity.

God gave Joshua His recipe for prosperity in two simple steps. First, never abandon the truth of God. God has given us some absolutes in His Word. These things are absolutely true, always. Second, let these truths dictate your life. Meditate on them, memorize them, and most importantly, live them. The result? You will live a life of prosperity in the eyes of the Lord.

Who are you really interested in impressing today? There are many you might want to impress, but the greatest is God himself. So, how do you impress Him? By living according to His Word. Joshua had no desire to be a "people pleaser." During his days serving under Moses he learned the absolute truth that you can't please everyone. So his goal was to please God, regardless. Not a bad goal!

RESPOND

Take a moment or two right now to examine your day. How can you please God today? Allow your mind to take a close look at every detail of your life today — your activities, your relationships, your thought patterns — and give each one to Him one at a time in prayer. Ask Him to sensitize you to His will in all you think and do. Read Joshua 6 and spend time meditating on God's Word.

REMEMBER

Make being a success in God's eyes your goal today.

Remember God

Read

After I looked things over, I stood up and said to the nobles, the officials and the rest of the people, "Don't be afraid of them. Remember the Lord, who is great and awesome, and fight for your brothers, your sons and your daughters, your wives and your homes." — NEHEMIAH 4:14.

Reflect

"Huftys never quit." This is a value we teach our kids over and over, because one of the easiest things to do is quit. It's too easy to walk away from a relationship or a project that demands more time and effort than it required in the beginning. Quitting is one of the biggest contributors to feeling defeated. As Nehemiah went into his project to rebuild the walls of Jerusalem, he probably had no idea how really complicated things would get.

Nehemiah was following God's plan for his life, but little did he know that his job description would be changing almost everyday. One day he would have to be a motivator. Another day he would be a builder. Eventually, he was faced with the decision of either quitting and leaving the project to protect the people or stay and fight. Nehemiah chose to stay and fight. And because he did, God rewarded his faithfulness.

Nehemiah's speech recorded in our verse today reveals the unflinching spirit of a committed servant of God. He saw and heard the opposition, but he didn't get so wrapped up in their attack that he forgot the One who called him into the project. Nehemiah knew that nothing took God by surprise, and that God always had a plan for victory. So he stood firm and didn't quit when times got tough.

Respond

Are you struggling today with a situation that you planned on completing, but now you want to quit? If so, ask yourself this question: Did God put me here and is time really up? He will give you the strength to do whatever is needed to calm any waters, if you simply ask. So ask, don't run, and God will give you the strength to fulfill His will.

Remember

God is not quitting on you, and He never will, so don't quit on Him.

FORGIVENESS ASAP

READ

And so, as those who have been chosen of God, holy and beloved, put on a heart of compassion, kindness, humility, gentleness and patience; bearing with one another, and forgiving each other, whoever has a complaint against anyone; just as the Lord forgave you, so also should you.
— COLOSSIANS 3:12-13 NASB.

REFLECT

Let's face it, most of us need an attitude change when it comes to instantly forgiving someone who has wronged us. We know we're supposed to forgive, but we like to savor it for awhile and have our own little pity party. We even tend to think that refusing to forgive for a time is justifiable. After all, we've been violated and hurt, and we deserve the opportunity to harbor our vengeful attitude. Sorry! As much as it might help get you off the hook, that attitude stinks biblically.

In today's verses Paul said that whoever has a complaint against anyone should be forgiven, just as the Lord forgave you. Now think about that for a minute. When the Lord forgave you, He didn't say, "Boy, I don't know. You know you really hurt Me. I'm going to have to think about this one." NO! He instantly forgave you, and that's what Paul is trying to get you to realize. You must make it a discipline of your life to forgive ASAP (as soon as possible). If you don't forgive immediately, feelings of malice and resentment will develop, which can lead to more sin.

Paul didn't "hang us out to dry" on this business of instant forgiveness. He gave us the characteristics that help us develop the right kind of forgiving attitude. Here's the list: compassion, kindness, humility, gentleness, and patience. If we make these characteristics a habit in our lives, we will develop the kind of forgiveness that God wants us to have.

RESPOND

How's your attitude when it comes to forgiving others? Have you been justifying your unforgiving attitude? Ask God to help you be an instant forgiver today. Then, forgive anyone who has it coming. When you do, He will release your forgiveness in return.

REMEMBER

When you need to forgive someone, you probably won't feel like forgiving, but forgive them ASAP anyway, and the feelings will come.

Stunted Growth

Read

For though by this time you ought to be teachers, you have need again for someone to teach you the elementary principles of the oracles of God, and you have come to need milk and not solid food. — HEBREWS 5:12 NASB.

Reflect

Do you know some people who just refuse to grow up? Maybe you're married to one. Or maybe you work with someone like that. Such people are playful and do the things they did as a child. They're usually a lot of fun to be around. They're childlike, and that's good.

But there are people who refuse to grow up in another way. They demand their own way. Instead of being childlike, they're childish. They blame others for their shortcomings. They're selfish and have a motto for every occasion: "How does this affect me?" Do you know anyone like that?

Just as many people are childish in their attitudes, many Christians are childish spiritually. They may be long-time Christians, but when they go to church, they are there to *get* a blessing, not to *be* a blessing. And when they pray, their prayers are selfish in content. They are the ones who need to be taught, as the writer of Hebrews indicates in today's verse. If a person is selfish, pessimistic, unproductive and talks about himself a lot, rest assured he isn't maturing. His growth has been stunted by the cares of life.

Respond

Now here's a tough question: Has your spiritual growth been stunted? Maturing Christians demonstrate God's love through a positive spirit, regardless of the circumstances. Is that you? Maturing Christians are persistent in prayer and their minds are wonderfully stable because they trust God as a habit of their lifestyle (see Isaiah 26:3). Still you? If so, take some time right now to thank God because of how He has blessed you. If that's not completely you, ask God to help you mature in the areas in which you still act a little childish. Ask Him to deliver you from selfishness and replace it with His unconditional love for others. None of us ever completely arrive, but we must be going forward to at least be headed there.

Remember

Your maturity is showing.

Faith When the Heat Is On

Read

In addition to all this, take up the shield of faith, with which you can extinguish all the flaming arrows of the evil one. — Ephesians 6:16.

Reflect

Just the thought of my dad brings memories to my mind that I'll cherish forever. If I could describe him to you in one word descriptions you would hear me say things like: faith, stability, poise, calm, strong, wisdom, listener, patience, persistence. As I look back I can see now that there were many times the "heat was on" him. He had to provide for a family of six, work a hundred miles from home, and manage a 300-plus acre farm. Add to this all of his children's extracurricular activities (I can't remember one he missed) and all the loving attention and support he gave Mom — and Dad was busy. It's funny how you never fully see the pressure your parents are under until you become a parent.

The challenge for us today is to be faithful to God when the pressure is on. Paul says that to do this, we must use the shield of faith. It was faith that kept my father coming home. He knew how faithful God had been to him, so he understood the importance of being faithful to what God had entrusted to him. Once as an electrical lineman he was electrocuted by 7200 volts. He hung lifeless on the pole with a hole burned into his leg, but God was faithful. The heat was on him then like you and I will never understand. Yet in all his pain and the inconvenience of his surgery and recovery, he kept the faith. I know now it wasn't him, but God working through him to show me the value of trusting God regardless of the circumstances.

Respond

Have you been tempted lately to give up? Has the pressure been too much to handle? Have faith. The shield of faith will protect you from the times when Satan whispers, "Cash it in. It's not worth it. Nothing will ever come of this." You may not see it now, but God is working to bring His plan to pass in your life. It may take you years (like it did me) to see the value of faith.

Remember

Without faith it is impossible to please Him, but with faith it is impossible not to please Him.

Expert Help

Read

Do not be overcome by evil, but overcome evil with good. — Romans 12:21.

Reflect

Imagine you are hiking in the mountains and come across a farmer lying in his field gasping for breath. You run up to him, and with his last breath he says, "S-s-s-some kind of poison." You bolt down the road to find help and run into some National Guard troops wearing masks. One comes up to you, gives you a gas mask, and says, "Put it on quick, there's been a leak of a fatal nerve gas nearby." Do you put it on? Of course you do! Why? Because you have seen the evidence of what the nerve gas can do and you have been offered help from an expert.

The same is true for overcoming evil in our lives. The unseen evil gas of sin lurks around every corner. We've seen many destroyed by its powerful attack. It has destroyed reputations and relationships. It has paralyzed many who never saw it coming. We have seen and been influenced by its overt and subtle influences in the world. But wait a minute, we know from expert advice — God's Word — how to overcome evil in our lives. By His Word and the strength of the Holy Spirit that works in us, we can be victorious over evil. And, we are some of the only chosen few who can really help others.

Respond

Paul says in our verse for today that we are to overcome evil with good. The question is: will we? Take a minute right now to praise and thank God for the goodness He has shown you this past week. Ask Him to forgive you for the times when you allowed Satan to trick you with evil. Pray for those you know who need God's protection and strength to overcome the attacks of the evil one. You are a bona fide "overcoming sin" expert because of your knowledge of the Scriptures and relationship with God. So make yourself available today to those in need.

Remember

Satan spreads evil like an invisible poison, but God's Word destroys every evil work.

Accepting Forgiveness

Read

Save me from bloodguilt, O God, the God who saves me, and my tongue will sing of your righteousness. O Lord, open my lips, and my mouth will declare your praise. — PSALM 51:14-15.

Reflect

He offended her. He handled the whole situation poorly. He yelled. She yelled. They hung up on each other. They didn't speak for weeks. Then he faced reality. Emotions settled down and he knew he was wrong. "I'm sorry, I was wrong. I handled the whole thing wrong. Will you forgive me?" were his words when he called. "Yes," she replied, "but I'm the one who should be asking for forgiveness. I don't know if I'll ever really be able to forgive myself."

Forgiveness means to *cancel* punishment. It doesn't mean, "I'll forgive you, but...." It means, "I forgive you, period." It means you may deserve punishment, but you're not going to get any from me. That is what Jesus did for you on the cross. Even though He had the right to punish us, He canceled it. That's forgiveness. But for some it is just as hard to receive forgiveness, as it is others to offer forgiveness.

I have found that too many people have problems accepting forgiveness. They feel they are unforgivable. And when they can't forgive themselves, they continue to punish themselves. The truth is, it's more important for God's forgiveness to be accepted than to be understood. Because without forgiveness, people can't move forward. They become paralyzed by their past. But when God's unconditional love and forgiveness are accepted, they are free to leave the past behind and move on to a better future.

Respond

Are you one of those who have difficulty receiving God's forgiveness? Have you been struggling with forgiving yourself? Forgiveness isn't some mind game. Jesus' blood is real, the cross is real, and the payment for your sin is real. It's a matter of putting your faith and trust in the hands of a faithful and trustworthy God. Take time right now to tell God how grateful you are for His unfailing forgiveness. Pray for Him to show you in His Word and through prayer that by the blood of Jesus, you are released from the sin of the past.

Remember

Forgiveness has no "buts" to it.

THE FATHER'S GRACE

READ

For it is by grace you have been saved, through faith — and this not from yourselves, it is the gift of God — not by works, so that no one can boast. — EPHESIANS 2:8-9.

REFLECT

My mom wrote me a letter like she had never written before. It was so sentimental it was scary. In her writing, she took me back to the time she brought me home from the hospital. She wrote of many events in my life — from crazy quirks I had to how she has seen God develop my personality. She shared in this five-page letter how much she loved me. And she pointed out how she had witnessed God bless me with a wonderful family and how I could now see her "parent side" of love. My, did that move me.

As a parent, you love regardless — as Paul wrote — by grace. You who aren't parents will be blessed in today's devotional, because you're probably somebody's kid. No truth in the Bible is more wonderful than this: Our Father's love gave us what we so desperately needed and didn't deserve — salvation from sin and death. As our Parent, He is compelled by unmerited favor (grace) to do it. He is saving us right now from the power of sin and the evil desires which controlled us before we accepted Jesus as Savior. And grace compels Him to do it until He brings us home to be with Him in heaven. As a father, I have experienced that with my children over the years...but how much more with our Father of grace!

RESPOND

Aren't you glad our heavenly Father saved you from death and hell, and that He is compelled to help you grow every step of life's way? Take a moment or two right now to praise and thank God for seeing your need of salvation and meeting it through His grace. Ask Him to forgive you for the times you have taken His love for granted. Pray that God will help you share His love today.

REMEMBER

You are not saved by what you do for Him, but by what He did for you.

Enjoying Success

Read

"Let not a wise man boast in his wisdom, and let not a mighty man boast in his might, let not a rich man boast in his riches; but let him who boasts, boast of this, that he understands and knows me." — JEREMIAH 9:23-24 NASB.

Reflect

I visited with an old friend of mine who was in town recently for a convention. We sat and talked for awhile about old times, and then the conversation moved to the future. "What are your goals?" I asked. "Where do you plan to be ten, fifteen years from now?" His answer was predictable. His goals, he said, were centered around being successful and influential in his field. And from that point on, his conversation centered around what he valued most — himself.

There is absolutely nothing wrong with wanting to be successful in our work. But when that becomes all we live for, we quickly lose perspective of what God's purpose is for our lives — namely, to know Him. Too often we become side-tracked, thinking our ambitions are the only things that matter.

In today's devotional passage, Jeremiah tells us the key to enjoying success: developing a proper value system. To place a high value on knowing and understanding God can make the greedy gracious. It can turn controllers into servants and make the faithless faithful. And when these powerful characteristics take root in peoples' lives, those who think first of God and the needs of others in every daily affair, there will be success — God's kind of success.

Respond

Have you dedicated a time each day to focus on getting to know God better? Are your eyes focusing on the Father instead of your own selfish ends? Focus on Him today. It won't take long for you to realize He is worth bragging about. Your conversations will shift from focusing on yourself to focusing on Him. And, you will find yourself enjoying success more.

Remember

A hundred years from today, all that will matter is what you did *with* God, not what you did *for* God.

OCTOBER 18

Surviving Life's Storms

Read

"And the rain descended, and the floods came, and the winds blew, and burst against the house; and yet it did not fall, for it had been founded upon the rock." — Matthew 7:25 NASB.

Reflect

One of the interesting things about foundations is that they are the most important part of the house, yet they are often the last thing we inspect. We focus on the aesthetics of the structure and not the hidden foundation. Many times we may have visible cracks in our walls, but the cracks are just symptoms of another problem — the foundation is moving. Likewise, when we suffer broken relationships or other crises, we often try to patch up the surface problems we can see, without looking at the foundational problem. Many times the foundational problem has something to do with the fact that God told us to do something, but we refused. And in time, our disobedience produced cracks in the walls of our lives.

A very interesting thing about foundations is that you pour them when it's raining. Notice Jesus said, "And the rain descended," not, "if it rains." Why? Because Jesus knew it would storm and rain. So He taught us to build a powerful foundation before the storms of life hit. What is your foundation made of? Who is the final authority in your life? If you are to survive the storms that inevitably will come, the final authority in your life must be the Word of God.

Respond

Is it raining in your life now? If not, get ready. For some it rains rebellious children. For others it rains the threat of divorce. For still others it rains the floods of Satan's confusion intended to produce poverty and bad health. And to survive those storms you must build the foundation of your life on the solid rock foundation of Jesus Christ. You can start now by spending time alone with Him. Praise Him for His protection and provision during the storms of life you have already experienced. Ask Him to forgive you for not trusting in the past. Then ask Him to help some people you know today who are weathering storms right now.

Remember

Be certain your life is founded on the solid word of Jesus Christ. Be prepared.

Confidence in a Crisis

Read

"But David pursued, he and four hundred men, for two hundred who were too exhausted to cross the brook Besor, remained behind." — 1 Samuel 30:10 NASB.

Reflect

Life is about 10 percent what you make it and 90 percent how you take it. What life does *to* you is determined by what life finds *in* you. Some people enjoy crises because they make them feel important. They don't want God to interrupt the storms of their lives because of the attention they are drawing from those who wish to minister to them. Therefore, like David's two hundred, they often miss out on the victory God has for them.

In today's verse we find that as David pursued the enemy to rescue his family and the families of his men, two hundred of his warriors became exhausted and couldn't go on. "But David pursued" because he was following the instructions of the Lord. He was as fatigued as his men. He had been through what they had been through and more. But at the heart of David's actions was his confidence in God's promise that he would overtake the enemy and rescue his family. He was in the midst of a crisis, but he had the promise of God. And to ignore that would have allowed the enemy to defeat him.

God always has a message for us in a crisis. It may be that we need to make an adjustment in some of the practices of our lives. But whatever the reason, God wants us to gain confidence through His Word. Only if we choose to ignore His Word and give up will we fail, because His Word is sure.

Respond

Stop and thank God today for all the gifts He gives you in the midst of a crisis. He gives you the Comforter, the Holy Spirit, who gives you strength, confidence, and wisdom to face tough times. Then confess the times you have ignored His way to go your own. Finally, ask Him to give you victory in the storms of life by speaking to you through His Word today.

Remember

Your confidence in God and His Word is what will see you through any crisis.

A Profile of Love

Read

"But the fruit of the Spirit is love." — Galatians 5:22 NASB.

Reflect

Making up a résumé or profile is one of the first steps you take to introduce yourself to the job market. You put down on paper all the things you have done or can do that make you a qualified applicant. If a Christian were to make up a profile that proved they were qualified as a Christian, it would have to be filled with outward characteristics that prove the inward presence of the Holy Spirit. These outward characteristics, called fruit, are demonstrated by love. Actually, all the other characteristics of the fruit of the Spirit mentioned in Galatians 5:22-23 are an outgrowth of love.

Do you know that life can be better for you than it is right now? Your resume profile can improve tremendously as you allow God's love to control you. When His love controls you, you can be free to love people you've found difficult to love. That's when our love (or lack of it) is most clearly displayed. You can overcome selfishness by allowing God's love to control your thoughts and behavior. How can this happen? It's simple. If you want His love to control you, just start praying in sincerity that it will. Start studying, memorizing, and meditating upon scriptures about His great and powerful love.

Respond

Our prayer time often gets side-tracked with how things *are,* rather than how we should *be.* Today, to improve your spiritual résumé, pray that God will help you to concentrate on His love flowing through you. When you start praying like that, you are praying for His will to be accomplished in your life, and He will honor that kind of prayer. Also pray today for those you know who need God's love. Ask Him to be real to them today. Make a list and pray for them consistently. Persistent prayers go a long way in accomplishing God's will.

Remember

The key characteristic of the Christian's résumé is love. Apply within...

"IT"

READ

"A man of many friends comes to ruin, but there is a friend who sticks closer than a brother." — PROVERBS 18:24 NASB.

REFLECT

"IT" is probably the worst thing that can happen to you while you are living. Many think it only happens when you get old, but the truth is, it can happen at any age. It forces you to tolerate things you never thought you would have to face, and when you do...you hate every minute of it. It produces an aching that visits and won't leave without help. It's a killer. It brings great despair. Crowds only make it worse, and activity becomes meaningless when it has invaded your life. But, it is one of the things friendship fixes. Not only does friendship fulfill your life, but friendship remedies the silent killer — loneliness.

Probably no one on earth was ever more lonely than Jesus on the cross. He had never been separated from the Father. Even while on earth He spent time alone with His Father. But, when He said, "My God, My God why have You forsaken me?" (see Matthew 15:34) He was alone, alone with the sins of the world on Him. He who knew no sin carried every sin on Him at that moment.

RESPOND

Have you experienced the anguish of loneliness lately? Are you isolated in loneliness? Do you long for a companion to share your interests and concerns? Because God knows how awful loneliness is, He gives us the promise of a friend who can be closer to you than a brother. And that friend is Jesus. He not only knows what loneliness is, He experienced it more than anyone who has ever lived. Not only did His friends desert Him, His Father turned His back on Him. But He did it for you. Spend some time right now to pause and thank God for His willingness to be your closest friend. Thank Him for taking loneliness out of your life through your intimate relationship with Him. Ask Him to forgive you for the times you haven't honored His friendship. Now go to church, and make a new friend.

REMEMBER

Friends are like medicine to those who are lonely. Be a friend today.

THE ROD

READ

Foolishness is bound up in the heart of a child; the rod of discipline will remove it far from him. — PROVERBS 22:15 NASB.

REFLECT

When I was growing up, "the rod" in our house was a hickory switch. Boy, how I remember it. A few switches across the calves of one's legs did wonders for rebellious notions and foolish young ways. "The rod" in our verse today means any form of effective discipline, but the hickory switch always worked with me. The sting of that little beauty did a world of good in my foolish young heart.

Sometimes when I got a spanking I tried to run away, which just made things worse. Then I finally woke up. Instead of running away from the spanking, I ran to it. That's right. When my dad started to spank me, I turned around and started hugging him. I'd say, "Oh Daddy, I'm sorry, I love you, I love you, I'm so sorry." And guess what? The spanking stopped. I hugged my dad and got as close as I could to him. And you know, when you think about it, that's what God wants when He disciplines us. He wants us to get as close to Him as we can, and when we do, the spanking stops.

All of us need a wake-up call from God now and then. He has to get our attention so we can get back on track in our Christian walk. God has a way of knowing what button to push. He faithfully uses various circumstances to interrupt our sinful wandering and draw us back to His course.

RESPOND

Do you need a wake-up call today? Do you know in your heart you've been wandering, at least just a bit? If you do, be encouraged in knowing the motive for God's discipline is always love. God always disciplines with the hope of better behavior as the goal — that's love. If you've been feeling His rod lately, try hugging the One who's holding it. Take some time to praise and thank God for disciplining you and bringing you closer to Him. Finally, thank Him for His loving concern to deal with the foolishness in your heart.

REMEMBER

God disciplines to draw us near to Him.

Being Led by God

Read

"The Lord is my shepherd, I shall not be in want." — Psalm 23:1.

Reflect

A long time ago I heard of a little boy who quoted verse one by saying, "The Lord is my shepherd and that's all I want." Even though he misquoted the verse, his interpretation was admirable. Oh, that we who are seasoned in the faith may adopt that attitude about following our Lord's leadership!

J. Vernon McGee says that Psalm 23 "is a He and me psalm." In other words, the emphasis throughout the writer's thoughts is that there is nothing between the soul of God and the soul of man. For God to be the Shepherd who leads our lives, there must be nothing between Him and us.

When we are in the Shepherd's care, He protects us from evil. When we wander from His protective care, we prohibit His leadership in our lives and become vulnerable to the enemy's attacks. Therefore, to be led by God, it is essential that we stay within His protective care and provision. He wants to lead us, and when we are being led by Him, we, like the psalmist, will feel that all we desire is found in Him.

Respond

The question today is not if we want to be led by God, but are we willing to put ourselves in the position to be led by Him. Are we willing to make the adjustments necessary to be led by Him. He is not interested in our plans and our direction. He is only interested in accomplishing His will through us. Therefore, we must take some time to seek His leadership. You can do that now, by thanking and praising God for His willingness to lead you and take such a great interest in your life. Ask Him to forgive you for the times when you have wandered away from His leadership. Ask Him to give you a listening ear and an obedient heart to do His will for your life.

Remember

Where God guides He provides, and where He leads He meets the needs.

The Power of Love

Read

When they had finished eating, Jesus said to Simon Peter, "Simon son of John, do you truly love me more than these?" — John 21:25.

Reflect

Going to the craft store is not my favorite thing. But I do it. Why? The power of love! No, I don't love crafts. They're okay, but I'd rather watch a Cardinals game. I love the one who loves the crafts — my wife. I know my wife likes crafts and I love her, so I go to those craft stores. You know, I'm even getting to the point that I can recognize good quality crafts. But what is even greater is that I'm falling deeper and deeper in love with my wife.

The same thing should be true in doing God's will. When you know what God wants, even if you're not crazy about doing it, your love for Him should motivate you to action. This is challenged today by many people who say, "You deserve to get your own way," or "Life is too short to do what you don't want to do." And because we listen to that kind of talk, we often fold and put God's interests on the shelf. In doing so, we show God the depth, or rather shallowness, of our love.

Peter knew what Jesus meant when He asked Peter if he loved Him. He knew the Lord was saying, "Show Me your love through your obedience to My will." No power in the world is greater than the power of love. When you stop and think about the depth and riches of God's love for you, it should motivate you to please Him regardless of what people around you say. The amazing thing about doing God's will is that as you are obedient to Him, even if you don't like what you are doing at the time, He reveals how His will can benefit you and others.

Respond

Take time right now to seek God's face regarding His will for you today. Ask Him to give you the courage to obey Him regardless of what it is. You'll begin recognizing the tremendous power of His touch in your life.

Remember

There is no power greater than God's love.

Make Up Your Mind

Read

"But Daniel resolved not to defile himself with the royal food and wine." — Daniel 1:8.

Reflect

Some people have trouble making decisions. Their favorite color is plaid! And if you ask them if they have trouble making decisions, they answer, "Yes and no." That can be frustrating! But Daniel was not in that crowd. He knew that the best thing he could do for God and for himself was to make up his mind to do God's will. He knew it was God's will that he not eat from the king's food and drink his wine. So, instead of making excuses to please the crowd, he "resolved" not to compromise God's will.

The first step in following the will of God is to make up your mind. If other people can get you to change your mind after you know what the will of God is, you haven't made up your mind to follow Him and let Him be Lord of your life.

Daniel made up his mind to stay pure, which is not optional for those who long to be in God's will. It's mandatory. To be pure is to go against the flow of the world's loose integrity system. We as believers are to be the purity pacesetters to a lost world. Then, like Daniel, we will find there is great power in purity.

Respond

In 1 Samuel 2:30, God said, "Those who honor me I will honor." You honor God by making up your mind on a daily basis to do His will. In other words, today you must choose to do God's will. When temptation intensifies, you must make up your mind hour by hour, minute by minute, and even second by second. It is a decision you will have to make over and over. Oh, and Satan won't give up when your mind is made up. So in order to do God's will, you must habitually submit your will to Him.

Remember

Make up your mind today, before the world system tries to make up your mind for you.

Hungry To Grow

Read

"From Him the whole body, joined and held together by every supporting ligament, grows and builds itself up in love, as each part does its work." — Ephesians 4:16.

Reflect

When I noticed that my oldest son was not satisfied with Happy Meals anymore, it bothered me. All of a sudden he wanted Quarter Pounders with cheese instead. He started coming to me — after we ate — to say those awful words that made me wonder if I had enough money in my pocket, "Dad, I'm still hungry." Now don't get me wrong, I was glad he was growing. But I also knew that the more he grew, the more it was going to cost. Actually, the cost didn't bother me when I compared it to the joy of seeing him grow into a fine young man of whom I am very proud. Every dollar I spend to help him grow is worth it.

That's the way it is spiritually. We only grow as we hunger for more of God and His Word. The more we grow, the more joy we find because God loves it when we are hungry for more of Him. It gets to the point where we don't even notice the cost in time, effort, and money, because the way God blesses us helps us see it is all well worth it. Developing a hunger for God's Word only happens as we spend time at His table eating the Word, time in prayer, time in praise and worship, and fellowshipping with other believers. What the world feeds us will never satisfy. Therefore, our diet must be filled with the things of God.

Respond

How spiritually hungry are you today? When you awake, do you rush through your morning routine of taking care of your physical needs in order to get to your spiritual needs? If this sounds pretty foreign, you're probably not very hungry. But it's easy to get hungry. Just draw near to God right now and ask Him to begin revealing Himself in a fresh way to you in Bible study, in prayer, in worship, and with other believers.

Remember

To grow as a believer you must cultivate a daily hunger for more of God.

TAKE THE ESCAPE!

READ

No temptation has seized you except what is common to man. And God is faithful; he will not let you be tempted beyond what you can bear. But when you are tempted, he will also provide a way out so that you can stand up under it. — 1 CORINTHIANS 10:13.

REFLECT

Whenever you work through a maze on a sheet of paper, do you immediately start drawing a line without considering the route you are going to take? Or do you look it over first and then start your way through it? If you are wise, you study the maze before you actually start writing. Why? Because when you look ahead, you can see the traps Not only that, you also can see the escape. The same principle is true for us when we deal with temptation. Every temptation has traps, but God also provides a way of escape. We must be faithful to look for that escape — and take it.

The problem many of us face is not in seeing the escape, but in taking it when we see it. Our flesh enjoys playing with temptation, so when we see the escape route, it frustrates us because we want to flirt with the temptation a little longer. We usually miscalculate the danger and the damage sin can do to our lives. And when we yield to sin, we get burned.

As God's child, you should hate sin as He does. Remember, it was sin that put Jesus on the cross. He was beaten, tortured, and mocked so you could be able to turn from evil and do good. Stay in the maze of temptation and you will be trapped, but go for the escape route and you will experience freedom.

RESPOND

As you pray today, praise and thank God for the escape route He has made available to you. Ask Him to forgive you for the times you have seen His escape plan and refused to take it. Pray for strength over the desires of the flesh to conquer that consistent temptation you face.

REMEMBER

God has provided an escape route for you to avoid sin today, look for it and take it.

OCTOBER 28

TRUE CONTENTMENT

READ

Keep your lives free from the love of money and be content with what you have, because God has said, "Never will I leave you; never will I forsake you." — HEBREWS 13:5.

REFLECT

I recently spoke with a rich man who had a history of many hurtful relationships. He had a hunger for something to fill the ache of previous relationships, so he struggled through one after another. "It sounds like you would just like a relationship where you could find genuine trust," I said. His reply was, "I'd give my house for a relationship like that." Material things weren't valuable to him anymore, because he knew possessions didn't fill the need deep inside.

People who are rich have an advantage over those who are poor, because they know that money can't buy happiness. It can make things more comfortable and perhaps more convenient, but it can't make them happier. The illusion of wealth is this: if you had more, you would have it made. You would be able to sit back and relax. But the truth is quite the opposite. If you had more, you would eventually want more, because you would recognize the more you had leaves you empty inside.

How content are you with your salary? The place you live? How about your possessions? The Scriptures teach us that contentment isn't found in the accumulation of things, but in the assurance that God will never leave or forsake us.

RESPOND

It is a proven fact that surrounding yourself with gadgets and doodads does not bring contentment. Spend some time right now praising and thanking God for the possessions He has entrusted to you. But thank Him even more for your relationship with Him. And if you know someone who has many possessions, yet they don't know Jesus Christ, pray for them now to know true contentment in Christ.

REMEMBER

True contentment is found in a personal, meaningful relationship with Jesus.

STOP WHINING!

READ

Do everything without complaining or arguing, so that you may become blameless and pure, children of God without fault in a crooked and depraved generation, in which you shine like stars in the universe. — PHILIPPIANS 2:14-15.

REFLECT

I remember as a teenager overhearing Dad say to Mom, "You know, Tom doesn't complain. He accepts things as they come and go." Well, I wish I could take credit for that attitude, but I think it had something to do with my parents' model. They never complained, and I followed their lead.

I never did like hanging out with squeaky wheels — they would tend to get on my nerves. It is true in life that the squeaky wheel gets the grease; but even after they receive the grease, they often still squeak. And when they squeak as Christians, they make Jesus look bad.

Paul wasn't a complainer. He urged the Christians at Philippi to refrain from complaining or arguing about anything. He had earned the right to say this because when he was encouraging them in this area, he was sitting in prison unjustly. It was Paul's attitude of refusing to complain in the tough times that made him a "shining star in the universe" who continues to shine today.

RESPOND

Isn't it interesting that those who don't complain are considered by Paul in today's verse as "blameless and pure?" What does that make those who do complain? Whining is manipulative. It may work for a while as people get tired of hearing you and let you have what you want. But after a while, they may just get tired, tell you to put a sock in it, and leave you alone. It is very unbecoming of a Christian to be a whiner. So if you are one: STOP!!! Become a shining star in the universe. Overcome this negative world with a positive attitude. Then watch how others will be attracted to your life. Spend some time praising God for His positive attitude toward you. Confess to Him the times that you have been a whiner and made Him look bad. Then pray that He will guide you to be an encouragement to someone today.

REMEMBER

Whining isn't shining. It is the result of a small, self-centered life.

Speak Up!

Read

I pray that you may be active in sharing your faith, so that you will have a full understanding of every good thing we have in Christ. — PHILEMON 6.

Reflect

The ability to share our faith is not unlike the ability of a football team. A football team has some players who specialize in handling the football — the backfield, the ends, and the center. But every player on the field knows what to do when the ball is fumbled. The same is true with sharing our faith. Every believer should know how to share their faith when the opportunity arises.

We all have different styles of sharing. Some are confrontational like Peter. Some are intellectual like Paul. Still others are relational like Andrew. But regardless of the style we use, the important thing is that we have a style and that we share our faith in an authentic way. Those who don't know Jesus will never care about what we know until they know that we care about them. So at the heart of every style of witnessing is the fundamental fact that we must care about the spiritual condition of others enough to share from our hearts.

Paul prayed for these people to actively share their faith. Do you actively share your faith? I'm not referring to letting people simply view your life and draw their own conclusions about Jesus Christ. That can be a step in leading someone to Christ, but it is only a step. The one who wrote this verse also wrote, "How, then, can they call on the one they have not believed in? And how can they believe in the one whom they have not heard? And how can they hear without someone preaching to them?" (Romans 10:14). You see, when the opportunity presents itself, you must speak up!

Respond

Take a moment or two to praise and thank God that you have THE message to share. Pray for strength and wisdom to know how to share your faith today, and ask God for open doors of opportunity to tell people about Jesus.

Remember

When you see someone in need of a personal relationship with Jesus, it's your opportunity to make an eternal score.

THE WORLD'S BIGGEST LIAR

READ

"Whenever he speaks a lie, he speaks from his own nature; for he is a liar, and the father of lies." — JOHN 8:44.

REFLECT

The name devil means *slanderer,* and his desire is to slander the name of Jesus Christ and mock everyone who follows Him. We hear the name of Jesus used by non-Christians in a derogatory tone often. If you work in the marketplace of our society, you probably hear people use His name as a swear word regularly, and it is accepted. But when was the last time you heard someone get angry and say, "Oh Buddha!" or, "Well Joseph Smith!" or, "Sun Yung Moon!" You never hear that. Why? Because it is the devil's purpose to slander the one name that destroys his work and plans — Jesus.

An acquaintance of mine tells a story about substitute teaching in a high school. One day he heard a student in the hall who was very upset say, "Jesus Christ." So my friend went up to him and said, "I can tell you are upset, but why did you use that name to express your anger?" The student replied, "What name?" You see the point? Satan has lied to our culture to the point that the King of kings has been equated to a swear word only. Satan has led our society to reduce the Lord Jesus to nothing. But Satan is the biggest liar of all.

RESPOND

What lies have you believed recently? Has the devil been able to slander the reality of Scripture to make you think you are worthless? Have you believed the lie that your secret sin isn't hurting anybody but you? Have you believed the lie that God could never forgive you or make your life new? God wants to expose all of Satan's lies to you so you will avoid believing them. Pray today for wisdom and strength to follow God totally!

REMEMBER

Embrace the truth in God's Word and you will never fall for the lies of the devil.

NOVEMBER 1

STANDING ON SOLID GROUND

READ

And with your feet fitted with the readiness that comes from the gospel of peace. —EPHESIANS 6:15.

REFLECT

The Roman soldier had spikes in his shoes to help him keep his footing while fighting in battle. These spikes served as a stabilizing factor so he wouldn't slip and make himself an easy target for the enemy. Likewise, the Christian soldier must be equipped to defeat the attacks of the devil that attempt to bring us down. The world system Satan designed can be slippery on the surface and cause us to easily slide into sin. In our verse today, Paul tells us to have our feet fitted with readiness so when the attack of our enemy comes, we will be able to stand. But we can't stand if we aren't prepared. And we prepare ourselves by embracing Jesus with our entire life.

It is important to realize this is not a theory. This is warfare against powers that we can't see. Satan uses old physical habits, mental laziness, and lack of discipline to trip us up. Then he goes in for the kill to completely disarm us. Because he is so serious about the battle and his methods are so refined, it is vital that we are ready at all times. One way we fit our feet with readiness is through prayer. When we pray, God can reveal to us His strength and our weakness. He can help us make decisions in advance that will help us keep our footing and avoid the traps of the enemy. He will protect and strengthen us as we seek Him.

RESPOND

Ask God to forgive you for the times you allowed Satan to influence you through temptation. Pray for those who are in the heat of the battle and on slippery ground. Finally, ask God to reveal the weaknesses that need to be submitted to Him. Pray for His help if you've slipped and fallen. Pray for His strength to stay pure, and make your footing sure.

REMEMBER

Satan has cleverly designed your fall, but you can turn the tables on him by having your feet planted securely in God's Word and the power of His Spirit.

Your Connection With God

Read

For there is one mediator between God and men, the man Christ Jesus, who gave himself as a ransom for all men — the testimony given in its proper time. — 1 Timothy 2:5.

Reflect

In the days of ancient patriarchs there lived a man named Job. If you are familiar with Job, you know he was a very wealthy, righteous man. And you know that through a rapid series of disasters, Job lost his wealth, his children, his possessions, and even his health. Then to top that off, he had three friends who came to "comfort" him. But instead of comforting Job, they spent most of their time accusing him of things he never did. One of Job's so-called friends, Bildad, said his sufferings were a result of God's judgment for sin in his life. So he counseled Job to confess his sins to be forgiven and restored to health. Notice part of Job's reply:

> "How can a man be in the right before God?...For He is not a man as I am that I may answer Him, that we may go to court together. There is no umpire between us, who may lay his hand upon us both" (Job 9:2, 32-33 NASB).

Job was sorrowful that there was no umpire or mediator to represent him before a holy God. A mediator is one who bridges the gap between two opposing parties. And Jesus is that mediator for you.

Respond

Do you ever feel like Job at times? You know, surrounded by opposing forces and circumstances to the point that it seems God is nowhere to be found? If you have received Jesus as your personal Lord and Savior, you have a great advantage over Job — you have a connection with God through the mediator of His Son. When the Father looks at you, He sees Jesus, the One who justified and forgave you when He hung on the cross. So spend some time with God praising Him and thanking Him for His forgiveness today. Then let Him speak to your troubled areas of life, because Jesus will always encourage you. He will never condemn you.

Remember

You have the best attorney in eternity representing you to God the Father, His Son Jesus. Rejoice in that today.

RELATIONSHIPS

READ

Bear with each other and forgive whatever grievances you may have against one another. Forgive as the Lord forgave you. And over all these virtues put on love, which binds them all together in perfect unity. — COLOSSIANS 3:13-14.

REFLECT

As a young minister in one of my first church settings I was just learning how to relate with church people. You know they can be difficult. There was this one older lady who taught me a lot...about me. It got to the point I was finding myself avoiding her. She was the worst. She smothered me. She never just had one thing to say to me, she had a hundred and one. Yet she was probably the most helpful and biggest supporter I had while I was in the ministry at that church.

In many cases what causes us the most joy in life, causes us the most pain. What am I referring to? Relationships. The Church, the body of Christ, is full of potential conflicts. Because the Church is filled with people who have been delivered from the eternal penalty of sin but are still dealing with the practice of sin, relationships can become strained. People can get hurt and fellowship can become difficult. So how are we to respond? We are to serve one another in humility. We are to care for each other and encourage one another to higher levels of love and obedience.

RESPOND

Perhaps from your perspective the Church may not be functioning properly today. You may be right. But let me remind you that even though it may be messed up in the way it handles some things, even though some of its members are not forgiving, even though some are sitting instead of serving, the Church is still the heartthrob of the bridegroom, Jesus Christ. Just as a bridegroom loves his bride and would die for her, so Jesus Christ still loves the Church — and He did die for her. Submit to Him today, for you are a part of His beautiful bride — the Church.

REMEMBER

Relationships are a big deal to God. Make them a big deal in your life today.

Be Comforted

Read

Your rod and staff, they comfort me. — Psalm 23:4.

Reflect

Probably no one is more caring than a shepherd. The shepherd in the Middle East carried two important pieces of equipment — the rod and the staff. The rod was used as a weapon, many times to ward off intruders who could harm the sheep, and also for discipline. When a sheep wandered off or got close to poisonous weeds, the shepherd used the rod to bring the sheep back to the flock. The rod served much the same purpose for the shepherd as the Word of God does for the Christian.

The second instrument the shepherd carried was the staff, a long, slender stick with a hook on the end of it. The shepherd used the staff to guide the sheep in the direction he wanted them to go. He did not use the staff to beat the sheep, but he laid it on the side of the sheep and applied just enough pressure to persuade the sheep to go in that direction. He also used the hook at the end of the staff to reach out and draw a sheep close to him for intimate examination. The Holy Spirit has much of the same function in guiding us in the direction of His will. He reaches out and nudges us in the direction He wants us to go.

Respond

Thank and praise God for the protection and comfort He provides you as He guides you to do His will. Thank Him for His Word and His Spirit. Ask God to help you recognize the times you do not follow Him and to forgive you for those times. Now pray for Him to help those you know who need the Comforter. Thank Him for sending the Holy Spirit to protect them and minister to them.

Remember

We're all just sheep who need the guidance of the heavenly Shepherd.

Nothing Gets Past Him

Read

To the angel of the church in Thyatira write...I know your deeds, your love and faith, your service and perseverance, and that you are now doing more than you did at first...Nevertheless...you tolerate that woman Jezebel. — REVELATION 2:18-20.

Reflect

Tolerance is a catch word today that can mean a lot of things. But to Jesus, when talking to the church at Thyatira, it meant "You're in trouble." Why? Because the church tolerated idolatry. An idol is anything that takes your heart from God.

The church at Thyatira was service-oriented and probably helped a lot of people. But it had allowed the world's system into the church through a woman. Jesus refers to her as Jezebel, a reference to the queen who promoted idolatry in the Old Testament. This woman claimed to speak for God and encouraged the believers to continue worshipping idols. Even after given the opportunity to repent, she willingly clung to her sin. Therefore, Jesus pronounced that judgment would fall on her, her family, and those who followed her. But those who stayed faithful and did not follow her would be rewarded. (See Revelation 2:18-29.)

Jesus is introduced in this passage of Scripture as the Son of God whose eyes are "like blazing fire," which means He does not tolerate immoral behavior. He looks at immorality with burning indignation and purifying judgment. The point is, nothing gets past God. Someone may think they're getting by with immoral thoughts or acts because they haven't been caught yet, but they're already caught. He sees, He knows, and their fall will happen if they don't repent. Like Thyatira, they may look good on the outside with all the good deeds they do, but they're like a broken clock — only right twice a day, and the rest of the time misleading!

Respond

As you spend time alone with God today, praise and thank Him for His patience with you, and ask Him to reveal any area that you need to set straight with Him. Pray for people you know who are caught in sin but don't know it. Ask God to reveal Himself to them so they may repent.

Remember

Don't tolerate sin in your life today.

SHARPEN YOURSELF

READ

Iron sharpens iron, so one man sharpens another. — PROVERBS 27:17 NASB.

REFLECT

I had a friend who was detailed, he dotted his "i's" and crossed his "t's." But I was the big picture, "spare me the details" guy. He was mostly all business; I was mostly all fun. He was totally focused; I was scatterbrained. He searched for ideas; I searched for one -liners. He loved to meet; I hated meetings. He was result-oriented; I was relationship-oriented. He drove me nuts; I drove him nuts. And our relationship was one of the most beneficial relationships I've ever had. Despite our differences, we were united by the same goal — to see people come to Jesus and let Him direct their lives.

Guess what happened over the years? I became more detailed and he became more fun. He actually got to the point that he could tell a joke without messing up the punch line. And I actually learned how to prioritize a "to do" list. But we would not have rubbed off on each other so much if we had not been committed to the same goals.

When you have a close friend, you can sharpen each other's mind and spiritual life. Sometimes this is painful, but the tremendous dynamic in this type of relationship is that you have a friend who knows you and still loves and accepts you. There's nothing quite like knowing you can open your heart and not be betrayed.

The eternal truth is that Jesus is the best friend you can ever have. He will not betray you or disappoint you. He wants to sharpen you so you can become all God wants you to be. The challenge is, you need to let Him rub off on you. And it is important to remember that friends make the biggest impact when they are close and consistent. So let your contact with Jesus be close and consistent.

RESPOND

If you don't have an "iron sharpening iron" friend, pray for God to send you one. It will be one of the most precious relationships you will know. In the meantime, let Jesus sharpen you.

REMEMBER

If you're friends aren't sharp, you'll become dull.

Worship in God's Word

Read

"Ezra opened the book...the people all stood up. Ezra praised the Lord, the great God; and all the people lifted their hands and responded, "Amen! Amen!" Then they bowed down and worshiped the Lord with their faces to the ground." — Nehemiah 8:5-6.

Reflect

Have you ever been to a worship service where all the people stood when God's Word was read? This scripture is the basis of that demonstration of worship. When Ezra read God's Word, the people showed respect by standing, and they stood for hours listening to His Word. They listened intently with the expectation that they were about to hear from God Almighty. This is the attitude and mindset we are to have as we open God's Word. We are to show respect and honor and expect to hear something vital for our lives.

When Ezra opened Gods' Word, the people knew they would hear the Word of God and not merely some man's ideas. They treated Gods' Word differently than man's words. These people were hungry for a word from God and they were willing to block out half a day to hear God speak to them. This resulted in worship. Praise broke out and people humbled themselves before God. They were not worshipping the book that was being read, they were worshipping the God who was speaking to them through the book.

When I have taken have a day to spend in God's Word, I always come home loving my wife and children more, and I'm more sensitive to them. I enjoy them more than ever. After I've spent an extended period of time with God, I better understand Jeremiah 29:13, when God said, "You will...find me when you seek me with all your heart." In other words, "If you are willing to block out the time and seek Me, I will be there to reveal Myself to you."

Respond

When was the last time you were so hungry for Gods' Word that you prioritized half a day to spend reading, studying, and expecting Him to speak to you? Spend some time in His Word and let Him guide you in your activities today.

Remember

Never forget that the Bible is God Himself speaking directly to your heart.

Daily Conversion

Read

And they entered into the covenant to seek the Lord God of their fathers with all their heart and soul. — 2 CHRONICLES 15:12 NASB.

Reflect

In our verse today, King Asa had the people enter into a "covenant to seek the Lord." Essentially, it was a national time of prayer, which called for serious measures and resulted in a time of peace and prosperity for the people of Judah. (See 2 Chronicles 15:15-18.)

Have you ever started praying, and before long your mind was ten thousand miles away? Or worse yet, you fell asleep? Aren't you glad God is patient with us? Oftentimes when we pray, we are like children who bug their parent for stuff at the grocery checkout line — and ten minutes later they have forgotten what they were asking for! To be serious about prayer is to be converted, which means to turn our wills entirely over to the will of God. He wants us to get up every day and experience conversion. He wants us to seek Him in prayer and submit to His desires so He can bless us and use us powerfully.

E.M. Bounds says, "God's acquaintance is not made hurriedly. He does not bestow His gifts on the casual or hasty comer and goer. To be much alone with God is the secret of knowing Him and of influence with Him." He points out that if you want to have an intimate relationship with God, you will not rush through prayer — too much depends on it. That's why it might be good for us to enter into a covenant with God to seek Him above all treasures. For when we are converted and make Him our daily treasure, we accomplish more than we know — namely, becoming more like Him.

Respond

Make an appointment with God so you can spend some time just seeking Him and His will for your life. Allow Him to convert your ungodly thoughts to righteous thoughts. Then upon conversion, go out in the power of the Holy Spirit and find someone else for Him to convert.

Remember

Praying for what God already wants is the first step in being converted to His way of thinking.

Light Exposes Sin

Read

"Woe to me!" I cried. "I am ruined! For I am a man of unclean lips, and live among a people of unclean lips, and my eyes have seen the King, the Lord Almighty." — Isaiah 6:5.

Reflect

When Isaiah saw the Lord like he had never seen Him before, something very interesting happened — he saw his sin. When you see God for who He is, seeing yourself for who you are becomes a glaring reality. When Isaiah saw how pure and holy God was, he immediately realized how impure and unholy he was. He saw his sin like never before, that he was a "man of unclean lips." Perhaps he had been dishonest and told lies. Perhaps he had been critical and sarcastic, tearing others down. Perhaps he cussed like a sailor. We don't know the specifics, but we do know there are many ways our mouth can hurt our relationship with God.

It wasn't just his unclean lips that hurt Isaiah's relationship with God. He had another problem. He hung out with people who were just like him. Did Isaiah influence them or did they influence him? We don't know for sure, but he was hanging out with those who were hurting his relationship with God.

When Isaiah saw his sin, God willingly cleansed him. To have fellowship with God, we must be right with Him. That's why it is so important to stay free of sin. We need to be like the psalmist and ask God to search us and see if there is any unclean way in us, so we can be cleansed and commit ourselves to a faithful relationship with Him. (See Psalm 139:23-24).

Respond

What do people closest to you say about your relationship with God? Do you hang around people who help you love God more? Take a close look at yourself. Let the light of God's truth shine into your life and reveal the things that hinder your walk with God. Then ask Him to forgive and cleanse you from all unrighteousness so that you can have sweet fellowship with Him today.

Remember

Guard your fellowship with the Father today and don't let any impure word escape your lips.

The Assignment

Read

Then I heard the voice of the Lord saying, "Whom shall I send. And who will go for us?" And I said, "Here am I. Send me!" — Isaiah 6:8.

Reflect

God desires to use *us* to accomplish the work of His kingdom. After He cleansed and forgave Isaiah of his sin, He asked him two questions, "Whom shall I send? And who will go for us?" Isaiah willingly volunteered for whatever God desired. In simple terms: God's assignment for Isaiah was to go and teach people everywhere about His ways, but to realize that when he preached and taught, no one would listen to him.

Isaiah asked the obvious question, "How long do I have to do this?" God's answer was, "As long as there are people to hear it." This response tells us how much God loves us. Even though there are times people are unwilling to listen to Him, He still pursues them with love.

Isaiah took God's challenge personally. He did not say, "Here am I, send my money." He said, "Send me." Our culture has been in a state of spiritual decline much like that of Isaiah's culture. But God is still calling, "Whom shall I send?" How will you respond? Can you willingly say to God, "I'll go where You want me to go and do what You want me to do?"

Respond

When you have a fresh encounter with God, you will want to serve Him like never before. You will be so grateful for His blessing and forgiveness in your life that service to Him will be a natural response. Take some time today to praise and thank God for His plan to reach the world. Ask Him to forgive you for the times you have not reached out to others the way you should have. Ask Him to help you witness to those God has allowed you to come in contact with each day. Ask Him to make you a clean vessel and use you to touch the lives of others today.

Remember

Regardless of your assignment today, the joy is in accomplishing it with God.

SUPPORTING YOUR FAMILY

READ

"From Him the whole body, joined and held together by every supporting ligament, grows and builds itself up in love, as each part does its work." — EPHESIANS 4:16.

REFLECT

One of the most traumatic times in my life struck during the first few weeks of my freshman year in high school. The upperclassmen were on a mission to publicly embarrass the new students. When an upperclassman came up to a freshman and said, "Button," the freshman had to bow down to him and say something to the effect, "I'm a green, green freshman, and you're a great, great sophomore (or junior or senior)." This rite usually took place in front of some freshman girls.

One day I looked down the hall and saw this entourage of heavyweights coming my way. I was trapped! But I had made up my "Arnold Schwarzenegger" mind (though it was in a "Steve Urkle" body) that I would not bow down to those heathens. They grabbed me and I felt pain. They pressured me and I felt tears. They yelled and I screamed. And then something took place that every freshman dreams of. My big brother grabbed the ring leader, threw him against the lockers, and said, "Don't ever touch my little brother again." From that day on I walked the halls like a rooster who ruled the barnyard. And I'll never forget what the bully said to my brother: "Oh, I'm sorry, Kent. I didn't know he was your brother."

RESPOND

Today's world is full of bullies, and the church family must take a stand. The world belches out threats and wants to embarrass the Church without realizing who our big brother is — Jesus. Take time right now to thank and praise God for His constant support of your life and your church. We as believers in the family need to be supportive of each other. Pray that God will give you an opportunity to support your brothers and sisters in Christ who need it this week.

REMEMBER

You have a big brother in Jesus who rescues you from the intimidation of the evil one.

BE PATIENT!

READ

It is better to be patient than powerful, it is better to win control over yourself than over whole cities. — PROVERBS 16:32 GNB.

REFLECT

I think God gives us kids to help us grow up. One of the things I've learned as a parent is that people, in general, are impatient. My kids have a difficult time understanding the word no. In fact, no doesn't mean no. It means "more negotiation is needed." Or, "Perhaps you didn't understand the urgency of my requests." And adults can be just as impatient.

When I'm impatient, all I'm concerned about are my needs, my desires, my rights, my wants, my goals, my schedule...and how everyone around me is messing up my life! It is very difficult to see clearly when my eyes are focused on me. And it is then that I need to grow up.

God often equates patience with maturity in the Scriptures. When we are impatient with others our spiritual immaturity — a lack of faith and trust in God — shows. If you trust God for every detail of your life, when you're stuck in a traffic jam and late for an important date, you will have peace. You know your heavenly Father will make all things work for your good. Waiting becomes another opportunity to lean on Him and seek His face for further direction.

RESPOND

How are you at waiting? Do people have to respond to your every whim at the snap of your fingers, or is your trust in God giving you patience and understanding? Thank God for His patience to see you mature. Ask Him to forgive you for the times you've acted impatiently with Him and others. Remember, God often sends people or circumstances into our lives that require us to practice patience! But don't worry, because, He will never put more on you than you can handle. And in the end, you will be more mature than before.

REMEMBER

Be patient with others today. It is one of the greatest witnesses to God's love working in your life.

Growing Stronger in Crisis

Read

When David and his men came to Ziklag, they found it destroyed by fire and their wives and sons and daughters taken captive. ...Moreover David was greatly distressed because the people spoke of stoning him, for all the people were embittered, each one because of his sons and daughters. But David strengthened himself in the Lord his God. — 1 Samuel 30:3,6.

Reflect

Imagine that you've had a very productive day, finished several projects successfully, and you're feeling pretty good about yourself. But when you get home, you find your home burned to the ground, all your possessions gone, and your family either killed or kidnapped. That would make everything you accomplished seem as nothing, wouldn't it?

That is exactly what happened to David and his men in today's verse. Notice the response of David's men: They were "embittered." Often that is what takes place when we go through a crisis. The storms that come into our lives drain our energies. Raging winds of resistance and the floods of negative news can capsize us if we don't anchor our lives in Jesus. The storms of life either make us bitter or better. The choice is up to us.

Has anyone ever been bitter toward you? David certainly experienced that. His men even considered stoning him. But David "strengthened himself in the Lord." He went immediately to God for comfort and direction. In the end, because he had God's wisdom and strength, David was able to lead these men to reclaim everything they had lost.

Respond

How can you get strength and encouragement from the Lord before, during, and after a crisis? From His Word and by listening to the Holy Spirit. Start your time of prayer today by praising and thanking God for the way He has blessed you. Confess any times you can think of when you became bitter in stormy times. Now, ask God to give you strength and wisdom from His Word to enable you to remain strong through any difficulty that comes your way today.

Remember

If you're going through a storm, hold on to your anchor, Jesus, then look for the rainbow!

Following the Right Plan

Read

"Therefore everyone who hears these words of Mine, and acts upon them, may be compared to a wise man, who built his house upon the rock." — Matthew 7:24 NASB.

Reflect

In today's verse Jesus refers to a builder who was described as wise because he not only heard the words of Jesus, but he also acted upon them. If you read further in this passage, you read about another man Jesus described as foolish because he heard the words of the Master architect but built his house (life) on the unstable sand of his own plans. The message is simple: we all build our lives according to some plan — and when we ignore His plan, our houses (lives) ultimately fall.

One of the tragic things for many Christians is that they set goals to achieve but they aren't Jesus' goals. Many go the wrong way because they have never consulted Him about the direction for their lives. Others actually do consult Him, but when they aren't satisfied with His plan, they go their own way instead. Both methods have the same result. Building on the unstable sand of their own thinking invites Satan's storms of destruction, and they never accomplish what Jesus had in mind for them.

Respond

Are you confident that you are building your life according to the rock-solid plan God has for you? Or have you gone your own way, asking Him to bless you? Do you consult God about the doors that are opening in your life? This process of following His plan is sometimes long, but it never fails. It takes wisdom and discernment. But if your commitment is to follow God's plan for your life, He will never leave you in the dark about it. Praise God now that He has a specific plan for your life. Ask Him to purify you so you may be able to follow His plan precisely. Ask Him to prepare those around you for the direction He is leading you. Now pray for courage to follow His plan.

Remember

God has a plan for your life that will bring prosperity and success to every area — so follow it today.

Healing the Wound

Read

"In Him we have...the forgiveness of our trespasses, according to the riches of His grace." — Ephesians 1:7 NASB.

Reflect

I have three scars on my left arm, and I can tell you every detail of how they got there. It was July 4, 1970. I was jumping over a woven wire fence pretending to be an Olympic hurdler, and I fell. I landed on a broken bottle and cut my left arm wide open. Well, before I knew it, Dr. Hanson was sewing me up with sixteen stitches. There are more details, but I'll spare you.

The point I want to make is that if you hit those scars today, my arm doesn't hurt. Why? Because I took care of it. The lacerations were sewed up, and the skin on my arm healed. The same is true of emotional scars from when you've been wronged. When you forgive immediately, there will still be a period of time when you will remember the hurt and feel the pain. But as you let the Holy Spirit and time do some healing, one day it won't hurt anymore. You'll look back and remember, but it won't hurt.

You may have been wronged, but you need to forgive or it will eat away at you until it affects you physically. To understand Jesus Christ's forgiveness personally, we must try to understand that His love is a love that won't let go. Regardless of what we have been or done, His love will never turn loose of us. (See John 10:28.) The love of God is a liberating love, healing and cleansing us continually if we let Him.

Respond

If you live under the pressure of old failures, they can cause you to think that you're still a failure. So spend some time reading Psalm 103:10 and thank God for His tremendous forgiveness. Search your heart for any old scars. Is there something there that you thought you had given to Him? A past hurt, offense, or shame? Give them to Jesus to sew up with His forgiving love. Forgive any offenders. Ask forgiveness for yourself and them. Then allow His unchanging, powerful love to help you heal.

Remember

The hurt of being wronged doesn't last if you forgive.

Praying Specifically

Read

They were all trying to frighten us, thinking, "Their hands will get too weak for the work, and it will not be completed." But I prayed, "Now strengthen my hands." — Nehemiah 6:9.

Reflect

My wife likes to tell the story of when she was a teenager, she told her mom there was nobody she was interested in dating because none were her type. She thought she might never get married. So her mom told her to pray specifically for her husband, and Rhonda made a list. As she prayed, the list changed and God refined her requests. Her prayer requests included: He had to be Christian, someone with a sense of humor, blue eyes, and blond hair. And guess what? God answered her prayers. I'm a Christian with blue eyes who loves to have fun, and she liked me so much, she dropped the blond hair (my hair is brown).

Praying specifically is very scriptural, because God is a God of details. So we shouldn't hesitate to pray specifically for the needs of others as well as our own. Notice in today's verse how specifically Nehemiah prayed when he faced opposition. He ignored the enemy's threats and sought the One who could strengthen the very part they said was weak: his hands. He knew that if his hands stopped, the work would stop. So he didn't pray for strength in general — Nehemiah prayed specifically for strength in his hands.

Respond

Do you pray general blanket prayers like, "God bless America...and all the missionaries in the world"? Or are your prayers usually specific regarding yourself and others? Some of the greatest prayers in the Bible are detailed prayers just like the one in today's Scripture passage. Praying specifically often indicates how serious you are about your request. Take some time to be alone with God right now and share with Him the detailed needs you have and some specific needs of others you know. Get a pad and paper if you need to.

Remember

God loves to hear your prayers. Share with Him the specifics of what's on your heart.

Discipleship

Read

He said to another man, "Follow me." But the man replied, "Lord, first let me go and bury my father." Jesus said to him, 'Let the dead bury their own dead, but you go and proclaim the kingdom of God." — Luke 9:59-60.

Reflect

"First." That word jumps out in these verses. It means priority. Jesus approached this man and said, "Follow me." So the man replied, "I'll be glad to...but first..." Don't you think this guy had a good excuse? His was a family commitment: to stay around and wait until his father died so he could take care of the burial arrangements. But Jesus said, "Let the dead bury the dead."

What Jesus meant by this was to let the spiritually dead (those who hadn't received His message) bury those who were physically dead. Jesus was telling this young man, "You have heard the message. I know you love your father, but don't expect Me to wait. My agenda is more important than yours. The kingdom of God must be proclaimed, and I've gifted you to do it."

When you ask someone to do something for you, don't you love a reply like this man's? Jesus knew this guy lacked the commitment to follow Him where He was going. It wasn't because the man lacked the ability to make a commitment. He had already shown that he could commit himself to something. But his priorities were messed up. So Jesus' reply was basically, "I refuse to be an addendum to your life."

Respond

Take a close look at your priorities today. Would Jesus be pleased with them? If He walked in your shoes today, would He have the same priorities? Take some time now to praise and thank Him for making you a priority. That's right. The God of all creation has made you His priority. Then let others see that, today, your priority is to follow Him.

Remember

Jesus isn't interested in your agenda — He *is* your agenda.

SUBMISSION

READ

Slaves, submit yourselves to your masters with all respect, not only to those who are good and considerate, but also to those who are harsh. — 1 PETER 2:18.

REFLECT

Ouch! Peter could have gone all day without writing those words. Submission is tough, especially when it's directed toward someone we don't like. Nevertheless, we must accept this verse with all the others. Obviously, Peter was referring to Christian slaves during the days of the early church, but the same is true for Christians today. We must be submissive to those who are over us, whether they are kind or unkind. It is natural behavior for the unbeliever to demand his rights. But the Spirit-controlled believer should be able to defer to God's will and let the Lord fight his battles.

The rules of submission are *still* intact when Christians work for Christians. In fact, even more so. Being employed by another believer doesn't give us the right to laziness or special privileges. So Peter was absolutely right in writing this verse, because God made the rules of submission with our best interest in mind.

Wherever there is insubordination there are problems. It leads to chaos and broken relationships, none of which honors God. And our verse today is God's attempt to protect us from these types of problems in the workplace. Just remember, getting along with the boss is important, but getting along with God is much more important.

RESPOND

You know, it is no surprise to God that you are where you are right now. He knows the authorities you are working for. Perhaps it is a grooming process for you to serve as someone's authority in the future. Are you submitting to the authorities God has placed in your life with your whole heart? Pray about that today. As you submit to God in this area, ask Him to show you how you may submit better to those authorities He has placed over you.

REMEMBER

You honor God when you submit to authority, and He will bless you for it.

DEFEATING TEMPTATION

READ

"No one is greater in this house than I am. My master has withheld nothing from me except you, because you are his wife. How then could I do such a wicked thing and sin against God?" — GENESIS 39:9.

REFLECT

Think for a minute what it would be like to "have it all." You have position, power, wealth, and everyone knows your name. Not only that, but you're good looking, and people listen to what you have to say because you have wisdom. But then comes the rub. You are tempted with something you don't have. It can be yours for the taking, but you know would be a great sin. Worse yet, if you don't go for it, you may be lied about and forced to lose everything you have gained. What would you do?

Notice what Joseph did. Our scripture today concerns his temptation by Potifar's wife to commit adultery. What a dilemma. So what did Joseph do? He resisted the temptation. He could have stayed there and justified his involvement with this married woman. He could have rationalized it and said, "Okay, just this once. I'll never do it again, but she has me trapped." But he didn't. Joseph knew he would never outlive the regret in his heart for one night of passion.

The key to the ability to resist temptation and flee it as Joseph did is found in his statement, "How then could I do such a wicked thing and sin against God?" Joseph may have had it all, but his heart belonged to God — not his power, position, or wealth. When believers have this level of surrender, they have no trouble resisting temptation.

RESPOND

Are you facing some strong temptations in your life today? Have you already given in to them? Have you made your situation worse by justifying your actions to minimize how bad they are? If that is the case, stop right now and give your heart completely and totally to God. Let Him be real to you. Then resist, and you will win.

REMEMBER

When you're tempted, choose to keep your "regrets account" at zero balance and your "integrity account" full.

No "I" in Selfless Love

Read

Do nothing from selfishness or empty conceit, but with humility of mind let each of you regard one another as more important than himself. — PHILIPPIANS 2:3 NASB.

Reflect

He had to have been one of the most selfish people I had ever met. He lived alone with his mother. She gave him everything under the sun, not to mention unending affirmation. He used personal pronouns a lot in conversation. "I" did this. "My" idea is this. This is "mine." How does this affect "me?" He was one of those "really great" guys, and if you didn't believe it, he'd tell you. Then out of the blue his mom died, leaving him alone. And that's when the change came. He saw what she had done for him, and realized that he had done nothing for her...nothing! So he changed. He became like his mom. He became a giver. He started taking time for others and spending time listening to them. He wanted people to look at him and see his mom.

The selfish life-style is an empty life-style. Selfish people don't think they're getting a fair deal. They always want more. And they usually keep their family in continual upheaval. Unselfish people, on the other hand, make life enjoyable for those around them. And as they persist in their giving, they produce the same attitude in others.

The man spoken of in this devotion was moved by his mother's selfless model, but he could just as easily have been moved by Jesus. He is the One from whom His children appropriate selflessness. His sacrificial life serves as an example of how you and I can live, if we only give Him our will.

Respond

What motivates you? The selfish needs of your personal welfare, or the needs of others? Maybe this man's mother was selfless toward him, but selfish toward others. That's why Jesus' completely selfless life is our role model. Pray about how you can serve another today. Ask God to forgive you and use you in service to others. Even if you don't feel like it, ask Him to help you submit. When you do, He will bless you more than you could ever imagine.

Remember

Unselfish people rarely use the word, "I."

No "Lite" Commitment

Read

And to know this love that surpasses knowledge — that you may be filled to the measure of all the fullness of God. — Ephesians 3:19.

Reflect

Several years ago a cartoon in a periodical caught my attention. The picture was of a church building with a marquee in front that said, "The Lite Church; 24 percent pure commitment; home of the 7.5 percent tithe; 15-minute sermons; and 45-minute worship services. We have 8 commandments (your choice). We use 3 spiritual laws and believe in an 800-year millennium. Everything you've wanted in a church and less." The sad thing about that cartoon is "The Lite Church" appeals to many believers today.

God wants us to experience His fullness which is found when we worship Him in spirit and truth together. We sing praises to Him and listen to His Word to know Him better. So attending worship services is not the issue. The question, is what or who we worship. When Jesus said, "Pick up your cross and follow Me," He didn't mean over to the local cafeteria after an "entertaining" service. No, He must be the focus of our services, whatever form they take.

Worshipping God in spirit and in truth requires a 100 percent commitment, whether you spend forty-five minutes or three and a half hours. He wants to reveal Himself to us so we can know His "love that surpasses knowledge" for ourselves, then go out and express His love to others. The church is the filling station. We get fueled up in love, wisdom, and power, then go out and be Jesus to a dying world.

Respond

Are you truly seeking to know this love that surpasses knowledge — that you may be filled to the measure of all the fullness of God? Spend some time alone with Him right now to worship Him. Allow Him to fill your heart and mind with insight about your life. Pray that God will enable you to always seek Him in a spirit of truth with all your heart.

Remember

Jesus is no church lightweight, so don't give Him a "lite" commitment.

A Revelation of You

Read

Even though I walk through the valley of the shadow of death, I will fear no evil for you are with me. — Psalm 23:4.

Reflect

What do you get when you squeeze an orange? Watch out, it's a trick question. You get out of it what is in it. What comes out of a Christian when they are squeezed? What's in them. Hopefully, what will emerge will be the fruit of the Spirit found in Galatians 5:22.

For the believer who is walking closely with God, there are two sides to going through anything in life. One is the comfort side, which is just knowing that God is with us. The second side is the revelation side. We cannot go anywhere with God without Him teaching us something, and our ears are listening their hardest when we are walking through the valleys of life!

God always wants to reveal His will to you, but sometimes He must first reveal *you* to you. A crisis has a way of making the real you come out. When you are squeezed and the pressure is on, you tend to drop your guard and what is really inside will come out. God shows you to yourself in the light of His Word. When you look into the mirror of God's Word, you see yourself as you are and can pray for cleansing and restoration. Once you are clean, you become a powerful vessel for His use.

Respond

Take a few minutes right now to praise and thank God for His constant presence and concern about your life. Ask Him to reveal to you — you — and to show you how to accomplish His will in your life. Finally, pray for those you know who are going through crises and need God's help. Ask God to reveal His presence and care to them.

Remember

When you get squeezed it is God's way of revealing *you* to you, so you can be cleansed by Him and then powerfully used by Him.

See Jesus As He Is

Read

I turned to see the voice that was speaking to me...and among the lampstands was someone "like a son of man," dressed in a robe reaching down to his feet and with a golden sash around his chest. His head and hair were white like wool, as white as snow and his eyes were like blazing fire. His feet were like bronze glowing in a furnace, and his voice was like the sound of rushing waters. — Revelation 1:12-15.

Reflect

John's description of Jesus in this passage of Scripture is very significant. First, we can tell John had never seen Jesus like this before. Even when He saw Him with Moses and Elijah on the Mount of Transfiguration (Matthew 17), He was not described like this or in this detail. Therefore, this was a tremendous spiritual experience. Spiritual experiences often happen when you see the Lord in a way you have never seen Him before. For John, this was incredible.

Notice how John described Jesus. His robe and sash tell of His royalty as the King of kings and Lord of lords. His hair was white, which speaks of His wisdom and purity. His eyes were like blazing fire, which represents His fiery holiness. His feet were like bronze, which represents His earthly suffering and judgment. And His voice, the voice John had heard years before, was like the rushing of waters, full of authority. Verse 16 says there was a double-edged sword in His mouth, which represents the living Word of God.

The vision that John saw in Revelation was nothing like the gentle carpenter's son he followed for three years. This was the risen, glorified Priest-King who has authority to rule over all today. Yes, this is how Jesus looks right now.

Respond

Is Jesus welcome in your daily schedule, or do you want to hide Him and just bring Him out on Sunday? Life-changing experiences begin when you start seeing Him like you've never seen Him before — as He really is! Look at Him today — you will never be the same!

Remember

Keep a living portrait of Jesus as John saw Him in your heart today and observe how it changes your perspective on things.

Appreciation as a Habit

Read

In everything give thanks; for this is God's will for you in Christ Jesus. — 1 Thessalonians 5:18 NASB.

Reflect

Nothing in the world is quite like a family. As I look back on the best days of my life, I see they were so good because of family. When God made the family, He put together a plan that would fill physical, social, mental, and spiritual needs. Obviously, only He can fill those needs, but He chooses to do it through the family. You may search other places to fill those needs, but when the family functions properly, you won't find love and care like that of the family.

On the surface, what Paul wrote in this verse about giving thanks seems like an impossible task. How can you give thanks in every situation? There must be a way, because the Bible says that giving thanks is God's will, and He would not command us to do something that was beyond our reach. Even when family situations are tense and tears of pain fall, we can thank God that He cares for our families. Even when evil strikes and we are under vicious attack, we can thank God that we have the power and wisdom to overcome and obtain victory through the blood and the name of Jesus.

Respond

What about your everyday life? Paul said that we are to give thanks for everything. So take time to express thanks first for your salvation and freedom in Jesus Christ. Then, even if you are single and you don't have a family close by, you can still give thanks for them. Thank God for the way He protects you and provides for you through your work. But then, as you go about your day today, be alert to thank your heavenly Father for all the little things He does to make your day go more smoothly.

Remember

When you have a heart of thanksgiving every moment of the day, it is hard for the cares of this world to get you down.

Expressions of Thanks

Read

This service that you perform is not only supplying the needs of God's people but is also overflowing in many expressions of thanks to God. — 2 Corinthians 9:12.

Reflect

I remember watching the offering plates being passed in the small church our family attended when I was growing up. I had no real concept of where that money went. I just accepted the fact that it went to God because I trusted those who collected it and those who gave. The church had earned my trust largely because it had earned the trust of my parents. So, understandably, I came to believe that it was a good idea to give. I also remember watching the offering tote board every Sunday to see the totals of offerings given. Because we were a small church and my dad was a tither, you could tell by the tote board if dad had sold any hogs or cattle the week before.

Respond

Along with learning how to give as a child, I also learned that you can't out give God. When Dad gave; God gave back. In today's verse, Paul was encouraging the Cortinthians to give, not only to supply the needs of God's people, but to be an expression of thanks to God. That's what offerings are: expressions of thanks to God. I like Max Lucado's comparison with writing a check that remind us of the things for which we have to be grateful when we give to God. Consider these components:

1. The Date: This reminds you that God is eternal and He has given you some time to honor Him.
2. The "Pay to the Order of" line: If you were honest, you would make it out to GOD. But instead you write it to the church that has gained your trust.
3. The Amount: A reminder that God owns it all anyway.
4. The Memo Line: If you're making it out to God, you can honestly say it's for you, because you're the one who benefits when you give.

Remember

When you give it frees you from the entanglements that tie you to this world and serves as an expression of love to God.

Giving Thanks

Read

The rest of mankind that were not killed by theses plagues still did not repent of the work of their hands; they did not stop worshiping demons, and idols of gold, silver, bronze, stone and wood idols that cannot see or hear or walk. — Revelation 9:20.

Reflect

A police officer stopped a young man in a new sports car one morning. The driver of the sports car said, "Officer, I'm in a hurry." The officer shot back, "Be quiet." The young man said, "But sir, if you'll just listen, I can save you a lot of trouble." Smiling, the officer responded, "Really. Well, maybe I'll let you think about that in jail." Several hours later the officer looked in on his prisoner and said, "Lucky for you that the police chief's daughter's wedding is today. He'll be in a good mood when he gets back." After a moment: "Don't count on it officer," the young man replied, "I'm the groom."

Some people just won't listen. Tragically, that will be true at the end of the age as well. With all the preaching and teaching, people will still be stubborn and choose hell over heaven. Can you imagine the hardness of heart that will be displayed by unbelievers in the Tribulation? Despite the warnings and sufferings, they will refuse to give their lives to Jesus.

How do you avoid hardening your heart? By taking time to give thanks. The great commentator, Matthew Henry, was once robbed on his way home one night. That night he wrote in his diary, "Lord, I thank you that I have not been robbed before. I thank you that even though they took my all, it was not much. I thank you that even though they took my purse, they did not take my life. I thank you that it was I who was robbed and not I who robbed."

Respond

Being thankful to God softens your heart so that He can speak to you, change you, and lead you into more blessing. Thank God for your daily joys and the grace He gives to you to overcome any circumstance you face.

Remember

Be thankful for every blessing you encounter today.

Time to Remember

Read

Write, therefore, what you have seen, what is now and what will take place later. — Revelation 1:19.

Reflect

June 14th is a special day in the Hufty family. So is December 19th. On those days our children, Zachary and Mackenzie (Zac and Mac) surrendered the rest of their lives to Jesus. So on those days we celebrate. There isn't a June 14th that goes by that Zac doesn't give us a play by play description of where he was, how he felt, and what he prayed. Mackenzie gives her story every December 19. Why do we do that? To remember.

There is power in remembering, especially when you remember who God is and what He has done. Over and over again in the Old Testament God instructed His servants not to forget Him. He told them to tell their children stories of all He had done for them. He instructed them to build altars of remembrance and to celebrate holidays to remember Him, much like we celebrate the 4th of July to remember His goodness to our country.

We are not to remember just for remembering sake, but to renew our love for God. Why do you think Jesus wanted John to write everything down? Was it that centuries later people could argue about what it meant? I don't think so. In keeping with the theme of the Bible from the start, Jesus was leaving this final message with His most faithful servant so that generations to come would remember Him.

Respond

Do you take time to remember God's goodness and celebrate His working in your life? Take a moment to praise and thank Him for His love and compassion and the blessings He has brought you. Renew your love for Him and ask Him to lead you to share all He's done for you with others today.

Remember

God has done great and mighty things for you. Remember Him today.

THE GOD OF TODAY

READ

He did this so that all the peoples of the earth might know that the hand of the Lord is powerful and so that you might always fear the Lord your God. — JOSHUA 4:24.

REFLECT

The lessons we heard in Sunday School as children help us remember who God is and what He is capable of doing. They remind us that if God can make giants fall at the hands of children; make city walls fall at the sound of trumpets; make hungry lions find praying Christians inedible; make a fiery inferno seem like an air conditioner to those who take a stand for Him; and even make donkeys talk; then He can handle the problems we face if we just trust Him. But sometimes we forget that the God of the past is still God today.

God didn't have the twelve stones put on the riverbank the day Israel crossed over the Jordan River just for Joshua and the nation to see. He put them there for future generations. God knew Joshua's generation would have children and that they would have grandchildren and great-grandchildren who would come to Gilgal. He knew they would walk along the banks of the Jordan River, notice the stones, and ask, "That's interesting, how many stones are there?" The elder would reply, "Twelve, one for each tribe of Israel." Then the youngest would ask, "Why?" And the elder would patiently explain, "So you would never forget the miracle that happened here."

RESPOND

You don't have to see stones piled up on a riverbank to worship God and give thanks. Neither do you have to wait until the weekend to have an intimate time with Him. He is at work every day in your life. But it is up to you to stop, take notice, and thank Him for His blessing on your life. Make your life a memorial to Him today by proclaiming His goodness to all those you meet.

REMEMBER

Remember all the wonderful things God is to you and thank Him for being your strength today.

Regular Times of Renewal

Read

When the Lord your God brings you into the land he swore to your fathers...a land with large, flourishing cities you did not build, houses filled with all kinds of good things you did not provide, wells you did not dig, and vineyards and olive groves you did not plant—then when you eat and are satisfied, be careful that you do not forget the Lord, who brought you out of Egypt, out of the land of slavery. — Deuteronomy 6:10-12.

Reflect

When I was a kid, my family would celebrate what we called "Hufty Holidays." These were days we set aside for the family to get away from the hustle and bustle of life and just enjoy each other. I'm happy to say that my family has continued that tradition today. In fact, the phrase "Hufty Holidays" is one of the favorite sayings around our house. The challenge is that my kids want to celebrate "Hufty Holidays" often, especially on regular school days!

Holidays are holy days. They are days we stop and remember what is important. One of the reasons for holidays is that God doesn't want us to get 365 days away from remembering who He is and what He has done. He wants us to have regular times of renewal because we need them. He knows that if we don't set aside time to remember Him and give thanks, we will fall into the trap of the world's selfish and ungrateful mindset.

How do you think you can avoid forgetting God in your daily life? Let me make a couple of suggestions. First, make a big deal about salvation. Try to remember the day you became a Christian and celebrate it as your spiritual birthday. If you can't remember the exact date, choose a day during that time of the year and make it a celebration. Secondly, share with others all God has done in your life. Recall the events and prayers that were involved.

Respond

Taking time to remember what God has done and giving thanks is important, because it gives you a heart of gratitude.

Remember

Stop ignoring God and start adoring Him — giving thanks for all He does for you during the day.

Thankful for What Is

Read

Be anxious for nothing, but in everything by prayer and supplication with thanksgiving let your requests be made known to God. And the peace of God, which surpasses all comprehension, shall guard your hearts and your minds in Christ Jesus. — PHILIPPIANS 4:6-7 NASB.

Reflect

My grandmother saw a lot of stress in her life! She outlived a husband and two of her children. She saw two world wars, the Korean conflict, the Vietnam war, the war in the Persian Gulf, and lived at home by herself until her death at the age of 99. A couple of years before her death I asked her, "What was the most stressful time you have ever gone through?" Without hesitation she said, "The Great Depression."

At that time my grandmother had five small children at home, and many times they wondered where they would get their next meal. When I asked her how they made it, one of the things she told me about God's provision really stood out. "We always thought of all the things we had for which we were thankful," she told me. What a message for stressful times!

In the midst of all her problems, my grandmother found peace. Where did peace like that come from? Being thankful for what they did have. Her gratitude helped her take her eyes off the difficulties and put them on Jesus, which resulted in inner peace.

Respond

When tension and anxiety rise up, put them down by naming all the ways God has blessed you and thanking Him. Get your eyes off what you don't have and commit to an attitude of gratitude. God's peace will rule in your life, because you have cast your cares upon Him. So make a new commitment today to give thanks for what is, not what isn't. Thank you, Grandma, for your wisdom in God's Word!

Remember

You can always find something to be thankful for, so choose to be thankful today.

The Blessed Hope

Read

The revelation of Jesus Christ, which God gave him to show his servants what must soon take place. He made it known by sending his angel to his servant John, who testifies to everything he saw—that is, the word of God and the testimony of Jesus Christ. — Revelation 1:1-2.

Reflect

When Jesus arrived on the scene in Bethlehem two thousand years ago, many did not notice. They were not looking for the One who could rescue them from the sin of this world. Many did not recognize Him for who He was even during His ministry years, and they rejected Him as a lunatic. But when Jesus returns, there will be no doubt who He is and what He is doing!

In the book of Revelation, Jesus takes center stage. He is the focus of the entire book, just as He is to be the focus of our entire lives. Revelation is the only book in the Bible that promises a blessing to those who read it and take it to heart. As you study this book, you will read about prophecies and symbols that may be difficult to understand. Don't get lost in the symbolism. The symbols stand for a reality that will soon take place — Jesus is coming back!

The return of Jesus to earth is our hope for the future. Just as He came, rose from the dead, and ascended to heaven; He promised to return. The book of Revelation revolves around that return. It is a testimony Jesus gave John, His most faithful servant, to share with us. Isn't it interesting that the only disciple recorded standing at the cross at the time of Jesus' death was the one selected to look into the future and see what would take place when He returned?

Respond

Take time right now to praise and thank God for the hope He gives us in the book of Revelation. Ask Him to forgive you for the times you have not been faithful in your Bible study, and pray for understanding and a new willingness to obey Him like never before. Who knows...He may return before you get finished!

Remember

Jesus is returning, and today could be the day!

Complete Acceptance

Read

Accept one another, then, just as Christ accepted you, in order to bring praise to God. — Romans 15:7.

Reflect

She was new to the youth group. Just moved in from out of state. Didn't know anyone. Didn't smile a lot at first. After the second Bible Study she had attended she came up to me and said, with all the confidence in the world and a smile on her face, "I need to talk to you sometime." I said, "Great, how about right now." She wasn't prepared for that response. Tears swelled up in her eyes and she said, "I don't have any friends. I'm just not fitting in." I smiled and said, "What's your name?" She replied, "Rachel." I said, "Well Rachel, I know some people right now who would love to meet you." I then motioned for some of our most faithful kids to come over. In a matter of minutes the tears were gone, names were exchanged, and plans were made for the next outing. What happened? Acceptance. No stipulations, no conditions, just pure acceptance. It's a beautiful thing to watch when you see unconditional acceptance take place.

One of the deepest longings that we all have is acceptance. We'll go almost anywhere to get it. Is it any wonder why gang participation is at an all time high today? They are made up of young people searching for acceptance. When you feel truly accepted, it makes no difference what you do or say, you know you will still be accepted. That is the atmosphere needed in the Church and our families today. This does not mean that all behavior is accepted. In fact, some unacceptable behavior requires painful correction. But each individual must feel accepted.

Paul said we must accept one another just as Jesus accepted us. It was many years ago that Jesus accepted me. My life has never been the same, and I have never ceased to be grateful. We've gone through some tough times, but I've always felt His security and love because I know I am accepted.

Respond

Spend some time praising God for His acceptance and the price He paid for you.

Remember

Everyone you meet today has a need to feel accepted.

Seeing Him Like Never Before

Read

In the year that King Uzziah died, I saw the Lord seated on a throne, high and exalted, and the train of his robe filled the temple. — Isaiah 6:1.

Reflect

Where were you when you first heard about the assassination of President Kennedy? How about the explosion of the Challenger space shuttle? Do you remember? The truth is, we often mark time by special events, and Isaiah marked time by the death of King Uzziah.

Uzziah was a great king and He was probably a hero of his day. But when he died, Isaiah did not panic. He didn't say, "What is this world coming to?" No, he went to the temple, and while there he saw the Lord like he had never seen Him before.

Isaiah had an encounter with God in the temple that day. Perhaps there were preceding days when he was on fire for God, and there were probably days he was cold. Perhaps on this day he was spiritually neutral, not expecting anything special from his visit to the temple. But as he humbled himself, God revealed Himself to Isaiah like never before. Has that ever happened to you? Have you come to worship, not really expecting anything, and God surprised you with His powerful presence?

Respond

Would you like an encounter with God like Isaiah experienced? Have you put yourself in a position to see Him? The Scripture says that you will find Him when you seek Him with all of your heart. (See Jeremiah 29:13.) So set aside a few moments today to praise and thank Him that He desires to have a fresh encounter with you too. Take time to confess to God the times you have fallen into the rut and routine of spiritual neutrality. Then let the Spirit of God flow through you to impact the lives of others. Pray that not only you would see God like you've never seem Him before, but that others will see Him living through you like they have never seen Him before.

Remember

Humble yourself and seek God with your whole being, then get ready to be amazed.

The Great Test

Read

By faith Abraham, when He was tested, offered up Isaac, and he who had received the promise was offering up his only begotten Son. — Hebrews 11:17 NASB.

Reflect

My sister was home with two sick kids, a three-year-old and a ten-year-old. She called me, and in the course of our conversation said she was really looking forward to going to the dentist. She said, "When you want to get away from the kids so badly that the dentist's chair looks good, you know you've got cabin fever." Nevertheless, she was faithful to care twenty-five hours a days for her beloved children. She was a straight-A mother, no matter the test.

Abraham faced a test I hope you and I never have to face. God wanted ALL of Abraham, so he tested him by telling him to kill the most precious possession he had — his only son. If he was willing to do this, he would prove that God's Word and will were far more important than any possession, even his son. Abraham knew God had given him his son and the promise that God would bless the nations through him. So he trusted God. Abraham followed His instructions. And God provided a ram to take Isaac's place as a sacrifice to God.

Respond

Who knows whether or not if baby Isaac's screaming during the night on occasion drove Abraham to look forward to a dental appointment? But when the time for testing came, he faithfully passed God's test. Why? Because Abraham made the decision to follow God long before Isaac was born. Have you made a decision to follow God's instructions regardless of the situation? In your time with God today praise Him for the fact that He desires to have a relationship with you. Ask Him to forgive the times you've looked forward to going to the dentist (just kidding), and for the times you have failed His tests. Ask Him to strengthen your faith today, so you can past the test.

Remember

God didn't want Isaac, He wanted Abraham's heart — and He wants all of your heart too.

Things That Burn and Things That Don't

Read

If any man builds on this foundation using gold, silver, costly stones, wood, hay or straw, his work will be shown for what it is, because the day will bring it to light. It will be revealed with fire, and the fire will test the quality of each man's work. — 1 CORINTHIANS 3:12-13.

Reflect

Jesus is the foundation of the life of every believer. But the believer is to build on His foundation with works, such as loving others, helping others in need, and witnessing to others about God's love. These compassionate works will be viewed on "the day" as gold, silver, and costly stones. In other words, they won't burn as they pass through the fire of God's purifying judgment; they will last for eternity.

Because God knows us, He can qualify our works as to whether or not they are genuinely for Him. And any works that are carnal, based on materialism, selfishness, and greed, will all burn like wood, hay, and straw on that day. Not only that, the works we do that were good, but not God — our idea and not His idea — will burn as well. God is interested in obedience to His Word and His Spirit.

So many times we have a great idea and never even consider whether it is something God would have us to do. We tell all our friends and get their opinion, and if they think it's a great idea too, off we go to the races — or a dead end street. The whole project might be so good that many come along for the ride, and it even blesses some people. But unless it came from the throne room of God, sadly, it was a distraction from what He really had for us and will burn up on "the day."

Respond

Take some time today to examine why you are serving in the areas you have chosen. Have you chosen them or has God? Ask Him to forgive you for the times you have done "your thing" instead of His will. Determine that from now on, He will run the show! When you do it His way, He calls that gold.

Remember

When we build on God's foundation of truth and love, our works are not in vain.

Don't Do as the Hypocrites Do

Read

So when you give to the needy, do not announce it with trumpets, as the hypocrites do. — Matthew 6:2.

Reflect

Motives are a big deal in the eyes of God. Jesus echoes the same phrase, "don't be like the hypocrites" continually because hypocrites are pretenders. They say and do certain things for outward appearances, when in reality they are something else entirely on the inside. In Jesus' eyes, the hypocrites had one big problem: their motives. Their hearts weren't in their deeds, and their motives were to make themselves look good. They were only skin deep.

The believer God honors, honors God first and takes no credit. The humble followers of Jesus do the things they do to please Him only — without any fanfare or discussion with others. You probably know some hypocrites. You probably haven't called them a hypocrite to their face, but you could identify the actions of a hypocrite easily. They are constantly doing things "for God" to draw attention to themselves.

Have you ever found yourself wanting to take a little glory for work you've done for God from time to time? Maybe you didn't start out that way, but when there was some credit to be taken, you took it. If you have, remember, Jesus said, "Don't do as the hypocrites do." Why? They make God look bad while trying to make themselves look good.

Respond

Take a moment right now to examine the motives of your heart. You don't want to be a hypocrite! Confess to God the times you have acted in such a way. Ask Him for strength to be what He wants you to be, to hear Him and obey Him faithfully and cheerfully, and to be real and authentic as a Christian. Finally, ask Him to help Him look good to those you come in contact with today.

Remember

The skin deep motives of a hypocrite are easy to see, so be genuine in your faith.

Practicing Your Gifts

Read

I praise you because I am fearfully and wonderfully made; your works are wonderful, I know that full well. — Psalm 139:14.

Reflect

In his book, *Twelve Things I Want My Kids To Remember Forever,* Jerry Jenkins tells a story about a former great basketball player by the name of Larry Bird. He asks these questions: Did Larry Bird work on his speed? Did he work on jumping? Did he work on his physique? The answer to all of these questions is, "No." In comparison to other professional basketball players, Larry Bird was slow. He couldn't jump more than a few inches off the ground, and his body looked softer than most of his opponents. Yet, he is a legend.

What do you think Larry Bird worked on the most during his great career? He worked on his shooting. He went to the arena every afternoon before a game and spent hours working on his host of shots. He would see if he could make a hundred shots in a row from all over the court, never stopping to wipe the sweat from his brow. This would wear most players out before a game, but it gave Larry Bird confidence.

Jesus has called everyone of God's children into a life of excellence, which requires dedication and discipline. He wants everyone of us to win His most valuable player award for dedicated service. So what are your gifts? Have you been working on them daily? If you are employed, have you been seeking to be the best worker in your office? If you are an employer, have you been seeking to be the best example of a manager and rewarder? If you are a parent, are you seeking to improve your skills as a loving educator who exemplifies the love of Christ?

Respond

In your prayer time today, make a new commitment to God in the area of your gifts. Ask for His forgiveness for not honing your skills as He would want you to. Then, hit the court!

Remember

You are fearfully and wonderfully made, and practice makes perfect as we give God our gifts.

A Burning Heart

Read

And they said to one another, "Were not our hearts burning within us while He was speaking to us on the road, while He was explaining the Scriptures to us?" — LUKE 24:32 NASB.

Reflect

The Christian life is filled with highs and lows. We all have our mountaintop experiences where we feel close to the Lord. But far too often these mountain top experiences are followed by times in a spiritual valley. This spiritual roller-coaster ride can be very discouraging and frustrating.

To stay out of the valley we must have a burning heart for Jesus. But first of all, we must understand that Christian's hearts have different temperatures, *depending on their walk with Jesus.* Some hearts are cold, possibly because circumstances haven't gone their way, or they haven't developed a meaningful relationship with Him. Some hearts are lukewarm. These are the ones who publicly claim to know Jesus, but never really trust Him privately in their daily lives. Then there are those who have burning hearts for the Lord. Why? Because they walk with Him!

Which kind of Christian are you? Do you consult God with a burning heart about everything and are committed to be loyal to Him whether things go your way or not? Or are you up now, down then, up again, down again because you have a cold or lukewarm heart? Burning heart Christians are convinced that God will bless them…come what may.

Respond

Is your heart burning for the Lord today? Or does your heart burn for other things that only bring temporary satisfaction? Take time to commit your whole heart and life to God. Confess the times you have allowed your heart to be lukewarm or even cold and ask God to cleanse you. Then go out and live with a burning heart for the things of God, and He will walk with you in a powerful way.

Remember

The burning heart experience comes to those who walk consistently with God.

His-Story Today

Read

Because he taught as one who had authority, and not as their teachers of the law. — Matthew 7:29.

Reflect

When I was going through my formal education, I loathed history. It was boring and monotonous to me. It was the necessary evil that hampered my GPA for years until my freshman year at college. Like any other year of school, I saw what courses I had to take, and history was one of them. So I signed up reluctantly and went to the first class. Like all first classes, the syllabus was passed out, and I found out how far behind I was on the first day. But something different from every previous history class I had ever took happened that day: my professor started teaching instead of merely reading from our book. He told us the story of Cortez. "So they decided to," he continued…and then the bell rang! Wow! What? I have to wait the whole weekend to find out what Cortez did?

What made the difference for me in history class that day? This teacher created in me an appetite to learn. Can you imagine what it must have been like to sit at Jesus' feet when He taught God's spiritual truths? Jesus taught with authority, and He used many stories, which created a hunger in His hearers' hearts to always come back for more. Multitudes followed Him to hear His words. Now we have nearly all of His words and most of His stories recorded in the Bible. None of us have an excuse for not being excited about studying God's Word.

Respond

Are you excited about God's Word? Do the stories Jesus teaches inspire you to faith? When the world starts caving in around you, do you find comfort in His teachings? The Law kills; but the Spirit gives life. So during today's devotional I invite you to take some time to let Jesus, the master teacher, inspire you with truth. Today, read His parable of the wise steward in Luke 16. Ask Him to show you the connections of this story with yourself. Then praise Him for the exciting history and practicality of His Word.

Remember

The Bible is His-story, which can make us all He wants us to be in His-story today.

Freedom From Flypaper

Read

Now the Lord is the Spirit, and where the Spirit of the Lord is, there is freedom. — 2 Corinthians 3:17.

Reflect

I once heard a story about a fly that was circling high above a piece of flypaper. As it circled, it saw other flies dancing on the piece of paper. He whizzed by a spider and heard the spider say, "Boy, it looks like they're having fun down there...you better join them before the party is over." The fly was hesitant, but the spider continued to persuade it by pointing out how he was missing out on all the fun that his friends were obviously having without him. After a moment of deliberation, the fly swooped down and landed next to his friends where he stayed...and died. What appeared to be true wasn't at all. What looked like freedom and fun was slavery and bondage.

Many times believers don't understand the freedom they have in Christ. The freedom He provides actually frees us from the flypaper of sin! We are all tempted, and the temptations are so appealing. But they are traps. So Jesus gives us His Word to avoid Satan's traps and temptations. He gives us His Spirit (see John 15:26) who strengthens and encourages us to avoid the traps. He also gives us an escape (see 1 Corinthians 10:13) to be delivered from Satan's traps.

There is really no reason for any believer to be caught in habitual sin. I believe the only reason we see so many Christians trapped on the flypaper is because they listened to the wrong voice, took the easy way — which turned out to be the hard way — and in the end they were too proud to admit they were in a mess.

Respond

If you are in a mess, don't be too proud to ask for help! We don't want another casualty on the flypaper. Then thank God for His Word and Spirit who keep you free from traps. Spend some time praising and thanking Him for the joy He deposits in your heart when you are free. And pray for those you know who are flying too low over the flypaper. Ask God to reveal His truth to them to avoid Satan's traps.

Remember

Satan only traps those who know no better.

He Lives In You

Read

And I will ask the Father, and he will give you another counselor to be with you forever. — John 14:16.

Reflect

On May 3, 1988, a United States jumbo jet was flying over the Pacific Ocean when it suddenly lost power. All three engines were powerless as the pilots prepared for a forced landing with 258 passengers aboard. Fortunately, no one was injured as they landed safely at Narita Airport in Japan. Why did the engines lose power? Three empty fuel tanks.

This story had a happy ending. However, many believers today are on a crash course to disaster because their fuel tanks are low and they are overcome by the pull of sin. Their downward spiral can only be changed by fueling up daily and letting the One who lives in them take the controls. They need to allow the Spirit to run their lives.

How are your fuel tanks today? Are they running on full or are they low on fuel? For God's Spirit to be revealed in our lives, we must set our minds on God, not just once in a while, but habitually throughout the day. We need to be running full in Him to navigate our daily lives in a victorious way. It's easy to see why our society is in a spiritual nose dive because of the world's rejection of Gods' Spirit and Word. But we as believers should be flying high and straight with our fuel tanks full, en route to God's destination.

Respond

Take some time during today's devotional to refuel with the Holy Spirit and God's Word. Ask God to give you the strength to do your work excellently today, in Jesus' name. Tank up on Psalm 1 and Luke 10. Then take off and fly the friendly skies with Jesus today!

Remember

God only teaches crash courses in submission and service.

THE SWORD OF THE SPIRIT

READ

Therefore put on the full armor of God, so that when the day of evil comes, you may be able to stand your ground, and after you have done everything, to stand.... and the sword of the Spirit, which is the word of God. — EPHESIANS 6:13,17.

REFLECT

Every soldier needs to be equipped with offensive and defensive weapons, and the "word of God" is our one offensive weapon. When Jesus was tempted, He relied on the sword of the Spirit to fight Satan's temptations in the wilderness and along every step of His ministry's way. For every out-of-context scripture Satan challenged Jesus with in the great "sword fight" of Matthew 4 , Jesus responded with, "It is written." And, Satan eventually fled.

The apostle Paul tells us in 2 Corinthians 10:4: "For the weapons of our warfare are not carnal, but mighty through God to the pulling down of strongholds." A stronghold is a tempting thought from our adversary intended to destroy God's will in our life. And the Word of God is the weapon that destroys Satan's deceptive work. Jesus modeled this truth for us in Matthew 4. The better we know the Word of God, the easier it is for us to recognize the lies of the enemy and reject them. So it is absolutely crucial that we know God's Word. The Word of God exposes the lies of Satan and slices his plans to ribbons.

RESPOND

Our verse today tells us the Word of God is the sword of the Spirit. Have you been wielding it against the assaults and deceptions of Satan? Take some time right now to seek God in the warrior passage of Psalm 144, because a weapon is no good without a warrior wielding it. Thank Jesus for going through all the temptations you will go through and for showing you how to handle them. Then read Ephesians 6:12-20 and thank God for His armor. Finally, make a new commitment today to go on the offensive and fight with His sword of the Spirit when Satan invades your camp to tempt you to fail.

REMEMBER

This is war; so fight to win!

Conviction Within

Read

Delight yourself in the Lord; and He will give you the desires of your heart. — Psalm 37:4.

Reflect

Our scripture today is probably one of the most misinterpreted scriptures in the Bible. Many people mistakenly think it says, "Delight yourself in the Lord and He will give you whatever your heart desires." But that is not the case. This verse carries with it a promise and a stipulation. The promise is: "He will give you desires." The stipulation is that you: "delight yourself in the Lord."

How do you delight yourself in the Lord? By disciplining yourself to spend time in the Bible, to pray, to seek His will, and to do His will. So here is the true meaning of our verse today: When you make the decision to delight in the Lord, you will want all of your decisions to be what He desires for you. Too often we make decisions on the basis of our desires, and not on the basis of God's desires. We make the decision we want, then pray that God will bless it.

Tragedy occurs when God is left out of our decisions, and when we leave Him out, Satan can come in. So the first step to making right decisions is to have a conviction within. But you must always beware to not mistake desire from without for conviction within. For example, suppose you face a decision to buy a new car. Ask yourself, "Is this a conviction I have in my heart or a desire from without? Am delighting in the Lord, or in the new car?"

Respond

Are you delighting yourself in the Lord today? Are you allowing His will to become your will in such a way that your heart's desires are reflecting Him? Pray for God's guidance and conviction of your deepest desires within. Ask Him to forgive past mistakes when your desires got in the way of His. Now, delight. Let the Word of God dwell in you richly, and express His desires to others today.

Remember

When we delight ourselves in the Lord: His desires become ours, not the other way around.

THE HOLY SPIRIT IN YOU

READ

We have not received the spirit of the world but the Spirit who is from God, that we may understand what God has freely given us. — 1 CORINTHIANS 2:12.

REFLECT

When Jesus left this earth, He knew His people would face challenges not only in the physical realm, but in the spiritual realm. So He sent the Holy Spirit to reside in the lives of all those who gave their lives to God and accepted the blood sacrifice of Jesus on the cross. The spirit of this world is in direct opposition to the Holy Spirit. The spirit of this world is dictated by Satan, and is in direct opposition to God's ways. As believers, we have been called out of this world, but live here to serve as a bridge to God. So while we are here on this earth, we are His representatives, to show the world the truth through God's Holy Spirit.

The apostle Paul discloses our freedom from Satan's worldly spirit and our privileged access into the wisdom of God. He has blessed us with the wisdom of His Word, and gives us His understanding of the fallen world around us. With this blessing and understanding we have much to be thankful for, but much responsibility comes with it. Jesus died to save the world, and He saved us to minister to it. So today as you seek Him in your devotional time, ask Him what He would have you do hand-in-hand with His Spirit who dwells in you.

RESPOND

Do those you associate with know you are a Christian? Have you been allowing the Holy Spirit to control your thoughts and actions on a daily basis? Because you have received the Spirit who is from God, God wants to use you to let Him speak where you go. So ask Him right now how He may want to use you to help someone get free from the spirit of the world. Ask Him to forgive you for the times when you've entertained the world's spirit. Then, go out today as His witness of power, love, and truth.

REMEMBER

The world wants to know Jesus, and the Holy Spirit who lives in you wants to speak through you today.

There's No Place Like Home

Read

"Be completely humble and gentle; be patient, bearing with one another in love." — Ephesians 4:16.

Reflect

Have you ever been away from home and become ill? Few things could be more miserable. You felt alone. And no matter how nice people were to you, all you had on your mind was home. You wanted familiar surroundings and familiar faces to give you a sense of security. Nothing provides security better than knowing you're loved and cared for. Jesus wants all of us to find our security in Him. When we become a vital part of His body, we understand that we are a part of a family who has found their security in Jesus and Jesus alone.

When you don't feel secure, you have no peace. That's why it is so important for you to be a part of the body of Christ — the Church. The church family is to be a place of security. Its members are to "be patient, bearing with one another in love." They care enough to provide a haven for others to find or renew their security in God.

A big bank account won't get it. A high-paying job will not provide it. Even a good marriage will fall short in providing security. The only way to have ultimate security that lasts through the storms of life is to allow Jesus to be the foundation of your life. And part of being in Christ is being a vital part of the Church.

Respond

How vital is "church" in your life — not only the universal Church, but the local church? The local church is the manifestation of the universal Church. Thank and praise God that there is no place like home in His family, the body of Christ. Ask Him to direct you in your involvement in His body, and thank Him for the security you find in being a part of it.

Remember

Ultimate security is only found in a personal relationship with Jesus.

We All Know

Read

For I know my transgressions, and my sin is always before me. Against you, you only, have I sinned and done what is evil in your sight, so that you are proved right when you speak and justified when you judge. — Psalm 51:3-4.

Reflect

Whenever I blew it on the baseball field growing up, guess who was the first one to know I had made an error? ME! The same is true when we sin.

King David knew he had sinned and acknowledged it in the verses for today. For years he had lived a righteous life. For years he had spent time alone with God as a shepherd, depending on God for strength to kill a bear, to take a stand and slay Goliath, and to lead a band of vagabonds and turn them into a group of "mighty men." He knew what discipleship was all about. He knew what it meant to walk with God, to be victorious in God's name, and how to humble himself. But he was also vulnerable. Like all of us, David had weak areas. And when he gave in to his weaknesses and sinned, he knew it. He tried to hide it, but he knew he couldn't hide from God.

Like David, we have no excuses for our sins and need God's forgiveness. Something always dies when we sin, so Jesus died once for all to destroy the power of sin. When Jesus paid the price for the sins of mankind as our sacrificial lamb, He provided the forgiveness we need. And today, He stands before God the Father on our behalf as He affirms for each of us who have received Him: "Price paid! Price paid!"

Respond

Whenever we blow it, we're always the first to know. All of us know deep down inside if we've sinned. Some try to make excuses, but they *know* nevertheless. You received Jesus as Savior because you knew. So take some time today to rejoice in the forgiveness of God. Pray for those you know who need God right now and ask Him to reveal Himself to them. Finally, ask God to help you make fewer errors on the field of life today.

Remember

We all know!

STRATEGY AGAINST THE WORLD

READ

Do not conform any longer to the pattern of this world, but be transformed by the renewing of your mind. Then you will be able to test and approve what God's will is — his good, pleasing and perfect will. — ROMANS 12:2.

REFLECT

One of the most troublesome parts of the ministry is to see someone make a meaningful commitment to Jesus Christ, then fail in their attempt to see that commitment through. They often experience depression, discouragement, and despair. Tragically, many refuse to make any more commitments to the Lord because of their fear of failing again.

I've noticed a pattern with many of these people. They start off well because they are sensitive to God's touch. But when they go back to the same daily pressures — and often old ways of thinking — they lose that sensitivity and thus the stability and strength needed to persevere. When this happens, they begin to feel overwhelmed and discouraged. Their downfall comes when they begin to think like the world again, instead of thinking like God. These believers need the support of other believers, encouraging them to continue their daily prayer and study time with God as a first priority. That is the only way they can keep their mind renewed to God's Word and remain stable.

Satan's strategies are so aggressive against the mind that we must have an equally aggressive strategy to overcome his pressure. Because the thought patterns of the world are contrary to the thought patterns of God, we must continuously yield our minds to God's Word. And we do this every time we read, study, memorize, and apply God's Word to our lives.

RESPOND

Spend some time filling your mind with God's Word right now. Read Mark 4 and expect that your life will consist of thirty-, sixty-, and one hundred-fold soil. As you spend time praying, ask God to give you His thoughts. Renewing your mind is the first step in living out your commitment to Jesus. No matter how long you've been living for Him, you can't do it without spending quality time with Him.

REMEMBER

Staying in God's Word and praying without ceasing is your strategy to stay faithful today.

Pray and Plan

Read

The king said to me, "What is it you want?" Then I prayed to the God of heaven, and I answered the king, "If it pleases the king and if your servant has found favor in his sight, let him send me to the city in Judah where my fathers are buried so that I can rebuild it." — NEHEMIAH 2:4-5.

Reflect

Nehemiah was a man who knew how to pray and how to plan. When he had something burning in his heart, he sought God for answers and got them. Here are some of the lessons we can learn from Nehemiah's success:

1. Before you talk to men about God's work, talk to God about men.
2. Before you talk to men about the little bit they can help, talk to God about the availability of His abundant provisions.
3. Before you listen to the opposition, listen to the Father.

When God gave Nehemiah the vision for rebuilding Jerusalem, He also gave him the plan to carry it out. So as Nehemiah went to prayer about his fervent desire to rebuild the city of Jerusalem, God gave him His plan for the project. In Nehemiah's mind, it was God's way without question, but so many believers question God's way or even disregard it altogether.

Nehemiah was faced with two thrones, the throne of the king and the throne of God. So are we when it comes to our decisions in life: our throne and God's throne. Each throne involves a plan. When we're on the throne, most of our planning is haphazard and need-oriented, based on supply and demand. But when God is on the throne, He gives us His perfect plan, and the supplies that are needed are provided on time as we obey Him.

Respond

What is God's plan for you today? Spend some quiet time with Him right now, praying for His vision to become your top priority. Then seek Him for the plan, because you'll need one to fulfill what He's calling you to do.

Remember

When you have an idea, go to God first.

A Sacrificed Life

Read

But even if I am being poured out like a drink offering on the sacrifice and service coming from your faith, I am glad and rejoice with all of you. — Philippians 2:17.

Reflect

I never look at giving of myself to my wife or children as a sacrifice. Why? Because of my deep love for them. In fact, when I'm not willing to sacrifice for them, it indicates how much more I love myself than I love them. That's when I repent! But when I give myself to them and see how it impacts their lives, I experience a joy that could never be achieved by putting myself first.

Sacrificing your life for others is the ultimate in giving. And Jesus is calling every Christian to live out what that means in practical terms. Paul was willing to pour out his life for the sake of the Church and do it joyfully. He was so in love with the Church that he was willing to give his all. Paul knew how much Jesus had sacrificed for him and that he could never repay the debt of His redeeming love. So to sacrifice on the behalf of others was a joy for Paul. Sacrificing himself for others was his way of paying the debt of love he owed to Jesus.

Respond

How much have you sacrificed for those you love? Have you consistently been willing to give yourself to help them in any way you can? How about your church? What is your attitude about sacrificing for God's people? Have you considered using your time and resources to enhance the ministry of your church to others? When it comes to the topic of sacrificing for others, we all pale in comparison to the love and sacrifice Jesus made for us. Take some time right now to praise and thank God for the sacrificial gift Jesus gave when He offered His life on the cross. Confess to Him the times you have been selfish and ignored the many opportunities to give others the gift of yourself. Finally, pray God will use you today in a sacrificial way to help others see Jesus.

Remember

Our families, church, and the world around us get a wonderful picture of Jesus when we choose to live a sacrificial life.

The Fruit of Repentance

Read

"Produce fruit in keeping with repentance. And do not think you can say to yourselves, 'We have Abraham as our father.'" — Matthew 3:8-9.

Reflect

The Jews of John's day thought they would go to heaven based on their standing as Jews, that they were the physical descendants of Abraham. But John assured them that it wasn't what their ancestors did that made them spiritual. And he warned them to "produce fruit in keeping with repentance."

Repentance means to have a change of mind. You can say you're repenting all you want, but unless you produce the fruit, or evidence, of repentance, it is difficult to believe any change has taken place. The fruit of a changed mind will blossom into actions such as the cessation of rudeness, immorality, laziness, drinking, doing drugs, exaggerating, lying, manipulating, and other nagging sins. In their place, you will notice godly actions such as forgiving, loving, praying, and serving.

Have you ever confronted someone after they mistreated you, and they assured you it would never happen again, but within a few days, they turned right around and did the same thing? When this happens, there probably wasn't true repentance. They didn't really change their mind, change directions, and begin to act according to God's Word instead of their flesh. John the Baptist said that true repentance is demonstrated by action.

Respond

In the stillness of your time alone with God today, let Him reveal the feelings, thoughts, and actions of sin that you have refused to repent from. Ask Him to give you the strength and courage to let go of them and let Him take control of your life. Then do it, whether you feel like it or not. He will honor your heart's sincere desire to be free and help you to overcome. You may have to repeat this procedure a few times before you begin to feel the difference, but don't give up before you see the victory — because you will see it!

Remember

The fruit of repentance reveals a godly attitude toward sin and a reverence for God.

The Cost of Selfishness

Read

But Elisha said to him, "Was not my spirit with you when the man got down from his chariot to meet you? Is this the time to take money, or to accept clothes? ...Naaman's leprosy will cling to you and to your descendants forever." Then Gehazi went from Elisha's presence and he was leprous. — 2 Kings 5:26-27.

Reflect

Elisha's servant, Gehazi, had great potential. He could have been the next great prophet of Israel. But he had a deadly inner problem — selfishness. He had followed the great prophet Elisha, just as Elisha had followed Elijah. So he had great mentors. He was probably very gifted, very persuasive, and well-liked. But when Naaman offered Elisha new clothes and treasures as a payment of appreciation for his healing from leprosy and Elisha refused, Gehazi couldn't believe it. So he pursued Naaman and lied to get the treasures for himself.

But Elisha knew Gehazi all too well. "Was not my spirit with you when the man got down from his chariot?" In other words, "When you were sneaking around and allowing your selfishness to control you, didn't you know the Lord would watch your every step and tell me?"

Respond

Selfishness can make us do crazy, unwise things. Gehazi, with all his potential and all the opportunities God had given him, was blind. What he *didn't* have blinded him to all the things he *did* have. Does that sound like you? Are you allowing selfishness and the desire for more to blind you from all the blessings God has given you? If so, stop. Spend some time praising and thanking God for His unselfish love and many blessings. Admit to Him the times you have allowed selfishness to get in the way of serving Him. Pray for those you know who are being burned by their own selfishness. Then ask God for creative ways to give to others today. You cannot be greedy and self-serving when you are busy giving to someone else.

Remember

The price of selfishness is too high. Ask Gehazi.

NOTICE HIM

READ

In those days Caesar Augustus issued a decree that a census should be taken of the entire Roman world.... And everyone went to his own town to register. — LUKE 2:1,3.

REFLECT

When you think of Christmas, you think of children's programs, manger scenes, wrapped gifts, and pine trees decked with colorful lights. You also envision long lines, impatient customers, and mall employees saying, "We just ran out!"

In the Middle East 2000 years ago, Bethlehem was in a similar chaos. Few people noticed the concerned young man leading a donkey, upon which sat his very pregnant wife. The innkeeper might have made a mental note of her condition, but he still didn't make room for the young couple. Today, things are much the same around Christmastime. People fill their lives with shopping and parties and never notice the Savior. They make a mental note that He was born around that time, but they have no place for Him in their lives.

We live in a hectic world in which our lives are dictated by schedules and deadlines. Joseph and Mary faced the same type of stress when Caesar Augustus issued his decree to report to their hometown to be counted in a census. The world was scrambling and everyone was headed somewhere. Today people scramble in search of something to give meaning to their lives — and they miss the only One who has that ability: Jesus.

RESPOND

Stop for a few minutes and think about Jesus. Look for Him and for His work in your life. Praise and thank Him for His active presence in your everyday affairs. Confess to Him the times you haven't made room for Him in your daily schedule. Finally, pray for those you know who need to see Him. Ask God to let you be a reflection of His love in their lives today.

REMEMBER

If you're feeling the pressure of schedules and deadlines today, discipline yourself to pause — and notice Jesus.

Jesus Puts You on the Map

Read

So Joseph also went up from the town of Nazareth in Galilee to Judea, to Bethlehem the town of David, because he belonged to the house and line of David. He went there to register with Mary, who was pledged to be married to him and was expecting a child. While they were there, the time came for the baby to be born, and she gave birth to her firstborn, a son. — Luke 2:4-7.

Reflect

Every Christmas we sing about the "little town of Bethlehem." This small town is now famous around the world because of one person who was born there: Jesus Christ. You probably know all the details of the Christmas story. You know that Jesus was born in a stable in Bethlehem, because there was no room in the inn. And after He was born, shepherds were divinely guided to come and see their Messiah. This was the beginning of Bethlehem becoming famous. This little town had a very important role in the history of mankind.

In the same way, we must realize that we aren't much without Jesus. Just as His birth made a great difference to Bethlehem, He comes into our lives expecting to make a great difference there too. But He can only make a difference to the degree that we will let Him. Often we say, "There is no room for you in this part of my life, Jesus." We divide our lives into different compartments and say, "I'll let You influence me in this area, but not in that one." If we will turn our lives completely over to Him, He will do for us what He did for Bethlehem — He will put us on the map — and give us a role in history only we can fulfill.

Respond

Have you given every part of your life to Jesus? Pray and ask the Holy Spirit to show you anything you have withheld from your Lord and Savior. Then turn it over to Him and watch what He does with it!

Remember

Surrender all to Jesus today and let Him put you on the map of human history.

SHELTER

READ

And she gave birth to her firstborn, a son. She wrapped him in cloths and placed him in a manger, because there was no room for them in the inn. — LUKE 2:7.

REFLECT

Can you remember the worst night's sleep you ever had? When our second child was born, even though it was a short labor, I was bushed when it was over. (Okay, ladies, my wife was a little tired too.) On that first Christmas eve, shelter was at a premium. Every bed, cot, blanket, and mat was taken. "No room!" were words that echoed in Joseph's mind as Mary's time of delivery drew nearer. The night Joseph entered Bethlehem with his nine-months-pregnant wife was probably the most difficult and yet most awesome sleepless night he ever spent.

Picture the scene for a moment: a stable for livestock. Can you smell it? The stalls reek; the wind whips through the cracks in the walls; the dirt floor is cold; filth is everywhere. Do you think it would be difficult to fall asleep? Yet in the middle of it all, a baby is cooing. It was God's perfect will that His Son would come into the world in the midst of this barnyard mess. And Jesus is still coming on the scene amid the stench and filth of our sinful lives. Just as He came into that smelly stable to save the world, He comes into our hearts to save us and deliver us from the stench of our worldly lives.

RESPOND

On that night shelter was hard to find, but we can experience the shelter of God's love and protection every day. Take some time right now to praise and worship God for the shelter of His love, which delivered you from the filth of sin. Then pray for those you know who need a visit from Jesus amid their mess of a life, who need shelter that only He can provide.

REMEMBER

Jesus is your shelter from stress and harm as you go about your busy day.

Keeping Watch

Read

And there were shepherds living out in the fields nearby, keeping watch over their flocks at night. An angel of the Lord appeared to them, and the glory of the Lord shone around them. — LUKE 2:8-9.

Reflect

There was really nothing special about these famous shepherds in the Christmas story. They were on their night watch the eve of Jesus' birth, keeping an eye on their sheep. Joseph probably wondered why they walked into the stable after Jesus was born. But stop and think about this situation for a moment. God reveals himself to those who aren't too busy to hear His voice — and these shepherds were certainly not busy.

Have you ever been so project-minded that you lost touch with everything else? Have you ever been so pressed by deadlines that you wouldn't answer the phone because you knew it would slow you down? If that sounds like you, shepherding is something you may want to consider as a career change! (Always very tempting at the Christmas season.) These shepherds weren't on a deadline to sheer their sheep when God's angels filled the skies.

It was during David's times of watching over his flock that God revealed Himself to him. And right after Paul became a Christian, he spent three years in Arabia under no pressure except to hear his Savior's voice. It was during this time that God spoke to him about his New Testament ministry. Throughout history God has delighted in revealing Himself to those who would take time to listen to Him.

Respond

Sometimes in our busy deadline-driven lives, God will cause interruptions to make us stop and to take notice, or keep watch, over His priorities. How much time do you allow in your schedule to listen to God? Do you make it a priority each day to spend time with Him? What projects are on your agenda for this week? Is keeping watch one of them? I hope so. Take some time right now to thank God that He speaks to ordinary, watchful men. Now, recommit your life to being one.

Remember

God speaks to those who take time to watch.

THE UNVEILING

READ

In the beginning was the Word, and the Word was with God, and the Word was God.... The Word became flesh and made his dwelling among us. We have seen his glory, the glory of the One and Only, who came from the Father, full of grace and truth. — JOHN 1:1,14.

REFLECT

Have you ever been to an unveiling? In this verse John unveils for us the Word of God becoming flesh. Remarkable! Jesus was with God in the beginning as the Word of God. He existed in the beginning with God, not because He had a beginning, but because He is eternal. He is the eternal Word of God. Before He was Jesus of Nazareth, He was the Word. While Luke reveals how Jesus got to the stable, John unveils how the Word was made flesh.

The whole idea of eternity is foreign to the natural mind, for we perceive everything in terms of a beginning and an end. Too often we want to think of God in the same way. But He wouldn't be much of a God if we could understand all there is to know about Him. The truth is, He unveiled Himself in the person of Jesus Christ, the eternal Word made flesh. And the Bible says that to see Jesus is to see the glory of God the Father, including all His grace and truth.

RESPOND

You may be thinking, "This is all very fascinating, but how can all this stuff about Jesus being unveiled as the Word of God help me today?" If you are hurting or going through a difficult time, you need to know the truth — and Jesus is the truth. He is the Living Word who happens to have gone through everything you are going through and more. Tell Him what you are going through and listen for His reply; feel His presence and the comfort of the Holy Spirit. There is nothing He cannot see you through.

REMEMBER

Jesus is the Living Word for you today.

Go Home Another Way

Read

And having been warned in a dream not to go back to Herod, they returned to their country by another route. — Matthew 2:12.

Reflect

The Wise Men were truly wise. Why? Because they followed God. God led them by the star to worship His Son, Jesus. Then afterward He warned them of Herod's treachery in a dream and redirected their route home. Take a look at James Taylor's rendition of this story:

> Those magic men in the Magi, some people call them wise, or Oriental, even Kings, well anyway those guys.
> They visited with Jesus, and sure enjoyed their stay.
> Then warned in a dream of King Herod's scheme, they went home by another way.
> Yes, they went home by another way.
> Maybe me and you can be wise guys too, and go home by another way
> ...Herod's always out there; he's got our card on file.
> It's a lead pipe cinch if you give an inch, then Herod likes to take a mile.
> It's best to go home by another way...
>
> *(Home by Another Way,* Manor House Music, 1988)

Herod symbolizes Satan. The wise men took God's instruction to go home by another way to protect themselves and the baby Jesus from the destruction of the enemy. God does the same thing for us today — if we will listen and obey. The truth is, Satan knows our weaknesses and our strengths, and if we give him an inch, he'll take a mile. He wants to talk us into a deal like he tried to fool the wise men. But if we stay in tune with God, through His Word and prayer, we can stay one step ahead of the evil one.

Respond

Do you want to be like the wise men? Take some time right now to pray and listen for God's instructions and wisdom for the day. Then thank your heavenly Father that by the blood of Jesus Christ you have authority over the enemy and every evil thing.

Remember

Satan is not passive when it comes to getting you off-track. So stay on your guard and be ready to go home another way.

The Light of Men

Read

In Him was life, and that life was the light of men. The light shines in the darkness, but the darkness has not understood it. — John 1:4-5.

Reflect

You would think that people in darkness would appreciate a light so they could see, but that is not always the case. All through John's gospel you can read about how many people did not receive Jesus or His teachings. They didn't understand what He was saying or what He was doing, so they opposed Him.

Jesus is the Living Word — the Light — and many people in both His time and ours today prefer to live in darkness. They enjoy their sin and are fascinated by themselves and their own thinking. The idea of absolutes and eternal truths — not to mention a God of *judgment* as well as love — is not their idea of fun. You see, they want to live life their own way and be their own god. The truth is, they are living Satan's original lie to Eve in the Garden of Eden, "You will be like God" (Genesis 3:4).

What is your attitude toward the Word of God? When the light of God's Word shines on a dark area of your life, do you react negatively to Jesus' claims on you? If you do, you must ask yourself if you believe Jesus is who He says He is. If you truly believe He is the only way to eternal life, you must give your whole heart to Him now. Don't withhold any part of your life from Him, because if you do, you are allowing darkness to reign in that area of your life.

Respond

Praise and worship Jesus as the light that shines in your heart and dispels all darkness. Thank Him for coming to earth to save you and give you a new life. Ask Him to forgive you for the times you have chosen to live in darkness, and make a commitment to live in His light.

Remember

If you allow the Light of God's Word to reign in your heart, you will be a light to all those around you today.

A Family Reunion

Read

Then Joseph said to his brothers, "Come close to me...I am your brother Joseph, the one you sold into Egypt." — Genesis 45:4.

Reflect

Family reunions can be special times. Just like baseball and apple pie, family reunions are quite American. However, the reunion of Joseph and his brothers was something special indeed. A scene that could have easily been a tragedy turned into a great reunion because Joseph has a spirit of reconciliation instead of vengeance.

We can learn from Joseph's example. He did five things that resulted in the restoration of his family.

1. He refused to air all the family's dirty laundry publicly. When he confronted them, he did it privately. (See Genesis 45:1.)
2. He refused to play the blame game. He didn't put a guilt trip on his brothers, but called to their attention the big picture — how God was at work the entire time. (See Genesis 45:5.)
3. He welcomed his brothers warmly. (See Genesis 45:9.)
4. He gave his brothers the gift of prime land in Egypt. (See Genesis 45:9.)
5. He showed affection in restoring fellowship. (See Genesis 45:14-15.)

Wouldn't you have loved to watch as Joseph embraced his brothers, beginning with Benjamin? The Bible says they wept and talked. What a beautiful family reunion!

Respond

Is there anyone in your family or do you have a friend with whom you need a family reunion like Joseph's? Have you been unwilling to take the first step toward reconciliation? Pray and ask God what He would have you do, and then do it. Ask Him to guide you as you seek full restoration with any family member or friend you have been estranged from — especially if they are your brother or sister in Christ.

Remember

True forgiveness is unconditional.

Don't Sleep With the Enemy!

Read

Therefore, brother, we have an obligation — but it is not to the sinful nature, to live according to it. For if you live according to the sinful nature, you will die; but if by the Spirit you put to death the misdeeds of the body, you will live. — ROMANS 8:12-13.

Reflect

Rose Greenhow was a secret agent of the Confederate Army. In fact, she once hid a message containing Union plans to attack Richmond in the curls of her hair. Interestingly, Rose lived within a rifle shot of the White House! Her house became the heart of a southern spy network that directed more than fifty agents. Isn't it amazing how spies could live so close to the home headquarters and go virtually unnoticed?

Unfortunately, the same is true for us. A battle over our minds is going on, and the old sinful nature spies on our weak spots and reveals them to the enemy commander, who is looking for any opportunity to attack us. If we do not resist and put to death the deeds of the flesh, we are in danger of being defeated by them.

Many of us have fallen into the trap of believing we have defeated the old nature for good after winning a few battles. The truth is, the enemy commander never gives up on using the old nature. He is always spying to see when we are weak and where. Our response must be to render the old nature dead and live for Jesus Christ — every minute of every day. We must not go to sleep and allow the enemy any foothold in our lives.

Respond

Begin your prayer time today by thanking and praising your Commander, Almighty God, who has already defeated the enemy. Give your life completely to Him and let Him give you His thoughts; allow Him to inspire your actions. If you stick close to God, the enemy cannot defeat you. Thank your heavenly Father that you can be secure in Him at all times through His Word and the Holy Spirit.

Remember

God has already defeated the enemy, so stay close to Him today and don't give the devil any ammunition.

THE LIGHT OF THE WORLD

READ

"You are the light of the world. A city on a hill cannot be hidden." — MATTHEW 5:14.

REFLECT

Jesus used the examples of salt and light to help us see what we are to do while we are here on earth. Just as we are to be salt in the world to help preserve lives from the decaying influences of the world system, we are also to be light to point people to God. As a ship coming into a harbor depends on a beacon to guide the way, so the Christian should be a light to those who are in darkness, to guide them through the seas of life. Many dangers lurk in the darkness, and only by help from the True Light can one safely maneuver to avoid the traps of the enemy and his evil world system.

How can you effectively point people to God? First of all, you do so through a consistent Christian lifestyle. Jesus said that if you lift Him up in your life, He will draw people to Himself. In other words, if you make Him the highest priority in your life, He will see to it that people will be drawn your way. If you maintain His attitudes of compassion and wisdom in your daily life, others will notice.

But that is not the only way. You are also to shine your light in the darkness. When you see a believer or an unbelieving friend going the wrong way, pray for them fervently. Your prayers release the light into their lives. And if God so leads you to speak to them, pray for the words to help guide that person to Him.

RESPOND

Spend some time thanking and praising God for His truth, the light that drew you to Him. Thank Him for the people He used to light the way for you to find Him. Confess to Him the times you have not let your light shine for Him, and determine in your heart that you will shine brightly all the time from now on. Finally, pray for those with whom you will rub shoulders today, that your light will shine on them.

REMEMBER

Jesus is the Light of the World, but He shines through you today.

Additional copies of this book and other book titles
from ALBURY PUBLISHING are available at your local bookstore.

ALBURY PUBLISHING
P. O. Box 470406
Tulsa, Oklahoma 74147-0406

In Canada books are available from:

Word Alive
P. O. Box 670
Niverville, Manitoba
CANADA ROA 1EO